D1738449

THE HAN

STUDIES ON ETHNIC GROUPS IN CHINA

Stevan Harrell, Editor

THE HAN

China's Diverse Majority

AGNIESZKA JONIAK-LÜTHI

UNIVERSITY *of* WASHINGTON PRESS | SEATTLE *&* LONDON

© 2015 by the University of Washington Press
Printed and bound in the United States of America
Composed in Minion Pro, typeface designed by Robert Slimbach
18 17 16 15   5 4 3 2 1

University of Washington Press
www.washington.edu/uwpress

Library of Congress Cataloging-in-Publication Data
Joniak-Lüthi, Agnieszka.
The Han : China's diverse majority / Agnieszka Joniak-Lüthi.
    pages   cm.—(Studies on ethnic groups in China)
Includes bibliographical references and index.
ISBN 978-0-295-99467-3 (hardcover : alk. paper)
1. Chinese—Ethnic identity.   2. China—Ethnic relations.   I. Title.
DS730.J657   2015
305.8951—dc23
2014036408

CONTENTS

Foreword by Stevan Harrell vii

Acknowledgments xi

Introduction 3

1 | Narrating "the Han" 19

2 | Contemporary Narratives of Han-ness 44

3 | Topographies of Identity 66

4 | Othering, Exclusion, and Discrimination 90

5 | Fragmented Identities, the Han *Minzu*, and Ethnicity 115

Epilogue 140

Notes 145

Glossary of Chinese Characters 161

References 167

Index 181

FOREWORD

STEVAN HARRELL

Are the Han Chinese in fact an ethnic group, the world's largest? If so, what makes them an ethnic group, and how are they similar to or different from others, particularly China's minority groups, who get the bulk of the attention when the question of ethnicity arises? Can we apply the same concepts and the same kinds of analysis to the 1.2 billion Han that we apply, say, to the 10 million Uyghur of Xinjiang or the 50,000 Mosuo or Na of the Sichuan-Yunnan border? How are the Han as an ethnic group different from the Chinese as a nationality? In what situations do people activate their identity as Han, and in what situations are local, national, or other identities more important? Agnieszka Joniak-Lüthi's *The Han: China's Diverse Majority* addresses all these questions and more.

Based on interviews in such disparate places as the great metropolises of Shanghai and Beijing, the small, Uyghur-dominated city of Aqsu in southern Xinjiang, and the remote Lugu Lake region on the Sichuan-Yunnan border, Joniak-Lüthi addresses several issues in ways that expand our understanding of what constitutes China and how the Chinese majority thinks of itself.

First, there is the nature of the Han as an ethnic group. Although other works have addressed the problematic nature of the category Han as officially constituted, none has taken such a close and detailed look at what constitutes Han-ness for individual Han people in varied locations; or taken such an enlightening look at what individual Han people think Han people are like, or at what they think they all have in common as a group.

Second, there is the relationship between being Han and being Chinese. Again, there is a lot of theorizing about how Chinese as a national category and Han as an ethnic category relate to each other, but in Joniak-Lüthi's study we find for the first time detailed examples of what individual Han interviewees in a variety of situations perceive as the relationship between the two identities.

Third, there are the internal divisions of the Han. Here, too, there are studies of particular subgroups, such as Hakka, Cantonese, or Subei people, but not until *The Han* have we had so clear a picture of the circumstances in which more local or regional identities, "home-place" identities as Joniak-Lüthi calls them, are more salient and those in which the unity of the Han is the more relevant concept. It is particularly interesting to know that regional stereotypes are pervasive among almost all groups of Han but that at the same time so many people can name characteristics of the Han as a whole.

Fourth, there is the relationship between Han and minorities. Although previous works have looked at the ways Han think of minorities, none has so thoroughly examined how Han identity fits into the general picture of ethnic-group identity in China. At a time when minority identities and conflicts between minorities and the state have become increasingly salient for our understanding of China and its politics, we need to pay more attention to the question of what Han identity means for the Han themselves and how conflict between Han and minorities is explained by the nature of Han identity. *The Han* makes an important contribution to this understanding.

Lastly, there is the question of ethnic groups and agency. Since we now know that China is not a totalitarian state where resistance is minimal and state-mandated categories are hegemonic in public discourse, but rather an authoritarian one where there is room to maneuver, even amid political repression and lack of democracy, it is important to know to what degree people accept the state's idea of how they ought to think of themselves. The answer to this question resounds in *The Han*: despite all the internal diversity and regional stereotyping, despite all the unofficial categories that supersede "Han" in certain circumstances, almost no one disagrees that there is such a thing as a Han and that it is an important category of ethnic identity in China.

The issues that Agnieszka Joniak-Lüthi addresses in *The Han* are thus complex, salient, and fascinating to any student of ethnic identity, nationalism, or the relationship between the two. *The Han* is only the third book in the Studies on Ethnic Groups in China series to address Han identity specifically (the first two are Nicole Constable's *Guest People* and Edward Rhoads's *Manchus and Han*), and the current volume is the first one to address the topic comprehensively. We are proud to introduce *The Han* as our nineteenth publication in Studies on Ethnic Groups in China.

ACKNOWLEDGMENTS

This book would not exist were it not for the support of numerous people and institutions who have accompanied me between Poland, China, and Switzerland for over ten years. First and foremost, I would like to thank my dear Polish and Swiss families for their love and support and for always standing beside me. It is indeed the greatest luxury to feel this support in everything one does in life. Particularly, I would like to thank Peter, with whom I conducted my fieldwork in China in 1999, who was my research assistant during my field study from 2002 to 2003, and who in the meantime became my husband. As the person most directly affected by my complaints, energy breakdowns, working crises, and all the bad moods and doubts one experiences during writing, he earns a very special thank you. I also would like to thank my friends: I am grateful that we can go through life together, sharing joys and sorrows and never forgetting to have a good laugh.

I have also experienced the warm help of tutors, colleagues, and friends at the graduate and postdoctoral level. First of all, I would like to thank Professor Alfred F. Majewicz from the Institute of Oriental Studies at Adam Mickiewicz University in Poznań for his supervision and for being fun, open, and motivating. I would additionally like to thank my former colleagues at the Institute of Oriental Studies for the fantastic working atmosphere and time spent together, during and beyond research and teaching matters. I still miss it! Next I would like to thank Professor Liang Deman from Sichuan University, my supervisor during my stay in Chengdu in 2002–3. Professor Liang welcomed me to her home every week with liters of green tea, and during hours of tutoring she introduced me to the complexity of post-1950s linguistic research in China. During my research in Beijing and Shanghai, I was helped enormously by Leszek Sobkowiak, who invited me to stay in his Shanghai apartment and provided me with everything I could possibly need. I also would like to thank Mieke Matthyssen; I was able to fine-tune my research design in her warm, snug flat in the middle of a Manchurian winter when she hosted me over the 2003 Spring Festival in Shenyang.

My research was enriched by the useful ideas of a large number of Chinese and foreign colleagues; I express my infinite gratitude to all of these individuals. I also send a big thank you to all of the informants in Beijing and Shanghai who shared their time and energy with me; and to my collaborators and informants in Zuosuo, where I conducted fieldwork in 1999, and in Xinjiang, where I conducted fieldwork from 2011 to 2012. This research greatly informed the ways I analyzed the data in this book.

The analysis and write-up of the fieldwork data took place at the Institute of Social Anthropology, University of Bern, Switzerland. There, I was greatly assisted by the helpful comments, motivating ideas, and literature suggestions shared with me by Hans-Rudolf Wicker, Ellen Hertz, Martin Sökefeld, Judith Hangartner, Sue Thüler, and other colleagues. Attending the institute's weekly colloquium together—and the exchange at a beer afterward—inspired me and gave me new energy to keep working. I am grateful to the Adam Mickiewicz University in Poznań, the Polish and Chinese Ministries of Education, and the Swiss Federal Commission for Scholarships for Foreign Students for financial support of my postgraduate studies and research.

While at work on this book manuscript in Seattle and Bern, I profited immensely from the knowledge, feedback, and comments of Pamela Kyle Crossley, Jeffrey Wasserstrom, Jonathan Lipman, Tom Mullaney, Mark Elliott, Dru Gladney, Cheng Yinghong, Nicolas Tapp, Madlen Kobi, Peter Lüthi, and Eric Schluessel. I am most grateful for the comments provided by the two reviewers of the manuscript, Stevan Harrell and James Leibold. The book was greatly improved by their suggestions and friendly critiques. Steve Harrell was a particularly attentive, helpful, and good-humored editor all along; thank you for that. Thanks also to Lorri Hagman of the University of Washington Press for her editorial assistance and most especially for so patiently explaining the nuances of writing styles to a nonnative English speaker. I am grateful to Jacqueline Volin, Tim Zimmermann, and Beth Fuget from the University of Washington Press and copy editor Julie Van Pelt for seeing the manuscript through the final stages of editing. Swiss National Science Foundation funded my stays at the University of Washington (UW). Stephanie Maher provided me with a great temporary home in Seattle, and Mike Caputi helped arrange my stays at the UW; my heartfelt thanks to both. I also would like to express my gratitude to Tomasz Ostwald and other Polish friends in Seattle who took care of me during my stays as a visiting researcher at the UW. Tomasz, your mojitos are unbeatable!

Further, I would like to thank the Adam Mickiewicz University Press and Cambridge University Press for granting permission to reprint parts of my articles published previously in *Linguistic and Oriental Studies from Poznań* and the *Journal of Asian Studies*. The Institute of Social Anthropology at the University of Bern provided financial support for the language proofs of the manuscript and assisted me in so many other ways all along. I would particularly like to thank Heinzpeter Znoj, Sabine Strasser, and Christiane Girardin for being uncomplicated, supportive, and encouraging. Michele Statz did the language proofs and greatly improved the style of the manuscript; thank you for that, Michele.

I am most grateful to all of these people and institutions and am well aware that without their assistance, this book would never have come into being.

THE HAN

INTRODUCTION

Being Han marks the biggest and most important difference between me and other people.

Hanzu are the center. . . . The country needs this strong center to be strong itself.

Minzu is not important; instead, it is that people from different regions have different characteristics.

Fieldwork interviews, Beijing and Shanghai, 2002–3

The Han *minzu—minzu* translated variously as "nationality" or "ethnic group" but generally used to indicate a state-recognized population category—officially constitutes 91.5 percent of China's population. The Hanzu are recognized by the state as the national majority and as the core of the Chinese multiethnic nation, which officially comprises also fifty-five other *minzu*, together referred to as "minor *minzu*" or "minorities" (*shaoshu minzu*) and often labeled with Stalinist vocabulary as "minority nationalities."[1] While critical research on the "minor *minzu*" and the Minzu Classification Project (Minzu Shibie) began to emerge in the late 1980s, critical studies on the Han as a *minzu* and the making of this category in mainland China seem to have lagged behind. The field is slowly gathering momentum, but the size, distribution, and internal variety of the Han *minzu* continue to challenge both anthropologists and historians. Some scholars have embarked on studies of localized Han communities.[2] Others have grappled with the Han from the perspective of broader historical or contemporary political and social processes.[3] This study is perhaps best situated in the latter category, because it does not focus on any specific localized Han community, instead considering identification and categorization processes among the Hanzu in the broader context of

3

state interventions in identity politics. At the same time, it is significantly different from most of this literature (but see Blum 2001), as the primary materials it draws on are not historical sources but interviews and observations. Moreover, this study refers to ongoing identity processes from the perspective of individual actors. As demonstrated by my research participants, these Han individuals are, on the one hand, agents who skillfully create and manipulate numerous identity options. On the other hand, however, their lives are simultaneously influenced by greater players, such as the state. As my research reveals, these dynamics significantly shape identity options and choices.

During my fieldwork, I was often struck by the ease with which identities are evoked and switched, by their situational nature, and by their dependence on scales of interaction and on "others." Han assume various identities deliberately to create the feeling of intimacy, to achieve something materially or symbolically, to evoke the feeling of belonging, to create the feeling of community, and to draw boundaries against "others." In other words, depending on their circumstances and interlocutors, Han individuals activate different identities, a process surely not unique to the Han but displaying specific characteristics in the case at hand. When confronted with people of other *minzu*, a Han will likely first evoke her or his Han *minzu* identity. When confronted with other Han, the options for self-identification expand. In these Han-to-Han interactions, Beijing People (Beijingren) may set themselves apart from Shanghai People (Shanghairen).[4] They may position themselves as Locals in relation to Migrants, Urbanites as opposed to Ruralites, and white collar as opposed to blue collar. At the scale of Han-to-Han interactions, the Han *minzu* disintegrates into myriad identity categories that depend on access to wealth, occupation, home place, place of temporary residence, kinship, *hukou* (household registration), and many other factors.

To draw attention away from such fragmentation, the Chinese government reiterates the significance of *minzu* boundaries. Often that occurs through the language of "*minzu* problems" or "ethnic conflicts," as when the government identifies unrest in Inner Mongolia or Xinjiang as "a *minzu* problem" as opposed to, say, a social problem rooted in job inequality. Such characterizations reestablish *minzu* as important categories of identification and perception. On the other hand, in parallel attempts to downplay the significance of the particular *minzu* boundaries that divide the Chinese nation (*Zhonghua minzu*), the central government also regularly reactivates its most significant external "others," namely Japan and the United States of America, relying on powerful catchphrases such as *nation, national independence*, and *national integrity*. Through this reemphasis on boundaries between Han and other *minzu* and between the Chinese nation and other nations, government agencies regularly mobilize and reinvent the identity categories they generated in the Minzu Classification Project of the 1950s and the category of nation as established in the nation-making processes since the late nineteenth century. Individual identity politics of the Hanzu are unavoidably greatly influenced by these workings of the state.

MAJOR CONTRIBUTIONS OF THIS STUDY

I launched the research for this book with a number of questions in mind: What does being Han mean to those classified as Hanzu? What are the narratives of Han-ness today? What other collective identities matter to the Hanzu? What are their roles and meanings? How do they relate to one another and to the *minzu* identity? In what analytical terms can we grasp *minzu* and other identity categories predominantly related to home place? Are they ethnic? Is the Han *minzu* an ethnic group? And finally, How can Hanzu seem so united in their Han-ness but at the same time be so fragmented and divided?

In order to discuss these questions, I explore narratives and discursive boundaries of Han-ness and then the boundaries that divide Hanzu into multiple, often mutually discriminating identity categories. In a majority of cases these categories are spatial, yet they exceed the conventional understanding of "native" place. I trace the meanings and roles of these identities, their relationships with the *minzu* identity, and the role of the state in determining these complex identity negotiations. Exploring the relationality of these various collective identities is necessary to understanding how the Han *minzu* is able to effectively accommodate such a great number of distinct identity groups.[5]

"The Han" as a Narration

Before moving on to an analysis of the research data, it is crucial to reflect on the very notion of being Han and the historical transformations of this identity. One of the central arguments of this study is that different eras have produced different categorical understandings of "the Han" as well as different "Han-nesses," or markers and enactments of the Han identity. Before the modern era of institutionalized, state-controlled, and state-enforced Han *minzu* as we know the category today, Han membership was more negotiable. Though Han-ness indisputably had boundaries in pre-modern China—*premodern* referring here most prominently to the Ming and Qing periods—these boundaries were relatively flexible. Han identity existed in an indistinct relationship with other identities such as Zhong-guo, Zhonghua, Xia, Hua, and Huaxia, all of which tend to be rendered in English as "Chinese." Moreover, territorial and lineage identities seem to have been much more significant for social mobilization, even if Han identity was meaningful in local contexts and likely provided some Han with a sort of community feeling beyond the more immediate kinship and place attachments.[6] Yet because the imperial biopolitical controlling mechanisms were limited, the boundaries of "the Han" could not have been set and guarded by state institutions to the degree possible today.[7] Imperial Han-ness was, accordingly, less regulated, and it likely claimed less of a person than nationalist-era identities. The increased capacity of the modern Chinese states—first the Republic of China and, in a much more pervasive way, the People's Republic of China (PRC)—effected an unprecedented institutionalization of Han-ness. It resulted in the reifica-tion of the Han category as a unitary and powerful national majority with a linear history of social and political consolidation. Since the turn of the twentieth century, the markers of Han-ness that both the first republic and the PRC relied on for projects of state and nation making have com-prised distinct products of the new nationalist symbolic order.

Because we can observe major changes in the ways Han-ness has been framed in the premodern and modern periods, I argue that, following the idea of nation as narration (Bhabha 1990; Anagnost 1997), "the Han" is a historically contingent narration dependent on those who "speak" it and on the ways in which they narrate it or imagine it (Anderson 1983). These narrations are generative in the sense that they generate the subject of which they speak; they are also historically contingent and creatively responsive to changing tasks and "others." Hence, most significantly, premodern and modern temporalities have produced different Han and distinct Han-nesses that have reflected contemporary understandings of the world. The premodern Han/Chinese were framed in terms of differentiation between culture and barbarism, and the premodern Han-ness/Chinese-ness was enacted with the help of certain rituals, family names, occupations, descent, genealogies, and customs (Watson 1988; Brown 1996; Ebrey 1996). The modern mode of Han narration has increased as a site of state intervention, with the Han imagined as a national majority that has developed in a linear process of historical growth. During the twentieth century, the Han became an institutionalized category (*minzu*), its boundaries guarded not only by members of the category itself but also by the state, an entity that depends on these very Han for the maintenance of social and territorial integrity. Still, although the mode of narration changed dramatically during the nationalism-motivated transition, my research shows that the roles assumed by the Han identity in individualized identity politics remain fragmented and diverse.

The Unity in Han-ness versus Fragmentation

Current representations in China tend to reify "the Han" as a coherent group that has evolved through millennia in a linear, progressive way to become the nation's core. While Western scholars of China have extensively discussed the impossibility of a linear history of "the Han" (e.g., Duara 1995; Elliott 2012), the Communist central governments have consistently represented the Han *minzu* as an outcome of a teleological process of national unfolding. In so doing, they have followed in the footsteps of early twentieth-century intellectuals and revolutionaries, individuals who created and popularized a vision of "the Han" as a unitary nation (*minzu*), with the intent to mobilize these very Han to rise against the Manchu of the last imperial dynasty of Qing.[8] Revolutionaries and nationalism-motivated intellectuals acted on a notion of the Han as a national community that originated from one ancestor (the legendary Yellow Emperor) and formed a singular, powerful national lineage.[9] The idea that the Han nation would become the backbone of the first postimperial state in China undergirded the Xinhai Revolution of 1911. As elsewhere in the world, nation building in China coincided with homogenizing attempts to create a national community, national history, national identity, national language, and national majority that would cement together the nation and the territory. Clearly, then, there is a strong state-related dimension of modern Han-ness. The Han category, in the form of a *minzu* as we know it today, is eventually the result of the massive state-driven biopolitical Minzu Classification Project launched in the 1950s. The Han *minzu* has since been officially shouldered with the role of national unifier, a narration specific to the process of nation and state making in twentieth-century China.

Although the Han *minzu* is a handy political category for nation- and state-making projects, the Han identity was not invented a century ago solely for nation-making purposes. Han-ness draws a significant part of its power from the local society and from the need for identification beyond the most immediate kinship and home-place community. It thus clearly predates any nation-making efforts. The reason that the identity is perpetuated has not changed: then and now, Han-ness—intertwined with Chinese-ness—has been maintained by the people who find it meaningful and useful in their fragmented identity politics. Though highly unstable in its scope and meaning, Han-ness/Chinese-ness was a significant identity in the pre-1911 period, widely utilized in negotiations on social positioning by those who identified with it in local as well as empirewide contexts.[10] Similarly, its meanings and roles today extend beyond national politics. Han-ness is a tangible and situationally important identity to people who are classified as Hanzu. My field observations demonstrate that this identity is also meaningful and viable to those who are excluded from this classification. However, this relationship is complicated by the fact that in contemporary China there are as many Han subject positions as there are people classified as Hanzu. Whereas certain ideas of "being Han" are common throughout China, the roles and meanings of this identity are fragmented and individualized by each Han in her and his identity negotiations. Han-ness concurrently exists in these two dimensions: as something private and enacted locally and as a link to state politics and state discourses (Harrell 2001, 295–96). Motivations for self-identification with Han-ness are fragmented, and the personal narratives collected during my fieldwork illustrate this. However, Han-ness also has a larger-than-individual dimension that links it directly to nation making, the official *minzu* policy, and the political discourse of ethnic diversity. Many of the Hanzu I talked with discussed not only how they feel as Han and what this identity offers them (or what it deprives them of) but also their awareness of how these state-generated and enforced dimensions of Han-ness influence their identity choices.

When discussed individually, Han-ness appears to be a powerful and meaningful identity. At the same time, the material collected proves that only by contrasting this identity with other collective identity categories can we contextualize its significance. Such contextualization helps reveal Han-ness for what it actually is, namely, one of a number of intertwined and relationally dependent collective identities relating to, among other things, ethnicity, nation, language, and place, between which Han individuals switch. Put differently, Han-ness is one component of complex topographies of identity. One of the central objectives of this study is therefore to demonstrate how the coherence of "the Han," as the category is conceived of and advertised by state institutions and by many Han themselves, disintegrates upon closer inspection, revealing multiple identity categories engaged in struggles over social positioning and control of both symbolic and tangible resources. Many of the identity categories that Han individuals put forth are related to home place. They are also constructed using more universal social boundaries—by dividing Urbanites and Ruralites, for instance, or Natives and Outsiders. These boundaries that divide the Hanzu are deep and multiple. On another level, Han-ness must also be contextualized in relation to the Chinese national identity—an identity even larger in scope and more inclusive. Some of my informants advocate Chinese-ness as a positive, egalitarian identity that incorporates *minzu* fragmentation and veils other social divisions. However, my observations in Beijing and Shanghai, as well as in China's multiethnic western borderlands, prove that both Han and people of other *minzu* have great difficulties in distinguishing between Han-ness and Chinese-ness. Chinese-ness seems too much like Han-ness to be a possible identity option for many non-Han people. A Uyghur man I became acquainted with in Xinjiang in 2011 perhaps best reflected this complex intertwining of Han and Chinese identities: he posited that China is not a Zhongguo (Central Country) but a Hanguo (Country of the Han).

To summarize, Han-ness has powerful competitors on the contemporary "identity market." These include home-place, occupational, and national identities that fragment or exceed Han-ness. In order to understand the complex topographies of collective identities, it is important to focus on the relationality and situationality of various identities, as well as their dependence on scales of social interaction. The notion of relationality highlights that Han-ness is merely one of many identities that people classified as Hanzu relate to, an identity entangled with others to form a mutually dependent network. When one identity is situationally mobilized, others become situationally less visible. In other circumstances, actors switch between identities relatively flexibly. Because the various identities have specific roles and relate to different scales of interaction, they are not mutually exclusive. Accordingly, one of the central arguments of this study is that the Hanzu, similar to many other large ethnic and even social groups, are concurrently united and fragmented. Each of many identity categories—Chinese, Han, Urbanite, Local, or Northerner, for example—actively creates and reifies categorical understandings of distinct "others." Because of this, such categories do not contradict one another. A Han can concurrently be a Hakka, a Zhejiang Person (by birth), a Beijing Person (by residence), a Chinese, a Ruralite, a Local, an Outsider, a Northerner, and a Southerner. Each of these identities is situationally meaningful, enacted vis-à-vis different "them," and has a specific social function. Depending on the situation, one or more identities will be activated. These identities are linked relationally and not in either-or terms, unless in instances of social and ethnic confrontation, when either-or discourses will likely prevail. Han-ness is thus perfectly compatible with other, even multiple, social, ethnic, and national identities. By assuming some of these identities the Han enact unity; by assuming others, fragmentation and division.

Home-Place Identities

The importance of home place (*jiaxiang, guxiang*)—rendered conventionally as "native place"—in Han topographies of identity is widely recognized by China scholars but has not been intensively explored within contemporary China studies (but see Honig 1992a; Leong 1997; and Xiang 2005). Thus, another major objective of this study is to explore the notion of home place and the attachments to it that contemporary Hanzu maintain.

Despite the past two decades of the extensive internal migration in China, the notion of home place and "home-place-determined mind-set" (*jiaxiang guannian*) remain critically important to the ways in which

Han individuals identify themselves and other Han. The majority of my informants described the centrality of home-place identities in their individualized identity systems. In contrast to Han-ness, home place was represented as more concrete, emotional, and familiar.

Still, as tangible and primordial as home-place identities feel to the Han, research results vividly demonstrate that the notion of home place is extremely unspecific and flexible. In a great majority of cases, Han individuals maintain attachments to multiple places they refer to as home. Some of these places are inherited (through either the patriline or matriline); others are based on the location of work or study or are connected to locations to which individuals feel bound through other personal experience. Han switch between these home-place identities situationally, depending on whom they confront. A person's birthplace (*chusheng di*), location of household registration, mother's or father's birthplace, ancestral home place, place of living, place of studying, spouse's place of living, and more were referred to as "home place" by my Han informants. Accordingly, home place, as it functions in contemporary China, is a *process* of negotiation between inherited, socially plausible, and individually desired place identities. Thus we must discuss the *politics* of home place and how places come to be claimed and practiced as "home." Some research participants fervently expressed that home place is assigned and unchangeable; others (though significantly fewer) argued the opposite with equal fervor. In social practice, when it fits a person's identity constellation and social-positioning strategies, a Han might emphasize her or his patrilineal ancestral home place and stress the primordiality and constancy of this identification. At other times, a Han may adopt different places as home. Additionally, because of the discrimination that results from association with some places, as well as a certain coerciveness of home-place identities, some Han reject the importance of home place entirely and turn instead to other social, ethnic, and national attachments. These Hanzu emphasize their identity as Han and Chinese, or they deny the importance of collective identities in general.

My research data confirm that place and particularly home-place attachments are strong and important for the Han. These attachments play the central role in identification and differentiation processes among the Han. At the same time, the data show that home place is an extremely flexible identity concept, lacking the stability ascribed to it in scholarly literature on China and by many Han themselves. While attachments to home place are surely emotional, some Han do not hesitate to switch between home-place attachments or to employ them purposefully and strategically. Furthermore, home place–related designations and stereotypes reveal social hierarchies of home places, where some are prestigious and socially privileged (large cities in general, Shanghai and Beijing in particular) and others (Henan, Subei, Sichuan, and Inner Mongolia more than others) provoke discrimination in the marital, job, and housing markets. Home place thus has significant influence on one's life chances. Because of this, despite the domination of primordial discourses, identity switching occurs often in practice, and competition and mutual discrimination take place to influence the positioning of "us" and to determine the positioning of "others."

In this research, home place emerges as a temporary, situational, and individually determined identity. The collected data demonstrate that many Han individuals feel attached to multiple home places and that a great variety of places may actually be referred to as "home." Obviously, every identity choice is restricted by its credibility to and recognition by both "us" and "them." Still, as one informant argued, the only time when individually constructed home-place identities lose their significance is when individuals confront state institutions. In these situations, it is solely the state-invented and enforced categories of *minzu* and household registration that matter for the categorization of an individual. Outside of this relationship, many options are open to skillful actors. The multiplicity, complexity, and intertwined nature of home places must be reflected in scholarly discussions of the potential of home place-related categorizations to oppose Han-ness and Chinese-ness and to possibly introduce political fragmentation (compare Gladney 1995). That many Han individuals have multiple home-place identities suggests rather that these have a centripetal effect, as each individual unites her or his attachments to a number of often distant regions, provinces, and cities. Moreover, although home place is important to how the Han identify themselves and other Han, the resulting identities should not be imagined as socially overwhelming. In numerous situations such identities will matter less than, for instance, being Chinese, Han, urban, or migrant. Or they will be concealed and downplayed to expose situationally more important axes of identification and differentiation.

Ethnicity, Degree, and Scale

The last major objective of this study is to explore whether Han *minzu* and other non-*minzu* identity categories to which Han express attachment (for instance Shanghai People, Urbanites, or Locals) are ethnic. Can we refer to these as ethnic groups? Are these processes of categorization and identification ethnic?

One conclusion is that the term *ethnic group* should not be introduced too early into analysis due on the one hand to its conceptual ambiguity and on the other to its reifying and objectifying power. Instead, locally pro duced identity categories that matter in everyday identification processes must be identified, as well as their mutual relationships and dependencies. In my research and the related literature, four generic terms manifest in many designations used by the Han to identify themselves and other Han: *minzu* (nationality, ethnic group, nation, as in Hanzu or *Zhonghua minzu*), *ren* (person, native of, as in Beijingren), *min* (people, a person of a certain occupation, as in Danmin), and *jia* (person, family, members of one family name group, as in Kejia).[11] *Ren, min,* and *jia* share the mean ing of "a person" or "people" and thus in some contexts are used inter changeably or form compounds, as in Hanzuren (Han Minzu Person) or Kejiaren (Kejia Person). At the same time, each of these terms has seman tically different connotations. *Ren* refers to identity as bound to locality, *jia* is kinship related, and *min* refers broadly to occupation. *Minzu*, on the other hand, belongs clearly to the nationalist symbolic order. It is critical to reflect on these semantic fields in order to understand the paradigms in which these identities are constructed and the ways in which they coexist.

Analysis of my research data suggests that ethnic and other social pro cesses of identification and categorization should be differentiated. While it is impossible to neatly disentangle these processes, they should be kept analytically separated as much as possible. In this way, we might avoid overextending the scope of ethnicity to cover all possible identifications, classifications, and exclusions. Moreover, this approach allows for more sensitivity to local forms of differentiation, forms that may be distinct from what Western scientific discourse defines as ethnicity or that may only partially or situationally overlap with this definition. The concepts "degree of ethnicity" and "transitory ethnicity" that I propose may be helpful in addressing this question.

Even though ethnic, national, and other social categorizations should be kept analytically distinct, ethnicity should not be turned into a stiff concept with neat, artificially drawn boundaries. The boundaries of ethnicity are obviously blurred. Thinking in terms of "degree of ethnicity" helps establish the flexibility of ethnicity without diminishing its meaningfulness. Although the size of the Han *minzu* demands respect and exceeds the scope of what scholars usually conceive to be ethnic, Han identity in this study emerges as ethnic to a much greater degree than non-*minzu* identities. Han identity is imagined as a historically evolved, given identity that binds people through common ancestors and shared destiny. As such, it can be explored using the theories and analytical instruments developed in the field of ethnic studies. At the same time, however, the Han *minzu* also has a clear national dimension. It is represented as the centerpiece of the Chinese nation and in some contexts as synonymous with Chinese-ness itself. Accordingly, it must also be examined with a nationalism-studies approach. That Han-ness appears *more* ethnic and national than the other collective identities maintained by the Hanzu is not accidental. Indeed, this draws attention to the fields of power in which these identities have been conceived and in which they operate. These fields of power determine which identity categories become a *minzu* or a nation and which are made into and represented as "regional" and "local." The state promotion of the Han *minzu* makes this identity very different regarding degree of "density," institutional recognition, and potential for mobilization. At the same time, the framing of non-*minzu* identities as "secondary" and "regional" symbolically indicates their ascribed place in the political order.

The second concept I propose, "transitory ethnicity," emphasizes the transient aspect of ethnicity, highlighting that social formations may become ethnic from time to time or may oscillate between being social and ethnic, as do many non-*minzu* attachments of the Hanzu. In regions where *minzu* "others" are not present in daily interactions, attachments to home place may emerge as transiently ethnic. In these contexts, the boundaries between Cantonese and Beijing People, but also between Urbanites and Ruralites or between Migrants and Locals, may become ethnicized for reasons of organization and mobilization. However, these forms of ethnicity weaken—though do not disappear—where their Han-ness, or Chinese-ness, is threatened, confronted, or mobilized. It is thus crucial to study these moments of confrontation and mobilization when individualized identity politics becomes explicitly entangled with ethnic and national discourses of belonging.

Han *minzu* identity on the one hand and home-place, occupational, and kinship-related identities on the other are parts of two distinct symbolic orders. While *minzu* originated in the nation-making projects of the late nineteenth century and was reinforced and invested with political importance during the project of Minzu Classification, other categories of identity originated with politics of differentiation that significantly predate these nation-making efforts.[12] As elsewhere in the world, the rise of nationalism in China introduced and induced new ways of categorizing the populace and was accompanied by large-scale homogenizing efforts to bridge prenationalist boundaries. *Minzu* is a product of this symbolic order of nationalism. *Ren*, *min*, and *jia*, on the other hand, are products and legacies of the prenationalist order. In the latter time period, significant regional and economic disparities were recognized and kinship played a central role in political, social, and economic organization. In this study I refer to these different symbolic orders as *scales*. The scale of occupational-, kinship-, and home place–based differentiation is inherently nonexclusive. This scale operates through multiple situationally activated identities. In contrast, the scale of *minzu* classification is a product of nation making; as such, it is discursively, if not always in practice, formulated in exclusionary, either-or terms.[13] Similarly, Chinese-ness is an identity that for Hanzu in mainland China is directly linked to state and citizenship and is located at yet another scale.[14] These scales are not hierarchical but coexist as parallel social dimensions belonging to different symbolic orders. Yet it is in the interest of the Chinese state to try to "verticalize" them and to ensure that, first, Han-ness prevails over the fragmented scale of non-*minzu* differentiations and, second, Chinese-ness prevails over *minzu*-related fragmentation.

RESEARCH LOCATION AND RESEARCH METHODS

The centerpiece of this book is material collected during field study in two major migrant destinations of Beijing and Shanghai between December 2002 and March 2003. Most of the direct quotes in this book are extracted from the almost one hundred semi-structured interviews I conducted in the two cities. Research participants came to Beijing and Shanghai from different locations, which allowed me to gather input on Han-ness detached from any specific locality. The majority of my interviewees came from urban areas in eastern and central China but some also arrived from distant regions such as Xinjiang, Guangxi, and Guangdong. Most had already experienced migration, either for work or studies, and quite a few had lived and worked in two or three other places before moving to Shanghai or Beijing for work or study. I obtained access to research participants through local contacts and notices that I posted at university campuses in both cities. Due to the nature of my project design, research participants were largely from my peer generation, between twenty and forty-five years of age. The informants were either students or university graduates. An overwhelming majority of research participants came to Beijing and Shanghai from other urban areas, and very few originated from rural families. Moreover, they all spoke fluent Putonghua, or standard Chinese (Mandarin).[15]

That this study's core interview material derives from predominantly urban, mobile, educated, and relatively young Putonghua speakers has important implications. This is especially true in terms of representations of rural Han and the urban-rural divide, the structure of individualized identity topographies (with multiple home-place identities), and the relatively small significance attached to local languages as a divisive factor. The relative mobility and young age of my research participants could imply that they are less rooted or, perhaps, that home-place identities matter less to them. Quite on the contrary, my data suggest that the experience of migration and leaving home actually made many of them more keenly aware of the importance of home-place attachments and the exclusionary and divisive discourses and practices that operate at the scale of place-based categorizations. Because all interviewees had at least fourteen years of state education—which particularly promotes the Han *minzu* and Chinese national identities—it can be expected that this schooling boosted participants' awareness of these identities. A population with fewer years of state education than my informants, then, may more strongly focus on "local," non-state-promoted identities. At the same time, siting research in Shanghai and Beijing—places where a *minzu* "other" is largely missing— likely enhanced the importance of Han-to-Han boundary-making processes. Had I conducted research in ethnic borderlands, the Han *minzu* identity would probably have been more prominent in identification and classification processes.

Semi-structured interviews constitute the core material from my research in Beijing and Shanghai. As I was interested in topographies of identity, narratives, and discourses, interviews emerged as the appropriate research tool. The interviews were "problem centered" (Flick 1998, 88–91), as I deliberately circled around the main issues of my study: identification, ascription, categorization, and differentiation. During an interview, which typically took two to three hours, my informant and I jointly wrote down on paper the responses to my questions. These sheets of paper lay between us on a table or desk. I found it important that research participants had control over and could correct what was written down. Moreover, when interviewees witnessed me writing down what they had just said, it made them more conscientious about what they were actually saying. This process also provided space for informants to reflect on their own opinions. Interviews were conducted primarily in standard Chinese, with the exception of two informants who insisted on speaking English. Much of the interview results are not directly referenced in this study, but they powerfully influenced my analysis and grounded many of my assumptions and interpretations.

Although my research in Beijing and Shanghai comprises the core of this study, the overall research context is much broader. My analysis is also based on data collected between February and July 1999, during ethnographic fieldwork in the village of Zuosuo, located in the multiethnic Yunnan-Sichuan borderlands, where the Han constituted a numerical minority. Through participant observation, semi-structured interviews, and short questionnaires, I collected material on interethnic relations and the position of the Han in this multiethnic village community. The material I collected importantly influenced my analysis of the data in the present study, especially in terms of the discourses of Han-ness and the ways they are transmitted across the country.

Finally, ten months of field research in 2011–12, primarily in the district of Aqsu in southern Xinjiang Uyghur Autonomous Region, also informed my analysis. Participant observation, hundreds of spontaneous conversations, and more than eighty semi-structured interviews illuminated identity politics and categorization processes among the Han living in Xinjiang, and also the interethnic relations between these different Han and the equally diverse Uyghur. This research significantly influenced my thinking about the importance of "scales" of interaction in identity processes, with the specific concept of "transitory ethnicity" being directly related to my research in Xinjiang. The major implication is that I may have reached different conclusions in the present study had I collected research data in an area less affected by violence and divisive identity discourses.

My aim during research in Shanghai and Beijing, cities to which Han migrate from all over China, was to collect data on Han-ness that would not be bound to any specific local community. The data from Zuosuo and Xinjiang add important localized insights to this material. Indeed, they illuminate interesting parallels and divergences between how Han-ness is articulated in Han-dominated locations of eastern China, an area where Han constitute a minority, and in western China, a region where Han have significant *minzu* "others." These data offer interesting insights into processes of categorization, identification, ascription, inclusion, exclusion, social positioning, and discrimination. With the combined interview data and observations of categorization processes in Shanghai and Beijing, Zuosuo and southern Xinjiang, I believe this book will provide valuable insights to the developing field of critical Han studies.

CHAPTER 1

NARRATING "THE HAN"

The premodern or imperial period in Chinese history, which ended in the late nineteenth century, and the modern, nationalist period that succeeded it needed and created different forms of "the Han" and different meanings of Han-ness. Despite some continuities, these two historical eras differ significantly with regard to how the Han category was imagined and how it functioned on local and statewide levels, highlighting its temporal variability and instability. In addition to variability in time, Han-ness has also been spatially fragmented. In the imperial era as well as today, various local communities have uniquely created their own Han markers and creatively explored the capacities of this identity. This variability, instability, and fragmentation contrasts with teleological attempts to narrate the Han as an evolutionarily developed category and with the linear narrations of national history (compare Duara 1995; Harrell 1996a, 4–5).

The contemporary category of Han *minzu* is not a product of an evolutionary development but an invention of the genealogization and nationalization processes initiated in the nineteenth century. However, Han identity—intertwined to be sure with Hua, Huaxia, and Zhongguo-ren identities—existed long before the rise of Han and Chinese nationalisms and is not a modern invention. The entangled nature of Han-ness has yielded diametrically opposed conceptualizations within and outside China. Organic, teleological, and diachronic representations have been suggested, most prominently by Fei Xiaotong (1989) and Xu Jieshun in his monumental 1999 work *Snowball: An Anthropological Analysis of Han Nationality* (Xueqiu: Hanzu de renleixue fenxi).[1] At the same time, Han-ness has been discussed in Western scholarship as an "invented tradition," an "empty" identity existing solely as an "other" to so many "minority nationalities" represented as particular, colorful, backward, and sexually exotic (Gladney 1991, 1994; Schein 2000).

This book proposes that Han-ness is neither an outcome of a consistent linear process of organic evolution nor solely an "other" of the minor *minzu*.[2] While contrasting with minority "others" is essential to the negotiation of Han identity at the scale of inter-*minzu* interactions, my data demonstrate that Han-ness means more to Han individuals than "being ordinary" or simply "not being a minority." Individual Han in their fragmented identity negotiations perpetuate this collective identity by investing it with locally significant meanings. The fictionality of a linear history of "the Han" does not make Han-ness less meaningful to Han individuals, nor to non-Han "others." In China's multiethnic borderlands, Han-ness is an identity that clearly matters in daily inter-*minzu* interactions. Although Han-ness loses some of its strength and becomes fragmented by other identification paradigms at the scale of Han-to-Han interactions, it is definitely not an "empty" identity.

At the same time, it is necessary to recognize the major historical shifts in the framing of Han-ness. The identity has been historically contingent, and administrative regimes have tried, with varying success, to determine its meaning and its scope. The Han signifier has obviously referred to different categories of people in different dynastic periods. The historical analysis in the present study focuses principally on the Ming (1368–1644) and Qing (1644–1911) dynastic periods, when the scope of Han denomination began to resemble that of today. In stark contrast to the preceding Yuan dynasty (1279–1368), the Ming meaning of the Han signifier included both southern and northern Chinese.[3] Beyond the historical instability of the Han category, major differences in the narration and "density" of Han-ness/Chinese-ness between the premodern and modern temporalities merit consideration. Significant differences in technologies of rule and claims to—but also capacity to—control the population resulted in different efficacies of the imperial and modern political regimes to control the boundaries of the Han category. Parallel to such administrative efforts, decentralized and localized attempts to determine the content and roles of Han-ness have occurred too and have had major influence on articulations of Han-ness.

HISTORICAL CONTINGENCY OF THE HAN CATEGORY AND HAN IDENTITY

The Han category derives its name from the Han dynasty (206 BCE–220 CE), which gained power over the unified Chinese empire after the short Qin rule (221–206 BCE). In the imperial tradition, the Han denomination applied not only to the dynasty itself but also to its subjects and did not vanish after the demise of the dynasty. The name continued to be used in some contexts for and by the subjects of later dynasties, along with earlier names such as Xia and Hua and subsequent dynastic names such as Sui, Tang, or Song. The Han identifier was unstable between the sixth and fifteenth centuries (Elliott 2012); at times and in some areas it was used in similar contexts like Zhongguoren (People of Central Lands, Chinese), and at other times it referred to categories of people divided by administrative borders of competing kingdoms. In the history of "Han-becoming," nomadic and seminomadic peoples north of the Central Plains played a key role in the fourth century in initiating the shift in the meaning of Han away from a dynastic designation to something of an ethnonym (Elliott 2012). Under the Mongols, the Han identifier was used to refer to one of the four classes of people into which Mongol rulers divided their subjects. Including the Mongols, who occupied the highest place in this hierarchy, these were Semuren (People of Various Categories, including other Central Asians, Europeans, and Muslims), Hanren (Han People, including northern Han/Chinese, Koreans, Khitan/Qidan, and Jurchen/Nüzhen), and Nanren (Southerners, referring to Han/Chinese and non-Han groups in southern China) (Gladney 1991, 18; Weng 2001).[4]

In contrast, the Ming employed "Han" as an inclusive designation for inhabitants of both northern and southern Chinese provinces, areas divided for two to three hundred years prior between different political regimes. The Ming are thus largely responsible for the popularization of Han as an empirewide identifier (Elliott 2012). Still, although the purview of the Han identifier came to resemble that of today, "Han" held a very different meaning, devoid of the racial overtones it acquired in the late nineteenth century with the introduction of the terms *zu* (racial lineage) and *minzu* (nation). Moreover, apparently even under the Qing, the Han identity was not the most often evoked one, not even in the multiethnic borderlands of Yunnan where the presence of "barbarian others" would seem to favor such identification (Giersch 2012, 191–209). On the contrary, until the nineteenth century, home-place identities were evoked most often for the purpose of identification. Only in the nineteenth century, in an interplay of empirewide and local developments, did the relationship between the unifying notion of Han-ness and home-place identities begin to reshuffle. The Manchu's increasing reliance on genealogies to differentiate themselves from Han subjects was one important impetus to this process. Growing connectivity, circulation, and mobility throughout the empire made up another.

The second half of the nineteenth century was a critical time in the transformation of Chinese culturalism into racialized nationalism, resulting in the formulation of a racially exclusionary understanding of the Han/Chinese nation (Dikötter 1996). Numerous studies demonstrate that Han-ness/Chinese-ness were meaningful in premodern China; to be identified as such was particularly advantageous in local power struggles.[5] Yet these identities were not compatible with the notion of the Han/Chinese nation put forth by Sun Yat-sen and other nationalism-motivated revolutionaries.[6] In his lectures, Sun repeatedly complained that the Han/Chinese lacked a national identity, that they were a "sheet of loose sand."[7] Reformulation and reinforcement of the Han/Chinese identity thus became a primary task for the revolutionaries. They set out to achieve this aim through inventing a legendary common ancestor of "the Han" (the Yellow Emperor), as well as by creating new national symbols and a national history.[8] In order to morally construct the revolution against the Manchu Qing, who had continued to cultivate many traditions associated with Chinese-ness, the revolutionary party strived to create a clear boundary between the Han and Manchu through constructing a racial distinction between the unitary Han race (*zhongzu, renzhong, zhong, zu*) and the race of the oppressive Manchu (Mullaney 2011, 23–24). By contrasting "the Han" with this powerful "other," especially in the pre-1912 period, the revolutionaries hoped that Han/Chinese, fragmented along strong kin and place identities, would begin to imagine themselves as one national community bound by a unitary national identity. However, despite the determination of the revolutionaries, and the later Communist Minzu Classification Project that further naturalized the Han *minzu* as a unitary national majority, Han-ness remains intertwined with other collective attachments related to, among other things, place, livelihood, occupation, and nation.[9]

Because Han-ness has been framed differently in various historical settings, has been fragmented and intertwined with other identities, and has been claimed by or denied to various groups, it is not possible to talk about "the Han" as a product of one continuous historical tide. Nonetheless, such linear histories thrive in Chinese governmental publications and in academic discourse. Xu Jieshun (2012, 118) offers an example of this narrative, arguing, "Like all concrete objects in the universe, all of which have origins followed by histories of formation, evolution, and development, the Han nationality underwent a similar process of formation, evolution, and development, during which its plurality gradually coagulated into a unity." Although the present study and other related scholarship posit that Han-ness is not a product of a consistent historical growth, Han-ness continues to be imagined as such by contemporary Han. Though de facto constructed and fragmented, it is today a primordially framed identity, just as it was in the communities that identified with it in the past. In this sense, Han-ness is both a new and an old identity. As a collective identifier, it has a long history; yet who was Han and what it meant to be Han has drastically differed from one historical frame to another, and from one location to another. Given, then, that its scope, meaning, and roles continue to shift, Han-ness is also a new and continuously reinvented identity.

The tools, instruments, narratives, functions, institutional backing, distribution mechanisms, and mechanisms controlling the meaning and boundaries of Han-ness changed dramatically in the twentieth century. Once conceptualized as a borderless "all under heaven" (*tianxia*), ruled by a moral ruler who was expected to follow his "way" (*dao*), the empire was much less omnipresent and pervasive than the modern state. The relatively fragmented nature of imperial control can be attributed to several factors, including slow communication channels, isolation from power centers, a heterogeneous administrative system (with vast non-Han regions of the empire ruled indirectly by ethnic chiefs), and the nonexistence of mass media. The empire did not possess the same penetrating power that modern states, and the modern Chinese state in particular, exercise over their citizens. Moreover, in the premodern period, Han-ness was only tenuously linked to a territory understood as a concretely delineated place.[10] This differs clearly from late nineteenth-and early twentieth-century China, when the link between Han-ness and the territorial state (*guo*) began to be massively promoted. Han-ness in the premodern and the modern periods must thus by definition be different. Without the pervasive power of the modern state, the unifying power of state institutions, and modern communication and governing technologies, Han-ness in imperial times could never achieve the degree of "density" and internal connectivity that it has today. An examination of these temporal lines of differentiation will help provide a foundation for the analysis of contemporary Han-ness.

PREMODERN HAN-NESS

What constituted Han-ness was subject to much change and contestation in the prenational period, including what the Han identifier implied and how it functioned locally—who self-identified as Han, who was identified as Han by others, who was denied Han-ness and for what reasons. Alternating between intertwined and distinct, Han-ness and Chinese-ness (represented by historical identifiers such as Zhongguoren, Xia, Hua, Huaxia, and the contemporary *Zhonghua minzu*, the "Chinese nation") continue to complicate historical analysis (Elliott 2012).[11] Moreover, when compared with the present day, premodern Han-ness appears to be a much more open identity category (Harrell 2001, 320).[12] Indeed, Han-ness historically could be acquired by assuming behaviors associated with this identity and by "documenting" descent from Han ancestors.[13] Hence, who identified as Han was rather flexible, even if identity choices were restricted by the recognition of these identities as socially plausible by both other "us" and other "them." The institutions that today create the impression of neat *minzu* identity boundaries in Communist China were missing from the premodern era; as such it is virtually impossible to draw a clear semantic boundary between the notions of Han-ness and Chinese-ness. This is compounded by the fact that these two English terms disintegrate into numerous designations in the Chinese language, designations that never had institutions to guard their consistent usage. These terms and these identities wander through history, at times united and at others times and locations distinct. Thus, in the analysis below, I do not artificially separate them; rather, I use Han-ness and Chinese-ness in an intertwined way to reflect their interpenetrations. When other scholars are quoted, I employ the identifiers they use. Observing how scientific naming conventions shift over time adds yet another critical dimension to this terminological complexity.

Markers of Premodern Han-ness

Much like contemporary Han-ness, premodern Han-ness/Chinese-ness was characterized by concurrent coherence and fragmentation. Through channels of imperial bureaucracy, as well as by population mobility motivated by sojourning, pilgrimage, and trade (Duara 1993, 7), some markers of Han-ness/Chinese-ness were distributed across the empire (e.g., the sequence of mortuary rituals [Watson 1993], or adherence to Confucian morality). At the same time, those who identified themselves as Han were divided by the boundaries of home place, lineage, occupation, family names, settlement patterns, migration histories, purported ancestors, language, and more. Each of these elements may have at one time been framed as more or less Han and thus more or less "cultured." Eventually, the most powerful groups usually determined locally what Han-ness was and then claimed the identity for themselves.[14] Similar to today, Han-ness in premodern China was an object of social bargaining. Through its intrinsic link to institutionalized power,[15] Han-ness/Chinese-ness offered resources to draw upon in struggles for social positioning and was thus an important stake in many local settings.[16] Belonging to the Han/Chinese world was made socially attractive through the category's claimed cultural superiority over the "uncultured" ones who lived beyond the boundaries of civilization. Given its advantages, some not-yet Han attempted to acquire Han identity in order to access the material and symbolic resources it offered (Brown 2004). In other situations, some Han/Chinese found it equally advantageous to assume non-Han identities, particularly when living in imperial borderlands under ethnic chiefs.[17] That identity switches in premodern China were much less restricted than today, however, does not mean that boundaries between the Han/Chinese and their "others" were insignificant in identification and categorization processes. Rather, premodern Chinese-ness emerged from an inherent tension. On the one hand, it was an inclusionary identity acquired by assuming certain markers. On the other hand, it derived from an intrinsic distinction between the "cultured" Han (or Huaxia, Hua, Zhongguoren) and the "barbarian" Yi (Leibold 2007, 22).

Drawing on studies conducted by historians, it appears that some Han markers were more universal and widely practiced, while others were local and meaningful only in specific communities. To accurately contrast contemporary markers of Han-ness with imperial-era markers of Han-ness/Chinese-ness, I turn now to some of these earlier markers. This discussion is not meant as a complete list of Han-ness/Chinese-ness boundaries in the premodern period. Rather, the discussion signals the complexity and multidimensionality of this identity that combined elements of descent with ideas of culturally negotiated belonging. The primary objective of identity markers was to draw the boundary between the Han/Chinese, who were imagined as cultured, and "others," who were imagined as exactly opposite. This practice of juxtaposition is at the heart of all ethnic and national boundary-making processes. While ethnicity in the premodern period was not affected by the institutions and penetrating presence characteristic of the modern Chinese state, the very processes of boundary making and maintenance were basically the same. Any "us" requires "them" for the purpose of identification; thus, the active reproduction of boundaries between "the Han" and their "others" has been a universal process, one not limited to the nineteenth- and twentieth-century nationalist transformations. Still, the identifiers, vocabulary, and images framing the Han/Chinese identity do differ.

At the heart of premodern notions of Han-ness was Confucianism-influenced imagery, which contrasted culture and refinement—associated with Han-ness/Chinese-ness—with wildness and primitiveness, or everything beyond the limits of Han/Chinese culture (Dikötter 1992, 2–3). This differentiation is vividly reflected in the designation of the Han dynasty's policy toward the non-Han as the "policy of reins and bridle" (*jimi zhengce*). Sima Qian's *Records of the Historian* (Shiji) reports that "four kinds of savages are governed by reins and bridle like the cattle" (Zhi si Yi ru niuma zhi shou jimi) (Gong 1992, 1).[18] Although not bound to any strictly delineated territory, the Chinese understanding of culture was inherently spatial by the late Zhou/early Han dynastic periods and imagined as a series of concentric squares.[19] The central square was occupied by the imperial domain (the so-called Jiuzhou, or "Nine Prefectures"), and territories further from this imaginary center were believed to be inhabited by uncultured "savages." These "savages" were distinguished by the Han/Chinese according to criteria of distance from "the center," cardinal directions based around the center, and degree of civilization as judged in relation to the center. The most distant populations were referred to as *wai* (outside), while those living closer to the center were *nei* (inside). The savages in the inside zone were further divided into *sheng* (raw, unfamiliar, uncultured) and *shu* (cooked, familiar, more cultured), depending on their perceived degree of integration to Han life ways, as discussed below. The "barbarians" were further divided as compass points into the Di (northern), Man (southern), Rong (western) and Yi (eastern) (Eberhard 1942; Müller 1980, 54–61; Heberer 1989, 17–18). Already by Sima Qian's time, however, the term Yi was applied as a more general label referring to non-Han/Chinese at the southwestern borders of the empire. It was also used as a broader identifier similar in meaning to the later term Fan, and sometimes it was combined with Fan, as in Fanyi.

Although the external wild space was believed to be populated by semi-human "savages," these were nevertheless viewed by some Han as potentially civilizable. This civilizing process was referred to as either *laihua* (transformation by proximity), Hanhua (Hanification), or *yong Xia bian Yi* (lit., "transformation of Yi savages by the ways of the Xia"). While scholars rightly argue that the theory of sinicization is largely a myth—one as willingly transmitted by the Han as by Western sinologists—the broad differentiation into cultured versus wild space, the contrasting of Han (or Hua, Huaxia, Zhongguoren) and Yi, and the belief in the transforming power of Han culture all offered handy tools for redrawing the boundaries around Han-ness/Chinese-ness and for constructing the ideas of cultural and political superiority.[20] In localized communities, this juxtaposition of culture and wildness was rendered graspable through mundane markers that directly referenced the lives of those who zealously communicated this identification.

Family names (*xing*) constituted a powerful marker of Chinese-ness and culture long before the Ming era (Ebrey 1996). Access to family names, especially monosyllabic family names, was limited by imperial law.[21] Theoretically, only the inhabitants of the imperial domain had family names, while the "uncultured" were referred to using general terms for whole groups or were given names that reflected the sound of their foreign self-denominations. Such general terms comprised character components such as "grass" and "dog" to emphasize these people's nonsedentary lifestyles and purported wildness (Müller 1980, 60–61; Thierry 1989, 78).[22] However, family names could also be acquired. One way to do so was through military service to the emperor. Many non-Han leaders accepted Han family names on the strength of imperial decrees. Such "convert" families would seek out alliances with Han/Chinese lineages that shared the same family name, thereby reinforcing their newly acquired identity (Eberhard 1962, 199–200). Clearly, then, the boundary drawn by limited access to family names was not very rigid. Also, the Han were never endogamous; as such, intermarriage was a popular means of entering the Han family-name groups (Yuan and Zhang 2002, 6–7).[23] Manipulations of genealogies, changes in the form of family names (from double to monosyllabic), and the invention of Han/Chinese ancestors were additional ways by which non-Han entered the Han family-name system.

Patrilineal descent from Han/Chinese ancestors as demonstrated through genealogies was a key claim to belonging to the cultured world. Even more than family names, this marker was clearly prone to reinvention. For instance, in genealogies from the Song period (960–1279), hardly anyone admitted descent from non-Han people in China's South (Ebrey 1996, 23), though such descent was highly probable. The altar with ancestral tablets—"evidence" of patrilineal descent from Han/Chinese ancestors—served to claim a legitimate place within the sphere of culture.[24] It was desirable for a lineage to have an ancestral home place within the Central Plains of northern China, where the first dynastic states came into being. A home place in the North made for an important stake in power negotiations, especially in southern China. Thus, powerful southern lineages deliberately traced their origins "back" to the northern plains in their genealogies, whether the connection was invented, actual, or both.

Rituals and beliefs were other markers that signaled belonging to the Han/Chinese world. It has been argued that in the late imperial and early modern eras, orthopraxy, or the form of rituals practiced, was shared by Chinese throughout the empire (Watson 1993, 87–89; Cohen 1994, 93). For instance, the funerary rites of Chinese elites and commoners were identical in basic structure, implying that the proper sequence of rites, or "anxiety over the practice of rituals," was central to people's validity as Chinese (Watson 1993, 87–89).[25] This arguably allowed for the creation of a basic unitary ritual system across the empire that at the same time retained local elements. In a similar vein, some scholars have argued that observing "forms" was always of central importance in the patriarchal and strongly hierarchical society of imperial China (Fei 1992, 132). As it was not morally permitted to rise against tradition and superiors in the social hierarchy, the only way for those within the hierarchy to subvert it was to continue in the forms while changing the content. The importance of forms or rituals (*li*), also translated as "propriety," "etiquette," or "proper behavior," extended far beyond funerary or life-cycle rites; indeed, rituals regulated virtually the whole world of social relationships.[26] The *Analects of Confucius* (*Lunyu* 1994), compiled by the disciples of Confucius around the fourth century BCE, repeatedly refer to the superiority of ritual, propriety, and etiquette over personal expression.[27]

Beginning in the second century BCE, the dynastic governments issued instructions for how to conduct rituals properly. With the help of other popular books such as *Family Rituals*, written by Zhu Xi in the twelfth century, the scholarly and bureaucratic elite successfully shaped popular practice (Harrison 2001, 24–25). Still, although properly performed rites were integral to late imperial Chinese-ness, the Chinese also shared common beliefs (Rawski 1988, 23–32). These included a belief in the absence of radical dualism of body and soul, characteristic of Chinese culture from at least the Bronze Age, and a belief in multiple souls, registered at least since the Han dynastic period. Moreover, imperial-era Chinese shared beliefs about the continuity of kinship links between the living and dead. Ancestors were believed to be capable of mediating with deities on behalf of their descendants. This translated into a broadly practiced cult of ancestors, despite the imperial ban on ancestral cults among commoners until the Song era (Rawski 1988, 29–30; Zheng 2001, 270–77).

The boundary between "culture" and "wildness," and thus between Han/Chinese and non-Han/Chinese, was also constructed and maintained through customs such as foot binding. In Taiwan, by the twentieth century, foot binding was "the most salient marker" that distinguished Han and aboriginal women (Brown 1996, 62). Other aspects of easier to attain Han-ness/Chinese-ness were also adopted on the island from Han/Chinese migrants and officials. Huang Shujing, a Chinese official who visited Taiwan in 1722, observed that some Chinese clothing, especially embroidered robes, had become popular among village headmen as a status symbol (Harrison 2001, 26). Fashion was also extensively used by mainland Han/Chinese in identity negotiations in the Ming, Qing, and Republican eras, as well as in Communist China (Finnane 2008). For instance, revision of Han fashions was an important element of Zhu Yuanzhang's (1328–98) attempts to rid the Ming empire of the "barbarian ways" of the preceding Mongol Yuan dynasty. These efforts included the campaign to abandon close-fitting tunics favored by the Mongols and return to the style of the Tang. Although the campaign was partially successful, the influence of northern peoples on clothing worn by the Han/Chinese proved difficult to eliminate (Finnane 2008, 44–48).

Wedding customs were additional opportunities to perform the distinction between Han and non-Han. For example, wealthy eighteenth-century Cantonese families often delayed the transfer of the bride to the groom's house. This custom was used to emphasize their Han-ness, in contrast to Boat People, who practiced an immediate transfer of the bride. At the same time, this "Han custom" would have been a shocking example of barbarism to the Han/Chinese in the North, who practiced the transfer of the bride as an integral part of the wedding ceremony (Harrison 2001, 31). Interestingly, the delayed transfer of the bride has a striking resemblance to the marriage practices of the contemporary Yao and She in Guangdong. Some southwestern non-Han peoples, including some Yi, also practice a delayed bride transfer (Stevan Harrell, personal communication, 2014; Harrison 2001). Thus, in an ironic twist, what was likely a non-Han/Chinese custom was adopted by those who claimed to be Han/Chinese and used as a marker of this identity. As evidenced by this example, while some customs and rituals were relatively universal and adhered to by Han from various social groups and geographical locations, others were invented and made meaningful only locally. In this sense, Han-ness was and remains both a local identity that has to be made locally meaningful through salient symbols and associations, and an identity that extends beyond the local community through its link to bureaucratic power.

The Confucianism-driven emphasis on writing and literature (*wen*) as central elements of Han culture (*wenhua*, lit., "process of becoming transformed into a literate being") also exercised fundamental influence on the idea of Han-ness. Non-Han/Chinese could assume some central markers of Han-ness by learning to write Chinese characters, read, compose poetry and essays, and recite Confucian classics. Although literacy alone did not make them Han/Chinese, it did facilitate links to Han/Chinese families and further socialization into this identity. From the perspective of twentieth-century nationalism-inspired intellectuals, the Han/Chinese script (Hanzi, Zhongwen) and its extensive body of literature were critical to the constructing of an unbroken continuum of "the Han," beginning with the first mythical ancestors and leading to the contemporary Han *minzu*.[28] In one scholar's account, the Chinese writing system "has bridged the past, present, and future of the Han, enabling this nationality to systematically record their entire history in documents written in Chinese characters" (Xu 2012, 120). Practices of glossing, citations, and "appropriation" of earlier terms by later commentators have been crucial in constructing this history (Chin 2012). Such efforts have helped create an impression of a historical movement as "produced only by antecedent causes rather than by complex transactions between the past and the present" (Duara 1995, 4).

From yet another angle, Han/Chinese script and literature contributed greatly to the constructing of "the Han" as a linguistic community, in spite of the extreme diversity of spoken languages. Since the Qin-era unification of script in the third century BCE, the Chinese script has arguably been one of the "most efficient instruments of political unification" (Gernet 1988, 37–39). A common written language certainly played a unifying role, especially among the Han bureaucratic elites recruited through the system of imperial examinations and appointed to positions in the centralized bureaucracy (Harrison 2001, 11).[29] Even if they were likely at first a class marker and not a universal marker of Han-ness, characters and written language as important Han/Chinese signifiers increased as the number of literate people grew. Currently, as my research data demonstrate, the script is one of the most often evoked symbols of Han-ness. Yuan and Zhang (2002, 7) argue that "without Chinese/Han script [Hanzi] there would be no Han." At the very least, it would be much more difficult to construct the Han category's temporal continuity.

Occupation was also a marker of premodern Han-ness/Chinese-ness. Occupations could be classified as more or less cultured and, accordingly, more or less Han/Chinese. The cultured way to live and work was to become a learned official, peasant, or artisan (Eberhard 1962). Pastoral and nomadic ways of living were disrespected; indeed, pastoralism as a lifeway was generally ascribed to "barbarians" (Thierry 1989, 76–78), likely due to its incompatibility with the Han/Chinese ideas of filial piety, territorial lineages, burial, and ancestral worship. Sea-bound occupations were also viewed negatively, for these jobs occurred in the liminal space between land and the sea, imagined as the realm of evil spirits. Han who engaged in pastoral and sea-bound occupations were regarded as "less Han," less human, and more barbarian. The Boat People (Danmin) of Guangdong, Fujian, and Guangxi are among the best studied of these categories. Although nominally Han, the Boat People—the majority of whom relied on the sea as their main source of income[30]—were excluded from imperial examinations and ascribed a much lower social status by Hakka, Hokkien, and Punti who inhabited the same areas.[31] The degree of separateness between Boat People and other groups in southern China's coastal areas was sufficient for some Boat People to apply for status as a distinct *minzu* in the 1950s. Following a 1954 field study conducted by a group of Chinese ethnologists, however, their application was rejected. Boat People then became "reconfirmed" in their Han-ness, together with the Punti, Hakka, and Hokkien, who had discriminated against them (Wang, Zhang, and Hu 1998, 120–21).

The Boat People were one of the groups involved in the empirewide division of dynastic subjects into the categories of *jianmin* (demeaned people, déclassé) and *liangmin* (commoners, decent people), categories to a great degree based on occupational specialization. "Decent people" consisted of landlords, farmers, craftsmen, and merchants. "Demeaned people," on the other hand, were associated with low or despised occupations; at least some of them were former slaves (Eberhard 1962). The déclassé, though Han, were legally excluded from participation in imperial exams and were registered as distinct from decent people. Even after they were emancipated from legal discrimination by a decree of Emperor Yongzheng in 1723, the demeaned people were socially discriminated against as "barbarian" well into the twentieth century.[32] Regarded as improper, their ways of earning a living excluded them from Han-ness by those who had the power to claim Han-ness for themselves and were in a need of an "other" to make their claims viable.

The premodern and modern periods have been characterized by significant differences in technologies of rule and capacity to control the boundaries of Han-ness/Chinese-ness. Although the imperial Han/Chinese marked the boundaries of their identity through family names, rituals, occupations, patrilineal descent, and certain customs, access to this identity group was institutionally restricted to a much lesser extent than in contemporary China. "Others" could typically try to assume some of the markers of Han-ness and strive to be recognized in this new identity by other Han. Clearly, then, before today's institutionalized Han-ness, membership in the category was more negotiable. Moreover, it appears that locality bonds, occupation, and territorial lineage identities were not only much more powerful but also much more salient than Han-ness as organizing principles among the Han/Chinese in the premodern period (Fei 1980, 1992; Lin 1998). Even into the Republican period (1912–49), for instance, home-place identities had a tremendous impact on the self-organization of Han migrants in larger cities (Naquin and Rawski 1987; Goodman 1992; Cole 1996). Hence, while Han-ness/Chinese-ness was certainly a meaningful identity that played an important role in processes of social and ethnic inclusion and exclusion, it coexisted with other powerful collective identities, including territorial and kin identities that were arguably more immediate and overwhelming. Also, because the reach of imperial control was limited, the boundaries of Han-ness could not be set and guarded by state institutions to the extent they are today, where almost every Chinese citizen has a personal ID that states her or his *minzu*. Imperial Han-ness was not only less regulated, total, and institutionalized than contemporary Han-ness; it also had a much smaller capacity as a paradigm of mobilization.

In the early twentieth century, the rise of the idea of a modern Chinese state effected a differentiation between the previously intertwined identity labels of Han and Chinese (Zhongguoren). With the formation of the first republic, the two categories began drifting apart in official political discourse but were never completely untangled. The Han category became one of the five major racial lineages (*zu*) that were expected to join their territories to form the first Republic of China. Besides the Han, these were the Manchu, Tibetans, Mongols, and the various Muslim groups subsumed under the term Hui. The term Zhongguoren (Chinese), on the other hand, gradually expanded in scope and, similar to *Zhonghua minzu* (Chinese nation), came to signify the national community of Chinese citizens.[33] This came to include the five major races as well as other non-Han groups who inhabited the extensive territory of the new Republican state.

MODERN HAN-NESS

The shift from culturalism to racialized nationalism, a shift that transformed the Han category from relatively open and inclusive to more exclusive, began gathering momentum in the second half of the nineteenth
century. The change followed the increasing reification of genealogies as
the central element of Manchu identity by the ruling Manchu dynasty.
While genealogies and ancestry as significant markers of Manchu identity were already being explored by the Manchu in the mid-eighteenth
century, in the second half of the nineteenth century, and paralleling the
rise of Han nationalism, the notion of genealogical descent expanded to
include the Manchu as a group, not as individual lineages (Crossley 1987,
1999).[34] Collective descent became the central component of a process that
contrasted the Han and the Manchu for the sake of identity building in
each of these two categories.[35] It was during the Taiping War (1851–64)
that the term *zu* (lineage) was introduced by the Taiping to refer to the
umbrella categories of Manchu, Han, and Mongols (Crossley 1997, 189;
Lipman 1996, 108–9). Still, in the reformist writings from the pre-1898
period, the social Darwinism–inspired rhetoric of the racial war between
the white and yellow races—with the Han and Manchu struggling jointly
as the yellow race against the white imperial powers—dominated how the
need for political change was articulated. The differentiation between the
Han and "Manchu oppressors" blamed for bringing about the demise of
"China" emerged more clearly only after the 1898 Hundred Days Reform.
In the wake of the failed reform, the rhetoric of the yellow and white races
was abandoned by the revolutionaries in favor of a more specific descent-
based distinction between the Han and Manchu (Chow 2001, 55).

 In order to construct the "national" (Han) revolution against "foreign"
powers (both Western imperialists and Manchu), diversified cultural
Han-ness had to be channeled into a more explicit and cohesive form. The
bond of and with Han-ness needed to be reformulated and reinforced;
accordingly, new terms, symbols, images, and rituals were invented to
focus people's attention on this identity. Although Han identity underwent some transformations during the late Qing era, the Han were still
far from the coherence that Sun Yat-sen and other revolutionaries deemed
necessary to become qualified as a nation. Han-ness was meaningful in
local settings, but it was not particularly compatible with the ideal of a

nation that Sun and others cherished, one defined in racial terms as a community of descent linked through common livelihood, spoken language, religion, customs, and habits.[36] To Sun, the existing attachment to Han-ness was insufficient for national mobilization. In many of his lectures, he complained about this unsatisfactory national unity: instead of a sense of a shared national past and future, the Han were fragmented by "clanism" and "native place sentiments."[37] Still, Sun viewed these territorial and kin attachments with possibility; they could constitute a useful foundation out of which a stable national community would grow quickly:

> If we are to recover our lost [sic] nationalism, we must have some kind of group unity, large group unity. An easy and successful way to bring about the unity of a large group is to build upon [the] foundation of small united groups, and the small units we can build upon in China are the clan groups and also the family groups. The "native place" sentiment of the Chinese is very deep-rooted too; it is especially easy to unite those who are from the same province, prefecture or village. . . . If we take these two fine sentiments as a foundation, it will be easy to bring together the people of the whole country. (Sun, n.d., 31–32)

The revolutionaries employed a variety of strategies to create a new, appropriate national identity for "the Han." Zhang Binglin was one of the first to recognize the need to establish the historicity of the Han in order to construct them successfully vis-à-vis the Manchu. In order to do this, Zhang elaborated the notion of Han as a racial lineage, expanding the concept of lineage to comprise all Han as constituting a descent group bound by blood and stemming from a common ancestor (Chow 1997). The invention of the Han as a blood-related group, the invention of a common ancestor for all Han (initially the Yellow Emperor, later Peking Man, and now Yuanmou Man),[38] and the creation of a linear Han/national history were among the key strategies for departing from culturalism (Chow 1997, 47). These nationalizing strategies also included the introduction of new chronologies, new national celebrations, a national anthem and flag, and the unifying cult of Sun Yat-sen himself as the "father of the nation" (*guofu*).[39] In addition to the existing written language, it was expected that the Han would also gradually adopt one spoken-language standard that would bridge existing linguistic divergences.[40] Though racialization of the

Han identity was partially a product of indigenous schools of thought and modes of representation, the rise of racialized Han/Chinese nationalism at the turn of the twentieth century must also be explored in the context of a larger international discourse on the evolution of human races. The articulation of Han/Chinese nationalism was particularly influenced by Thomas Huxley's *On Evolution*, translated into Chinese in 1898 (Dikötter 1997, 13–14; Chow 2001, 53–54). The introduction of this and other racial theories "provided the timely coloration of modernity to an anti-Manchu . . . ideology" (Chow 1997, 52).

The genealogization of the Han and Manchu as large descent groups, the nationalization of the Han/Chinese identity, the replacement of the category of imperial subjects with the Chinese nation, and the process by which these identities were racialized all occurred in quick succession. Hence, new terms loop and fall out of use during this period, used by intellectuals to render equally intertwined and wobbly notions of lineage, race, and nation. During the nationalizing of the Han, imperial notions of "all under heaven" and *datong* (great unity) were abandoned as incompatible with the new national symbolic order. They were replaced by imagery of a Han race/Chinese nation inhabiting a state territory with clearly demarcated borders. This territorial state ultimately had a determining role in the making of the Chinese nation: "In the Chinese revolution, the state was not just midwife at the birth of the nation but in fact its sire. . . . The state not only delivered the nation into the world but determined what form it should take" (Fitzgerald 1995, 77). As this state was extremely heterogeneous, during the establishment of the first republic the inherent tension in the pre-1912 revolutionary rhetoric that interchangeably employed the terms *Han racial lineage* (Hanzu) and *Chinese nation* (Zhonghua minzu) had to be addressed. Accordingly, the notions of a multiracial Chinese nation and the Republic of Five Races (Wuzu Gonghe) were conceived. Through the idea of five founding races, the government worked to ensure the integrity of the territory it claimed for the new Republican state.

Still, the five races were not conceived of as equally important; throughout, the Han were reified as both the backbone (*gugan*) and the core (*zhuti*) (Leibold 2012, 215), into which "the others" were expected to gradually assimilate. Sun posited that the dying out of singular races—the Manchu, Tibetans, Mongols, and Muslims—or rather, their melting with the "mass of the genuine Chinese," must be facilitated (Heberer 1984, 43).

Ten years after the establishment of the first republic, Liang Qichao continued to discuss the central role of the superior Hua culture and people in assimilating neighboring people to form an organically evolving Chinese nation (Leibold 2012, 226–27). Hence, even though the umbrella concept of a multiracial nation was developed, in a parallel rhetoric the role of the Han as the core of that nation was ensured.

The priority of nationalist intellectuals and revolutionaries was to create the notion of the Han as a racial community and to mobilize its resources against foreign invaders. But group boundaries cannot be established overnight; "boundaries must be underpinned by a suitable apparatus of myth and legend which cannot be generated spontaneously" (Horowitz 1985, 70). With regard to the Han, this meant that the category needed to be gradually reinvented to fit into the new historical order of nationalism. Although Han/Chinese shared some ideas of Han-ness/Chinese-ness before the arrival of nationalism, this attachment was not territorial in the sense of modern territorial states. The spatial opposition between culture and wildness on which Han-ness/Chinese-ness was founded had come to be powerfully challenged, especially since the nineteenth century. Several factors, among them defeat in the war with Japan (1894–95), the severing of Vietnam and Korea from the sphere of symbolic allegiance to the Qing throne, and the encroachment of foreign powers onto the Chinese territory, demonstrated the incompatibility of the Confucian idea of world order with the contemporary system of increasingly powerful nation-states. The nationalism-motivated revolutionaries believed that the only way for China to survive was to thoroughly redefine both "China" and "Han" using a vocabulary compatible with Western notions of state, nation, sovereignty, territory, borders, and government. Accordingly, the new framing of the Han was put forth, as a huge lineage stemming from a common ancestor and bound to a concrete state territory within which their interests could be secured and realized. This notion then needed to be distributed and popularized as broadly as possible to mobilize the "masses" for the national revolution. New media such as newspapers played a critical role in the mobilization process.[41] Yet because the Republican state was relatively weak, the implementation of nation- and state-making projects encountered significant institutional limitations. This changed in the aftermath of the civil war between the Nationalists and the Communists, which was followed by the establishment of the new Communist state and its successfully constructed mechanisms of control.

The Communist state approached nation- and state-making projects with unprecedented zeal. Exhausted by decades of war, the millions of farmers and workers through whom Mao built the Communist base longed for a government that promised stabilization. With the substantial assistance of Soviet advisors, the new regime quickly expanded its power, including into the non-Han areas of southern, western, and northern China. Government and party officials traveled through distant borderlands, trying to draw non-Han leaders to the Communist side, either through negotiation or by force, and to gradually integrate their territories in a unitary administrative system. In areas inhabited by the Han, Land Reform was introduced during the 1950s; landlords were deposed and land was gradually collectivized between 1953 and 1956. In 1958 collectives were consolidated into People's Communes by the increasingly totalitarian regime. In the cities, economic relations were redefined and urban enterprises were nationalized in 1956. While the establishment of a national language had not achieved substantial progress under the Nationalists, it was relatively quickly carried out by the Communists; in 1954 the national language standard, Putonghua, was introduced to unite the Han and prospectively the non-Han. The Communist government tackled other nation-making and Han-making projects with similar energy.

Like Sun Yat-sen, Mao Zedong regarded the Han as the core of the Chinese nation. In fact, in his writings he refers to the Han as embodying the Chinese nation itself (Mao 1968–69, 354–55). In contrast to the Republican government—which only officially acknowledged the existence and importance of the territorially crucial Mongols, Manchu, Tibetans, and Muslims—the Communists were determined to get a better idea of China's ethnic complexity, including granting state recognition and the nominal right to equality to other ethnic groups in China. Accordingly, in the 1950s the Communist government launched the Minzu Classification Project, which aimed to identify what *minzu* inhabited the territory of the new Chinese state.[42] Official recognition of these *minzu* would help the government extend its control over the multiethnic "borderlands", areas that in fact constituted about 60 percent of the new state's territory. The principle of the Minzu Classification Project was inspired by and partially modeled after the nationalities policy implemented in the Soviet Union under Stalin during the 1920s (Hirsch 2005). However, by emphasizing the primary role of language in the classification of non-Han peoples, the categorizations this project produced in fact closely followed the Republican-era taxonomies (Mullaney 2011).

Beyond systematizing knowledge about multiethnic areas, teams of ethnographers, anthropologists, historians, and linguists aimed to classify the prospective *minzu* "scientifically"; this was done with respect to their historical, social, and material "advancement" on evolutionist scales borrowed from Josef Stalin and Lewis H. Morgan. That the project was carried out by social scientists lent a scientific aura of reason to what was in fact a political undertaking to enforce the leading role of the Han in the national community and to systematize society in order to expand the spaces of state control. In the aftermath of the project, the government officially recognized fifty-six *minzu* as living within the Chinese state territory.[43] The Han were recognized as the largest *minzu* and were officially confirmed as the leading national majority. The other *minzu* in China were expected to "catch up" with the Han in socioeconomic terms, eventually forming with them a proletarian class devoid of nationalist sentiments. Until this happened, the Han were to be, in Stalin's words, the "unifier of nationalities."

Stalin argued that while in Western Europe, nations developed into independent nation-states (*samostoiatelnye natsionalnye gosudarstva*), in Eastern Europe inter-national states, or multi-national states (*mezhdunatsionalnye gosudarstva*) were the dominant state form, the Soviet Union being one of them. In these states, the most politically advanced nation (*natsiia*) played the role of a unifier of nationalities (*obedinitel natsionalnostei*) (Stalin 1948, 13–14). Nationalities, Stalin (1950, 278) posited, were "underdeveloped nations" in the precapitalist stage of historical development.[44] As such, they had to accept that leading posts in the nationalities states were already occupied by the leading nations that had "awakened" to political awareness earlier and advanced at a faster pace. This idea of state and nation was flexibly adopted by Mao for China.[45] As were Russians in the Soviet Union, so were Han in China "shouldered" with the role of the "unifiers." The fifty-five minority *minzu* were to assume the role of the underdeveloped "nationalities."

The position of the Han *minzu* as the leading actor was further "scientifically" reinforced with the help of the Stalinist and Morganian models of social development. Stalin proposed that all societies follow the same path of historical development, from primitive commune to slavery, feudalism, capitalism, and finally, to socialism.[46] Morgan's model, which complemented Stalin's in the Minzu Classification Project, was similarly linear and evolutionary.[47] Morgan argued that all societies must pass through three main stages of development, from savagery to barbarism to civilization. He framed these periods in terms of material change and changes in marital form (Morgan 1976, 33–34).[48] Though the labels of savagery, barbarism, and civilization were not explicitly implemented in the project of Minzu Classification, Morgan's evolutionary classification of marital forms did significantly inform how researchers discussed the marriage and family structure of the ethnic groups they studied. In a prominent example of this evolutionary discourse, the partially matrilineal Na (Mosuo) from the Lugu Lake region in Yunnan and Sichuan were labeled a "living fossil." [49] Further, the form of sexual union (*tisese* in Na and *zouhun* in Chinese) practiced by some of the Na was in this evolutionary framework labeled a "backward group marriage" to be overcome by a more "hygienic" and "civilized" monogamous marriage (Yan 1982, 1989). The Minzu Classification Project compartmentalized the population of China with the help of Stalin's and Morgan's schemes and assigned the Han *minzu* to the most advanced, socialist stage of historical development. This effectively made "the Han" a model for other *minzu* to imitate. While in premodern China the notion of Han cultural superiority was spatial and largely based on the distinction between a cultured center and the wild space beyond it, modern notions of Han superiority were constructed linearly and temporally.

The presumed a priori existence of "the Han" as one coherent *minzu* was not addressed in the classification project. The scientists in the field were expected to find "the Han" and their "others," and they surely did. The political underpinnings of the Minzu Classification rendered all challenges to the existence of a unitary Han *minzu* unwelcome. Moreover, the project "scientifically proved" that the Han *minzu* was historically and socially most advanced. But Mao did not stop there. He also ascribed to the Han rich revolutionary traditions, a devotion to class struggle, and an intrinsic resistance against the "dark forces of feudalism" (Mao 1968–69). In slight contrast to this revolutionary rhetoric, Mao simultaneously represented the Han as creators of a superior cultural tradition, an exquisite literary tradition, and the oldest and continuous civilization. Mao's narration of the Han was deliberate and selective:

> Developing along the same lines as many other nations of the world, the Chinese nation (chiefly the Han) first went through some tens of thousands of years of life in classless primitive communes. Up to now approximately 4,000 years have passed since the collapse of the primitive communes and the transition to class society. In the history of Chinese civilization, agriculture and handicraft have always been known as highly developed; many great thinkers, scientists, inventors, statesmen, military experts, men of letters and artists have flourished, and there is a rich store of classical works.... China, with a recorded history of almost 4,000 years, is therefore one of the oldest civilized countries in the world. The history of the Hans, for instance shows that the Chinese people [sic] would never submit to rule by the dark forces and that in every case they succeeded in overthrowing or changing such rule by revolutionary means. In thousands of years of the history of the Hans, there have been hundreds of peasant insurrections, great or small, against the regime of darkness imposed by the landlords and nobility.... All the nationalities of China have always rebelled against the foreign yoke.... In thousands of years of history of the Chinese nation many national heroes and revolutionary leaders have emerged. So the Chinese nation is also a nation with a glorious revolutionary tradition and a splendid cultural heritage.[50] (Mao 1954, 3:73–74)

In this new Communist framing, the blood kinship that the Nationalists promoted was overshadowed *in the political rhetoric* by an emphasis on unity in class struggle, both within the Chinese society and internationally. The Han were now framed as socially and historically progressive, as revolutionary and proletarian.[51] They became reified as a unified national majority and reinforced as such institutionally on an unprecedented scale. Still, Mao's semantic swapping of "Chinese people," "the Han," and "Chinese nation" in his speech demonstrates a perpetual tension. The Communists necessarily aimed to reinvent and strengthen the Han as a national majority, but they simultaneously had to reinforce an even newer and completely unfamiliar construct of the multiethnic Chinese nation, one composed of fifty-six *minzu*. The question of whether it is possible to promote the two simultaneously, without making Chineseness appear too much like Han-ness, remains real and unresolved today. So, too, does a related problem: how to make Han-ness meaningful when many of the markers of Han-ness are at the same time "things Chinese."

Despite new elements in the Communist narration of the Han, in practice the government maintained the Nationalists' emphasis on blood kinship by reinforcing descent as the only channel for transmission of Han-ness. Through this the government further strengthened the "genealogical mentality" among the Hanzu and the link between kinship and nation (Pieke 2003). In the aftermath of the Minzu Classification Project, descent became the only officially viable criterion for the transmission of Han identity.[52] In official discourse and the enactment of *minzu* policy, Han identity, similar to other *minzu* identities, can only be inherited. It cannot be acquired. The acquisition of markers of Han-ness by a person of another *minzu* has no impact whatsoever on the official *minzu* status of that person. Through the classification project, the boundaries of Han-ness, like those of other *minzu*, were institutionalized and stiffened. The resulting classifications are either-or; the only options are to be Han or to be another *minzu*. The question of degree, compatible with the imperial notion of Han-ness as a cultural identity, was made irrelevant. After the Minzu Classification, almost all citizens of the People's Republic of China were issued an ID that states their *minzu* status.[53] The state machine has reproduced and reinforced these categories of identity ever since.[54]

Although the meaning and roles of Han identity extend far beyond the domain controllable by state agencies, the Minzu Classification Project contributed immensely to the reification and objectification of "the Han" as a coherent *minzu* (Gladney 1999, 48–50). By juxtaposing the progressive, revolutionary, and socially advanced Han majority with the fifty-five "nationalities," the leading role of the Han *minzu* became "scientifically" justified, rhetorically objectified, and enforced institutionally. In spite of, or rather, *because of* the numerous boundaries dividing those classified as Hanzu, the central government has since persistently promoted the Han as a powerful united national majority with a long-standing territorial bond to China.

CONCLUSION

Because we can observe distinct changes between the framing of Han-ness in different historical periods, "the Han" should be understood as a narration. This understanding follows Ann Anagnost's (1997, 2) notion of nation as narration as well as Benedict Anderson's (1983, 15) idea of imagined community.[55] Ethnic groups, like nations, can be seen as narrations; they are generative narrations that adapt to tasks, challenges, and the "others" to whom they are exposed. While the notion of narration highlights the generative aspect of ethnic and national narratives, Anderson emphasizes the agency of those who "imagine," or, as Anagnost describes, "speak" those narrations. Drawing on this scholarship, we should understand "the Han" as a formative narration remolded by those who imagine. Every temporal and spatial frame generates its own national narrations (Anagnost 1997, 2). Likewise, every such frame generates its own Han-ness, thereby producing a synchronic "series of moments" rather than a teleological history of unfolding.[56] And yet, although a scholar's job is often to deconstruct and de-teleologize, the actors tend to "speak" in continuities.[57] This schism, between deconstructive scholarship and actors comfortable with continuities and teleologies, is manifest in the material explored in the present study.

CHAPTER 2

CONTEMPORARY NARRATIVES OF HAN-NESS

Premodern and modern temporalities have produced distinct Han categorizations and very different and multiple versions of Han-ness, making it
impossible to frame the contemporary Han *minzu* as a singular product of
progressive national development. Yet Han-ness should not be understood
as a randomly invented identity imposed on state subjects by the imperial,
Nationalist, and Communist governments in a purely instrumental way.
Rather, Han-ness draws its vitality from its place at the interface of the
need for identification and differentiation that extends beyond kinship
and locality bonds, and the need for a politically handy population category at the level of national politics. These two dimensions of Han-ness
are mutually dependent. The way that Han-ness is narrated and framed
in large-scale political processes has a great impact on individual scales
of narration. Powerfully influenced by state-invented and state-enforced
Han-ness, Han individuals employ these Han representations in their personalized identity politics and reproduce them in social and ethnic interactions. In interactions with locally specific "others," Han-ness acquires
fragmented and localized meanings. This fragmentation, in turn, exer-
cises a significant influence on state-driven discourses of identity.

The analysis below moves from a comparison of premodern and
modern temporalities to an exclusive focus on contemporary China and
explores questions of what Han-ness, or being Han, means today. Unlike

most scholarly publications about "the Han," which tend to discuss the category's ethnogenesis or the processes of othering formative to it, my approach here is different.[1] I focus on analyzing contemporary markers and narratives of Han-ness elicited from interviews, discussing what Han individuals themselves imagine Han-ness to be. This has implications for the contemporary debate on the meaning and roles of Han identity. My research data reveal that Han-ness, although to a certain extend conceived vis-à-vis its "minority others," greatly exceeds majority/minority bifurcations. Han-ness is equally constructed, for instance, in relation to home-place identities. The emic notions of Han-ness analyzed here not only illustrate processes in which "the Han" are constructed vis-à-vis their multiple and differentiated "others." Han individuals also invest the Han identity with meanings that make sense in their localized identity politics.

In the present chapter, I throughout place "the Han" and their most often evoked "other," "the minorities," in quotation marks. I do this for the same reason James Ferguson (1994) places "development" in quotation marks in his study of "development" in Lesotho. Quotation marks remind us to remain alert to possible reifications, ensuring that we do not begin to presume that "the Han" and "the minorities" exist as objective and unquestionable realities. Various markers of Han-ness analyzed here should not be taken to suggest that there is a coherent category of "the Han" that these markers objectively describe. On the contrary, the markers are generative and conflate to *form* a narration of "the Han" that must be analyzed in order to understand the category's political and social effects. Although quotation marks may negatively influence the readability of this chapter, the narrative quality of "the Han" must be emphasized for the sake of scholarly clarity.

DISCURSIVE MARKERS AND BOUNDARIES OF HAN-NESS

Discussions about what it means to be Han, about what characterizes Hanzu, and about the symbols of Han-ness formed the central axis of the interviews I conducted in Beijing and Shanghai. I refer here to the collected characteristics (*tedian*) and symbols (*biaozhi*) as "markers," as they *mark* the boundaries of Han-ness and its meaning.[2] My aim in asking questions about such imaginary markers was to observe how individuals reacted to my queries and to identify any contrasts drawn by the research participants between "the Han" and their "others." The later analysis of interview materials focused on identifying the main narratives that the collected markers revealed and the corresponding images of "the Han" they objectified. Hence, my aim here is not to engage in a detailed analysis of all of the ascribed characteristics and symbols content-wise and argue why "the Han" are, for instance, believed to be "cunning" or "to have mastered many modern technologies." My interest is also not in discussing whether these statements are "true" or "false." Instead, the logic that motivates my analysis is to view these statements as part of identity negotiation processes. My goal is to extract from them the underlying narratives and discourses. The very act of ascription and the ways in which research participants conducted it is also instructive: it offers important clues about which identities matter, as well as when and for whom they matter.

During the interviews, conversations about markers of "the Han" and what it means to be Han today were particularly vivid. Many interviewees engaged in long monologues about what "the Han" are like and why. A great majority needed almost no time to consider the question; most responded immediately and thoughtfully. In a clear contrast to this overwhelming majority, a small minority of informants argued that it was not possible to talk about Han markers. Some of these individuals commented that boundaries between "the Han" and other *minzu* are difficult to draw. One individual argued, "The Han have intermingled with other *minzu* through intermarriage," and another claimed, "All the Chinese *minzu* are united and their cultures assimilated." A different informant stated, "It is difficult to draw a boundary between the Han and minorities [because] these have become similar to the Han." Others argued that "the Han" constitute an extremely fragmented category, one that renders attempts at generalizations about Han-ness impossible. Comments from these interviewees include that "Hanzu are a large category and there are various groups within it," and, "Hanzu lack the feeling of unity [and] lack the group spirit." Instead of emphasizing the boundaries between "the Han" and their "others," these informants stressed either the absence of boundaries or fissures within the category itself. Still, the overwhelming majority of research participants engaged with the question about Han markers without hesitation and with much verbosity. Han-ness seemed an obvious identity category to them, one that was meaningful and had clear boundaries that neatly separated it from its corresponding "others."

The queries about the meaning of Han-ness and about Han markers were among the opening questions in the interviews. At this point in the conversation, an overwhelming majority of research participants identified "the Han" in relation to other *minzu* of China. In these large-scale, nonlocalized juxtapositions, the Uyghur and the Tibetans figured most often as the salient "others" of "the Han."[3] One interviewee also contrasted "the Han" with Americans and Japanese, "others" who exist beyond China's borders. In these relationships of internal and external othering, Han-ness is clearly perceived as a meaningful and important identity. Table 2.1 gives a representative sample of the markers collected. The left-hand column presents fifteen narratives identified by the markers; these are narratives synthesized from the hundreds of markers ascribed by the informants. The right-hand column lists concrete examples of markers quoted directly from the interviews.

A great majority of these markers reproduce specific power relations that bind the Han *minzu*, its "minority others," and the state. These markers are used not only to draw boundaries around the category but also to objectify the asymmetric power relationships in which it is engaged. A large number of these asymmetric markers pertain to the population size and distribution of Hanzu in China. Almost half of the research participants pointed out that Hanzu are the largest population and have the widest distribution of all *minzu*. "The Han" were accordingly represented as numerically superior and spatially encompassing. They were framed by the informants as being "at home" throughout the whole territory of China and thus distinct from "the minorities," who, with the possible exception of the Hui, are perceived to be spatially restricted to one region of the country. While one could argue that this is clearly not "true" or that China's territory comprises large regions where "the minorities" actually constitute local majorities, these markers nonetheless demonstrate that there is a firm *belief* in China as the land of "the Han," with the Han *minzu* "embracing" the entire territory.

Markers relating to "the Han" as a standard category devoid of unique characteristics were referenced by every fourth informant. Some informants also described "the Han" through negation, as those *not* having certain features associated with "minority" *minzu*; they argued, for instance, that "the Han" cannot dance and that they have no eating taboos. When contrasted with "minorities"—who have abundant characteristics and

TABLE 2.1. Narratives of Han-ness and examples of Han markers ascribed

Narratives of Han-ness	Examples of Han markers ascribed by research participants
Han are the largest population and have the widest distribution	Han are a large population. Han are a large population that occupies a wide territory (*ren duo di guang*). Han are most numerous. Han are a large *minzu* (*da de minzu*). Han have wide distribution (*fenbu guang, fensan guang*). Han are omnipresent in China.
Han do not have any characteristics or symbols	When compared with minorities, Han do not have any characteristics. Han have very few eating taboos, unlike Huizu. Compared to minorities, Han do not have any special customs. Han do not have any privileges on university exams, unlike the minorities. Han cannot dance. Han do not have any beliefs. Han do not wear any characteristic costumes. Han are ordinary (*yiban*). Han do things in a common way (*yong putong de fangfa lai zuoshi*).
Han are modern and open	Han have mastered many modern technologies (*zhangwo le xuduo xianjin jishu*). Han are the most modern *minzu* (*zui xiandai*). Han have a feel for modern times. Han are the vanguard (*qianwei*) of the nation. Han develop the fastest. Han are receptive to new things (*shanyu jieshou xin de shiwu*). Compared to other *minzu*, Hanzu are open in thinking (*sixiang geng kaifang*). Han are more open toward external influences than minority *minzu*. Han stick less to their own tradition (*chuantong*).
Han have a long history and a strong cultural foundation; Han culture has assimilated other cultures	Han have ancient culture and customs (*gulao de chuantong wenhua he xisu*). Cultural greatness (*wenhua shang de qiangda*) is a characteristic of the Han. Compared with other *minzu*, the cultural atmosphere among Hanzu is stronger (*wenhua fenwei nong yidian*). There are more Han scholars. Hanzu have a long human history (*guangfan de renwen lishi*). Han have assimilated (*ronghe*) the cultures of various *minzu*.

Narratives of Han-ness	Examples of Han markers ascribed by research participants
Confucianism has had a determining impact on Han-ness	Hanzu are profoundly influenced by Confucianism. Confucian morality (*Rujia daode*) is the symbol of the Han. Han respect authority (*zunzhong quanwei*) and practice filial piety (*xiaoshun fumu*). Han ascribe importance to the Doctrine of the Mean (*jiangjiu Zhongyong zhi Dao*). Han advocate the rule of virtue (*dezhi*) and not the rule of law (*fazhi*).[a]
Family and personal relations are of great importance to the Han	Hanzu attach a lot of importance to the "five relationships"[b] and the patriarchal family system (*jiazhangzhi*). The importance of family is reflected in the worship of ancestors. Han have a saying: "The more sons, the more happiness." Han have a lineage-determined mind-set (*jiazu guannian*).
Han are "better" than other *minzu*	Han are the smartest. Compared to minorities, Han are quick thinking, industrious, and hardworking. Han are clever in the event of conflict. Han have willpower. What is special about Hanzu when compared with minority *minzu* is their enterprising spirit. Han are full of ambition and courage. Han have a sense of responsibility.
Han are patriotic and have dominated China politically for a long time	Han are patriotic (*aiguo*). Han regard themselves as the Chinese nation (*Zhonghua minzu*). Han have a long history of controlling China. Han have been governing China for a very long time.
The Han language is the symbol of Hanzu	Han speak the Han language. The Han language is the symbol of Hanzu. Han language and writing have the broadest usage and biggest influence in China and the whole world. Compared with minority *minzu*, what is special about Hanzu is the culture of language (*yuyan wenhua*). The Han language divides into numerous branches.

(continued)

[a] In the report to the Sixteenth National Congress of the Communist Party of China, Jiang Zemin argued that "ruling the country by law and ruling the country by virtue complement each other" (DNC 2002, 47).
[b] The five principal relationships are those between ruler and minister, father and son, husband and wife, older and younger brothers, and friends. They are all regulated by certain rights and obligations.

TABLE 2.1. *continued*

Narratives of Han-ness	Examples of Han markers ascribed by research participants
Han share a set of common characteristics	Han are kindhearted, honest, modest, gentle, docile, and easy to get along with. Han hide strength under the appearance of gentleness. Han have a round-about way of saying things. Han do not like to show off their individuality. Han advocate peace and harmony. Han have a relatively weak conquering spirit. Han are sly and crafty.
Han have unique dietary habits	When compared with minorities, Han have a miscellaneous diet. Han spend a lot of time cooking and eating. Han eat four dishes and one soup.
Han have unique festivals and customs	During the Spring Festival, Han eat dumplings (*jiaozi*). During the Spring Festival, Han call on relatives and exchange gifts. Han wear red clothes on festival occasions. During the Dragon Boat Festival, dragon boat races take place.
Han wear unique clothing	Han wear different clothing than minorities. Han wore special clothing in the past.
Han have a unique appearance	Han have different facial features. Han appearance is different from that of minorities. Han have small eyes, a flat nose, yellow skin, and single-fold eyelids.
Han are agriculturalists	Han live in the flatlands. Han are agriculturalists. Hanzu culture is founded on agriculture, not commerce.

Source: Fieldwork interviews in Beijing and Shanghai, 2002–3.

peculiarities—"the Han" in these statements appear invisible in their "thusness" (Harrell 2001, 295). While it could be argued that "the Han" have as many peculiarities as other *minzu* or, from the other end, that all other *minzu* are ordinary to their members, this is insignificant in narrative terms. Differentiation between those who are "ordinary" (*yiban*) and those who are "special" (*you tese*) reflects a specific relationship in which "the Han" become an unmarked category, an implicit standard constituting a reference point for others, similar to whiteness, maleness, and other "invisible" categories of identity.[4]

The next large group of markers linked Han-ness with modernity, advancement, and openness. Research participants repeatedly argued that "Hanzu are the most modern *minzu*." In this narrative, "the Han" are represented as the "vanguard of the nation" in both a technological and cultural sense. As those who "have mastered modern technologies," "the Han" are objectified as predestined to lead others indirectly constructed as less modern and open, in the pressing pursuit of progress and advancement. While "the Han" are here naturalized as modern and striving forward, other narratives additionally situate them as strongly rooted in the past. My informants claimed equally often that "the Han" have a uniquely long human history and powerful culture. A few interviewees further underscored that "Han culture" has successfully assimilated other "cultures." Here, then, the discourse of technological and cultural modernity is accompanied by a discourse of cultural and historical potency. The former looks forward, arguing that "the Han" embody the qualities needed to move forward and thrive; the latter argues that the reason for "the Han's" current power is historical—the backward and the forward views arguably comprising the necessary components of all ethnic and national narrations.[5]

Markers that less obviously refer to national narrations and power asymmetries are those related to Confucianism. Every third interviewee pointed out that the influence of Confucianism on "Han culture" could not be overestimated. While Confucianism could arguably be classified as a cultural marker, its intrinsic link to imperial power structures renders it clearly political as well. Even though the relatively anarchist Daoism has a similarly long and well-established history—and in the West is perhaps even more often associated with "Chinese-ness" than Confucianism— none of the research participants ever mentioned it as a symbol of Han-ness. Likewise, none of them mentioned Chinese Buddhism. That only Confucianism was singled out as a "Han symbol" suggests that its significance has less to do with Confucianism as a philosophical system per se and more with its promotion by political configurations as an official state cult for over two millennia and as a foundation of the system of imperial examinations. Confucianism significantly contributed to the creation of the "culture"/"barbarism" paradigm (Dikötter 1992), which continues to influence how Han imagine inter-*minzu* relations as well as how state power over ethnic borderlands is understood in contemporary China. Also, the representation of "Han culture" as able to assimilate other cultures is closely connected to the Confucian discussion of the acculturation of "savages" to the culture of the Central Countries. Despite the political ambiguity of Confucianism in the High Communist Period under Mao Zedong, many research participants surprisingly pointed to Confucianism as a marker of Han-ness, reflecting the revival of Confucianism in contemporary China.[6] Likewise, the importance ascribed to family relations and kin obligations by additional interviewees appears to stem from Confucianism and the system of hierarchical social relations it put forth.[7]

The largest category of markers, referred to by a clear majority of informants, constructs "the Han" as "better" than "minorities" in a number of ways. These markers objectify "the Han" as more "industrious," "hardworking," "clever," and "enterprising" than "the minorities." Significantly, none of these qualities were ever ascribed by Han informants to other *minzu* in China. These characteristics powerfully signal that "the Han" locate their own *minzu* ahead of other *minzu* and demonstrate how this leading position is objectified through the continual characterization of non-Han *minzu* as lagging behind or "less than" (i.e., as less industrious, less hardworking, and less enterprising). This narrative constructs "the Han" as the driving force of the Chinese nation and state—a representation earlier formulated and utilized by both Sun Yat-sen and Mao Zedong—and reinforces specific imageries of inter-*minzu* relations.

Another group of interviewees ascribed markers that directly linked "the Han," the nation, and the state. These markers classified Hanzu as patriotic (implying that others are not?) and singled them out as having a history of political control over China. Although Manchu or Mongols could claim a history of political control over China too, the achievements of the Mongol Yuan and Manchu Qing dynasties have been somewhat veiled in Chinese historiography. The Han research participants variously characterized these dynasties as periods of cruelty, moral and material corruption, foreign oppression, and/or increasing isolation and marginalization of China. Considering that China governs the territory that was significantly expanded by the Mongols and Manchus, such narratives are somewhat surprising. Still, these formulations obviously do constitute part of the popular fragmented Han nationalism (see Leibold 2010), likely so because they have continued to facilitate the construction of the Han/ Chinese dynasties and the Han/Chinese people as those who created and repeatedly restored political power and cultural order in the empire and the modern state.

Markers referring to language were the last main category intrinsically involved in power asymmetries. The informants who proposed them argued that the Han/Chinese language (Hanyu, Zhongwen, also Putonghua) is the symbol of "the Han."[8] Indeed, it is "the culture of language" (*yuyan wenhua*) that makes "the Han" unique in relation to other *minzu*. "Han speak the Han language," it was argued. This normalized statement reflects, obviously, a massive linguistic asymmetry when we consider that in China, Naxi cannot just speak Naxi, or that Mongols cannot just speak Mongol, but must also be able to speak the Han language. Under the present linguistic status quo, "non-Han" need to acquire this national standard before they are able to access the national "linguistic market" (Bourdieu 1991, 45) and the resources available to those who speak it.[9] Thus, a language-related marker like "Han speak the Han language" points directly to the political powers that locate "the Han," and specifically the northern Han, whose speech was selected as the foundation of the spoken standard at the very center of Chinese national narration.[10]

Unlike the markers discussed above, all of which reflect, imply, and naturalize certain power asymmetries, the final six narratives in table 2.1 do not narrate "the Han" through vertical relationships with other *minzu*. Rather, they reinvent "the Han" through horizontal comparisons, as a community that shares certain characteristics, physical traits, and cultural codes. These narratives include what the informants identified as typical character traits shared by "the Han:" a "kindhearted" nature, for instance, as well as a propensity to be "sincere," "indirect," but also "sly." Some research participants further highlighted the uniqueness of Han dietary habits and the link between Han-ness, agriculture, and life in China's flatlands, and they referred to specific festivals and celebrations as symbols of Han-ness. A small number of informants emphasized Han clothing and appearance as different from that of "minorities."[11] Racialized notions of Han-ness and references to "two blacks and one yellow" (i.e., black eyes, black hair, and yellow skin), to "the Han" as "Descendants of the Dragon" (Long de Chuanren), or to "the Han" as a blood community were marginally popular with research participants. Despite the apparently growing resaturation of Han/Chinese nationalism with racial symbolism today (Sautman 1997; Cheng 2011, 2012), very few interviewees referred to these racialized attributes to express their idea of Han-ness.[12] Racialized Han-ness was less often articulated than the Han-ness expressed through specific power relations and the contrasting of characteristics and cultural markers.

Historical Shift in Markers of Han-ness

Historical studies suggest that in imperial China, rituals, the patriarchal family structure, family names (especially monosyllabic ones), descent from Han ancestors "proven" through genealogies, and agrarian occupations (among many others) were all markers popularly associated with Han-ness/Chinese-ness. Accompanying the rise of Han/Chinese nationalism at the turn of the twentieth century, narratives of shared national descent, common ancestors, linear national history and national language, and the political bond between the Han *minzu* and the Chinese state began to be zealously promoted as new markers of Han-ness. This narration of "the Han" signaled a departure from imperial culturalism and the shift to a nationalist symbolic order. The popular narratives of contemporary Han-ness, as my research results suggest, are in many ways similar to those promoted in the Republican period, but expanded and enriched through new elements. These contemporary narratives not only reproduce "the Han" by delineating the category and differentiating it from other *minzu*; they also convey a number of asymmetric spatial imageries. First, these imageries objectify "the Han" as located *ahead* of others in an assumed linear progression via the Han category's associations with modernity and advancement. Second, narratives of numerical superiority and nationwide distribution create an understanding of "the Han" as all encompassing, located *everywhere*. Last, markers that relate to the Han language and script, which became the spoken and written national standards, locate "the Han" in the very *center* of the Chinese national narration and symbolically also *above* other *minzu* who must acquire the language of "the Han" in order to function successfully in the national community. Having their *minzu* first generated and then empowered by the political processes of the twentieth century, individual Han feel entitled to reproduce this Han narration in their individual identity politics, contributing to its maintenance and further perpetuation.

In the premodern period, Han-ness/Chinese-ness was a matter of degree of acculturation to empirewide or locally understood Han/Chinese lifeways and the ability to prove descent from Han/Chinese ancestors (Ebrey 1996). With the nationalizing project of the late nineteenth century, Han-ness became increasingly institutionalized. Since 1949, together with other *minzu* identities, it has been subject to Communist state planning and has been a domain of state interventions. The acquisition of identity markers and recognition by other Han, once essential elements of identity politics in premodern China, are insignificant to the official distributors of *minzu* identity labels today. Whatever similarities some "minority" people may share with "the Han" in terms of cultural codes, behavior, or language, they have no impact on a person's official classification. In the aftermath of the Minzu Classification Project, which effected a new ordering of the entire state population, institutionally confirmed descent is the only legal channel through which *minzu* identity can be transmitted.

This institutionality of Han-ness makes it appear very distant from the processes of ascription, flexibility of boundaries, and negotiability of identities associated with the notion of ethnicity in Western anthropological discourse. Still, this apparent rigidity of *minzu* boundaries does not prevent Chinese citizens from switching identity labels and reinventing genealogies and ancestors, just as they did in imperial times. Mette Halskov Hansen (2005) describes such inventions and switches in Xishuangbanna/ Sipsongpanna in southern Yunnan, where some Han villagers acquire non-Han identities by inventing non-Han ancestors. Because "minority" *minzu* profit from a number of preferential policies—including access to higher education, employment in local government, and permission to have more children than Han are allowed to bear—non-Han identities have a high practical value and are worth acquiring in contemporary China.[13] Consequently, some "minority" populations have grown at a much higher rate than the Han population. For example, the Hanzu population increased by 20 percent between the 1982 and the 2000 censuses. During the same time, the Bai *minzu* population grew by 64 percent; Miao, 77 percent; Xibe, 125 percent; and Manchu, 148 percent (Gladney 1998, 12–13). Obviously, being a non-Han today has its advantages. More and more Han are becoming parents of non-Han, as children of mixed-*minzu* couples are increasingly choosing to assume the *minzu* of the non-Han parent for themselves (Harrell 2001, 307). This indicates that although power relations reflected in the narratives of Han-ness seem to be clearly asymmetric, and the symbolic resources attached to "the Han" label immense, in practice other factors mitigate the attractiveness of this identity. The preferential policies of the past thirty years make it attractive for some Han, especially those living with non-Han in economically disadvantaged border regions of China, to assume non-Han identity labels.[14] It would be worth exploring what effects such changes in *minzu* identity labels have on self-identification and identity negotiations of these naturalized Han.

DISTRIBUTION OF NARRATIVES:
EDUCATION AND LANGUAGE

During analysis of the data I collected in the Han-dominated cities of Shanghai and Beijing, it became clear that great similarities existed between these data and those I collected during my fieldwork in the non-Han dominated village of Zuosuo in the southwestern borderlands of Sichuan in 1999. At that time, Zuosuo was inhabited by seven identity groups: the Na, Nahi, Nuosu, Prmi, Bo, Gam, and Han. These groups were officially divided into five *minzu*: the Mongol (Na), Naxi (Nahi), Yi (Nuosu), Tibetan (Prmi, Bo, Gam), and Han. One of my central questions was how local Hanzu defined their position in relation to other *minzu* villagers and what it meant to be Han in this multiethnic setting.

Among the locally significant markers of Han-ness ascribed by both Han and non-Han in the village were "Han burn incense," "Han have an ancestral tablet on the wall where the incense is burned," "Han raise chickens," "Han women wear embroidered clothing,"[15] "Han marry," "Han worship the house spirit [*jiashen*]," "Han use mortars to grind grain," and "Han celebrate the Spring Festival." Further, in Zuosuo, where Hanzu constituted a clear minority, Han informants described "the Han" as having a "high level of culture" (*wenhua shuiping gao*) and an "advanced culture," as being "most numerous," and as "living all over the country." Han respondents also thought of "the Han" as having the "most advanced technology" and as being "more intelligent" than "minorities." The members of six other ethnic groups, in addition to using the locally significant markers, described their Han neighbors as unfamiliar strangers, people without markers (*mei sha tedian*) and without religion (*meiyou zongjiao*) but also as "most advanced" and "most numerous."

Besides the very specific, locally significant markers, there are great similarities between the narratives of Han-ness put forth in Zuosuo, a remote, non-Han-dominated village, and those articulated in the Han-dominated cities of Shanghai and Beijing. This invites us to consider the channels through which these markers are transmitted and popularized. Mass media, particularly television and radio, were inaccessible in the village in 1999, as there was no regular electricity. This seems to point to the propagating power of another channel for the distribution of ideas, namely centralized education.[16] Significantly, the markers of Han-ness that were virtually identical to those collected in Beijing and Shanghai were almost exclusively reproduced by those Han and non-Han villagers who had received some years of official education and were able to speak Putonghua. Interestingly, not only elderly non-Han but also some elderly Han villagers who received very basic or no education at all, who lived among the Na in smaller hamlets on the Zuosuo plain, and who grew up in pre-Communist and early Communist power constellations speaking local dialects were unaware of the narratives of Han superiority. It is also possible that these people rejected such narratives as too distant from social practice. Even more significantly, some of the early Han settlers and their children ascribed superior position in the village to the Na, who were power and wealth holders in pre-Communist and early Communist times. In 1999, the Naru language—native language of the Na—was the lingua franca for all ethnic groups in Zuosuo, with the exception of more recent Han immigrants. This raises two questions: What is the role of language in the transmission of narratives of Han-ness and the corresponding narratives of "minorities"? And what is happening in schools?

Scholars from multiple disciplines—including history, sociology, educational sciences, and social anthropology—have proposed several answers to these questions. Some argue that schools play a crucial role in determining the workings of power in society, as they produce docile, self-disciplining bodies (Foucault 1991). Others additionally posit that schools encourage students to "accept a subordinate position in the centralized bureaucratic world of the . . . nation-state" (Keyes 1991, 89). In a class-focused analysis, state schools and examination systems reproduce and perpetuate class relations by favoring certain forms of examinations, transferring certain kinds of knowledge, and emphasizing the use of one legitimate language (Bourdieu and Passeron 1977). Schools also play a critical role in nationalizing projects, with curriculum serving as a transmitter of the imageries of state and nation as well as a discourse of national belonging and territorial integrity (Bass 1998; Hansen 1999). Yet while schools may attempt to reproduce class relations or national imageries, there are numerous examples of "schooling for citizenship" turning into "schooling for resistance," challenging the very structures and relations that education was expected to reproduce (Harrell and Ma 1999, 217). Although perspectives differ, attempts to theorize the workings of schools clearly demonstrate that state schools play a central role in the making of national communities and the reproduction of power relations in a society. Because of this, and because of their tentative potential as spaces of contestation, schools and other educational institutions are thus sites of increased state intervention and control.[17]

The school curriculum in China is centralized and relatively standardized, even in such distinct areas as Beijing, Xinjiang, or Sichuan. Though some freedom to develop supplementary teaching materials and select textbooks was introduced in the 1999 curricular reform, in all these locations education still popularizes uniform ideas and values, a centrally approved historiography, and state-approved national imageries (Chu, n.d.). Additionally, in the second decade of the twenty-first century, schooling continues to promote a *minzu* classification based on the outdated evolutionist models of Stalin and Morgan as well as on specific representations of majority-minority relations. Fei Xiaotong's (1988, 223–24) thesis that "the Han" are economically and culturally more advanced than other *minzu* and that only with the assistance of "the Han" will the "minorities" be able to successfully overcome their backwardness, still reflects much of what textbooks contain. The recently published fifth-grade *Moral Education and Society* textbook further reproduces this narrative by telling a story of Princess Wencheng of the Tang dynasty, who moved to Tibet to marry the king Songtsen Gampo: "Princess Wencheng brought grain seeds and vegetable seeds from inner China and taught Tibetan people farming and other techniques, such as flour-milling. . . . Princess Wencheng also introduced into Tibet the carriage, horse, mule, and camel, production technologies, and medical books. All these advanced the social progress of Tubo" (Chu, n.d.).

State schools play a key role in disseminating such progressive classifications, asymmetric representations, and specific national imageries and in shaping popular discourse about the *minzu* in China. Indeed, elementary-school textbooks still distribute images of "the minorities" focused on their embeddedness in nature, unique costumes, food, architecture, festivals, customs, and most importantly, dancing and singing (Chu, n.d.). "The minorities" are represented as dancing and singing away their time, while "the Han" focus on production, modernization and increasing the gross domestic product. The government's control of school curriculum, an education increasingly conducted in the Han language in ethnic areas (Johnson and Chhetri 2002; Clothey 2005; my fieldwork in Xinjiang, 2011–12), and the establishment of broad access to mass media in these areas (ZZWY 2010, 466–69; my fieldwork in Xinjiang, 2011–12) are of great importance in the perpetuation of majority-minority power asymmetries and their composing elements.

In Zuosuo, a community where Han constituted about 20 percent of the total population, there were twenty-four teachers at the junior high school. Seventeen of them were Han, four were Na, and one was Nuosu. Among the twenty teachers at the central elementary school, ten were Han, eight were Na, and two were Nuosu. In both schools, the sole language of instruction was standard Chinese.[18] Although the Han teachers in these schools were devoted to teaching, tried hard to offer good-quality classes, and worked to improve their pronunciation with regular training in standard Chinese (as all spoke with a strong Sichuan accent), the narratives of Han intellectual, cultural, and technological superiority and the corresponding "minority" inferiority were nevertheless manifest in almost every conversation we shared. Somewhat unsurprisingly, I experienced a number of awkward moments when twelve- or thirteen-year-old Na pupils from the local school welcomed me to their homes and explained in standard Chinese that their *minzu* was "feudal" (*fengjian*) and "uncivilized" (*bu wenming*). Acquired most likely in school, such representations of "minorities" have enormous impact on identity formation. Larger political, legal, economic, and social effects of such narratives are equally significant. The popular perception (especially among Han in eastern China) of ethnic areas as thoroughly dependent on help from the "center," along with notions of "the Han" as agents of development and progress, are only a few examples of the discourses that these narratives fuel.

While Chinese textbooks formally stress equality and national unity, students are also sensitive to what is left out of the curriculum and to the very structure of the educational system (Hansen 1999, 258). When the curriculum does not discuss local culture, history, and ethnicity, and is not taught in locally used languages, it becomes an important sign of nonrecognition, a void that official textbooks implicitly endorse. Such "silences" are as instructive in the analysis of discourse as that which a discourse vocalizes (Foucault 1990). Nonetheless it is equally important to recognize that what schools *try* to do—distribute specific "knowledges," specific narratives of "the Han" and representations of "minorities"—is also contested. The high drop-out rates of "minority" students, as reported by Badeng Nima (2008) in Tibetan areas and also registered in Zuosuo, can be read as a form of resistance to these attempts. Furthermore, the incompatibility of the knowledge conveyed by the school curriculum with the actual lifestyles, occupational specialization (e.g., herding), cultural context, or religion of "the minorities" also motivates some parents to keep their children out of state schools, instead selecting monastic education (Davis 2005). Others may send their children to state schools for only a limited number of years to acquire basic reading and writing skills (my fieldwork in Xinjiang, 2011–12).

Moreover, the reception of narratives encoded in the curriculum is not uniform. Among Zuosuo residents who received education in standard Chinese, narratives of Han advancement and superiority were most openly challenged by the Nuosu. In conversations and in short written questionnaires distributed among the students of the junior high school, some Nuosu resolutely negated these narratives of Han-ness. They argued that there is actually a lot that Hanzu can learn from them. What "the Han" should learn was not always specified, but the respondents' sentiments were nonetheless clear. Interestingly, the Nuosu were perceived by all other ethnic groups in the village as "backward" (*luohou*) and "remote" (*pianpi*). Indeed, apart from the relatively few Nuosu who lived on the Zuosuo plain, most lived in mountainous locations, away from schools and other government and Communist Party agencies.[19] The Nuosu from mountain villages said they chose to live in the mountains because the air is much better there, unlike the air on the plains, which reportedly makes them prone to diseases. This narrative is likely much more than an expression of health concern. The Nuosu community's geographic distance from the Party, government, and education agencies was of great significance in their contestation of the bureaucratic power located in the valley. This distance, along with other factors such as family education, a history of separation from the local community, and perhaps also the Nuosu being the nominal masters of the Liangshan Yi Autonomous Prefecture where Zuosuo is located, enabled the Nuosu to contest narratives of Han-ness popularized by the centralized education system, with Putonghua as the dominant language of instruction.

Today, fifteen years later, the power of education-transmitted representations of "the Han" and "the minorities" has likely waned in Zuosuo, owing to the influence of the area's booming tourism industry. Other ethnic areas in China demonstrate that "doing tourism" can lead to "minorities" formulating new ideas about their ethnic groups and repositioning themselves in ways at least partially independent from the evolutionist classifications and the modern/Han versus backward/minorities bifurcations (Chio 2014). Revalorization of "minority" cultures, at least in the self-perception of the affected "minority" people, is thus possible. The question remains, however, whether and how much this self-revalorization has changed the popular discourse of "minorities." It seems that Han tourism's age-old game of reification of "the exotic" and "the primitive" in ethnic areas continues, albeit perhaps in a more transactional and symmetric way in some communities (Chio 2014). Still, the insights from my fieldwork in Xinjiang demonstrate that narratives of backwardness, low cultural quality (*suzhi di*), superstition (*mixin*), chaos (*luan*), feudalism (*fengjian*), lack of civilization (*bu wenming*), and lack of hygiene (*bu weisheng*) in relation to "minority" lifestyles, marital practices, religions, and inhabited places remain prevalent. The use of the Han language, especially by young and linguistically inexperienced speakers, almost automatically activates these narratives, as in the example discussed below.

One evening during a family dinner in Aqsu in 2011, in a context similar to Zuosuo more than a decade earlier, two Uyghur *minkaohan*, students at a Chinese-language high school, discussed with me the "backward" Uyghur who practice "feudal" marital customs. In this case, the custom in question was the "chain marriage," a marital form in which Uyghur men and women marry, divorce, marry, and again divorce in *relatively* short intervals. It was clear that the Communist nomenclature used to discuss nonstandardized ethnic marital practices was already part of these teenagers' vocabulary, ready to be applied. It was also clear that the "backwardness" and "feudalism" rhetoric was as uncomfortable to their mother, herself a graduate of Uyghur-language schools, as it was to me, a foreigner. Embarrassed, she corrected her daughter in standard Chinese, saying that these customs are not feudal but are a Uyghur "tradition" (*chuantong*) in some areas of Xinjiang. This distinct linguistic sensibility draws attention to the role of the language of instruction and the influence of linguistic socialization on the reception of narratives of both "the Han" and "the minorities."

Like the selection of curriculum content, the selection of language of instruction in schools with a large share of non-Han students is obviously a political issue. First, it reveals which power holders are capable of determining the language of public schooling. Second, in multiethnic states, national language and the language of instruction are important political stakes that give one group an enormous advantage when compared to others. With its use of standard Chinese, China is an example of a state where political domination and language domination are closely intertwined and reinforce one another. National language that is "known and recognized (more or less completely) throughout the whole jurisdiction of a certain political authority, . . . helps in turn to reinforce the authority which is the source of its dominance" (Bourdieu 1991, 45). Even more significant to the material discussed above, a national language is never simply a means of interethnic communication. Instead, it is a transmitter of specific narratives, norms, and values that are encoded in every language (Kymlicka 1995).[20] With the declaration of the northern variety of the Han language as the sole national spoken-language standard, and of the Chinese written language as the sole national written-language standard, the historical and contemporary narratives of "the Han" as well as of "minorities" became part of the legitimate national language. This national language standard, in turn, became the language of instruction for "the Han" and is becoming the sole language of instruction for many non-Han too. Through these processes, the asymmetric power representations and narratives of "the Han" and "the minorities" have acquired the power of being self-evident, which makes them difficult to trace and challenge, especially from within the system. Still, as some Han research participants from Shanghai and Beijing prove, along with some Han, Na, Nuosu, and Uyghur from Sichuan and Xinjiang, it is not impossible.

CONCLUSION

With their distinct power structures, objectives, ideologies, and world-views, two major temporalities in Chinese history—imperial and modern—have in discursive and practical ways produced different categories of "the Han." Historically and still today, the exact markers used to construct the boundaries of Han-ness are of secondary importance to the processes of boundary making and maintenance. Yet identification of these markers is helpful in locating the narratives that invest Han-ness with subjective meaning for the members of the category.

My research material demonstrates that Han-ness today is not conceptualized in terms of one or two key markers. Indeed, no single marker was proposed by the majority of research participants. Instead, most described what they understood as "being Han" using several "characteristics" and "symbols." Still, the narratives that motivated respondents were quite repetitive. In contemporary China, Han-ness is narrated in terms of numerical superiority, long history, cultural dominance, and character attributes that narrate "the Han" as hardworking, responsible, modern, and patriotic. Han-ness is also powerfully represented as an unmarked category, as "the ordinary" constructed as the reference point for other *minzu*. Also, great importance is attached to Confucianism as shaping the Han worldview. Finally, the Han language and script are referred to as markers of "the Han" and are represented as legitimate national standards.

The collected markers point to an inherent contradiction in defining Han-ness. Nearly a quarter of my research participants discussed the "invisibility" of "the Han" as those who do not have unique characteristics. Yet somewhat contradictory to this "invisibility," these same participants—and many others—proposed hundreds of "visible" markers of Han-ness. This suggests that Han-ness is invisible in some contrastive relationships, most prominently when juxtaposed with orientalized and exoticized "minorities," but not in others.[21] Han-ness also exists beyond these majority/minority bifurcations. Contrasting Han-ness with "minorities" is merely one axis of comparison through which Han identity is constructed today. Its relationships with Chinese-ness, home-place identities, and lineage identities are other relevant axes. Although Han-ness may situationally "disappear" in these relationships too, this disappearance occurs in very different ways and for different reasons. While situationally invisible in some relationships, Han-ness is elsewhere an important and viable identity, one appreciated, for example, for its unifying potential. The identity's strength lies in the fact that it offers unitary space for Han who are otherwise divided in everyday life by discriminatory boundaries of occupation, spoken language, home place, or access to wealth. The large number of markers collected, and the zeal with which many Han discussed them, demonstrate that Han-ness is a well-established and powerful identity concept; one could even say it discursively "flourishes" when contrasted with its salient "others," the "minority" *minzu* being but one.

Han-ness connotes various symbolic resources that make it a worthwhile identity. Specific power relations ingrained in the discourse of Han-ness permit individual Han to reproduce these relations in their fragmented, individualized identity politics. As this discourse deploys power, those who are empowered by it further reinforce the discourse (Foucault 1972, 1990). In the same logic of entanglement, the political authority that produces and popularizes the discourse of Han-ness and objectifies the Han *minzu* as a dominant majority, is in turn reinforced by the very Han it empowers. As an additional twist, the state is also dependent on "the Han" as a national majority to maintain its territorial and institutional integrity. It is in this relationship of mutual interdependence that the Han narration is reinvented, maintained, and reproduced. The state educational system and the national language are two important channels through which this reproduction occurs. The now almost universally accessible mass media, but also word of mouth via the increasing number of migrants, also play a role in this process of distribution.

Because narratives are embedded in language, the Han language that became the national standard is an extremely important component of the Han narration. The language is intrinsic to the vertical and horizontal imageries of progress and advancement against which other *minzu* are measured. Together with the centralized education system, the Han language is thus largely responsible for the transmission of specific narratives of "the Han" and "the minorities" throughout the entire country, including its multiethnic regions. In these regions, the narratives influence local processes of identity negotiation, social positioning, and power distribution. The example of Zuosuo demonstrates how these narratives influence young people in particular through the process of school education and contribute to the gradual reshuffling of power relations in the village. As the centralized education system in ethnic borderlands becomes increasingly reliant on the Han language as the language of instruction, demand for Han teachers is growing. In many areas of Xinjiang and Qinghai, school job openings favor Han over "minority" teachers to fulfill the quotas for Han-language classes set up by regional and provincial governments. Consequently, the number of Han teachers in ethnic regions is on the rise, particularly in urban and semiurban areas and in secondary education. Besides the curriculum and the language of instruction, these migrating teachers are a third important transmitter of narratives of Han-ness throughout the country. While the narratives are certainly not uncontested, they are nonetheless embedded in the national language, which invests them with the potential to become self-evident and thus have continued influence on processes of power negotiation.

Han-ness is a vital and important identity. Yet however influential, it has not replaced other collective attachments maintained by Han individuals. Moreover, the situationality of identity choices and localized identity politics continue to blur neat boundaries of *minzu* classification. Thus, although the influence of the state on identity formation is substantial, it also has its limits. As "tangible" as the boundaries of Han-ness may seem in the markers analyzed above, these boundaries do not keep "the Han" narration from fracturing into dozens of non-*minzu* identity categories when the angle of observation is changed. On the other hand, Han-ness is also restrained by Chinese-ness, which as a national identity should nominally mitigate divisions and rifts caused by *minzu* and other categorizations. Thus, as concrete and powerful as it appears here, Han identity must be contextualized and related to other collective identities maintained by Han individuals. In so doing, we can trace when, how, and whether the category matters in individualized topographies of identity.

CHAPTER 3

TOPOGRAPHIES OF IDENTITY

The roles and functions of Han-ness are most apparent when Han identity is contextualized in relation to the other collective identities that matter to contemporary Han. In a situationally dependent way, Han individuals switch between a number of collective identities, including *minzu* and nation but also, commonly, place-related identities.[1] Observations of these identity switches give rise to questions of how Han frame these identities, what roles they ascribe to them, and where they situate their *minzu* identity in relation to the other collective identities they maintain. In order to trace this relationality, I asked my research participants to discuss these attachments and explore their significance in their individualized identity topographies. Although the responses are only a snapshot of the moment-by-moment identity choices in the overall process of identity negotiation, these representations are nevertheless particularly informative. They demonstrate the reasoning behind and the "making sense" of identities, however fluid they may be. The first focus of the analysis below is thus on this "making sense" of identities and on their relationality and interconnectedness.

The second aim is to explore in some detail the Han attachment to *jiaxiang* and *guxiang*, conventionally translated as "native place." As the research data demonstrate, native place assumes a prominent role in identity negotiations of Han individuals. At the same time, these data show that the notion of native place is anything but well defined. Although most Han informants claimed attachment to one native place when asked about it directly, further inquiries and observations revealed that the majority of them actually referred to more than one place as native. Furthermore, while they concealed or diminished the importance of certain native places, other places were clearly a source of pride. In addition to the notion of native place and other understandings of place-based identities, the complexity of native-place attachments clearly merits investigation.

HOME-PLACE IDENTITY

Place Attachments of Han/Chinese: A Brief Introduction

Individual and collective attachments to place are critical to identity formation due to "shared cognitive maps and embodied social practices that make place meaningful for a community" (Dautcher 2009, 50). Both Chinese and Western scholars widely agree that place-based attachments play an important role in how the Han identify themselves and others. Several studies demonstrate the influence of place-based bonds in economic, social, and even, as some argue, ethnic organization and differentiation among the Han.[2]

The most common concepts in discourses of place-based differentiation are *jiaxiang, guxiang,* and *jiguan.* In their dictionary definitions, the first two terms, *jiaxiang* and *guxiang,* have a similar meaning; they indicate "hometown" or "native place." *Guxiang* is also translated as "birthplace."[3] In the third term, *jiguan, ji* stands for "record," "registry," and "register," while *guan* literally means "being linked together" and "following in the continuous line."[4] Although *jiguan* is translated as "native place" too, it refers more specifically to the locality identified as ancestral land along the patriline, the place where the family's name originates and where, especially south of the Yangzi River, the ancestral hall is located.[5]

Fei Xiaotong (1992, 121–27) argues that the Han bond with a place, and more broadly with a region of origin, should be understood as an extension of consanguinity into space.[6] In premodern China two kinds of bonds, blood kinship and spatial kinship, were the determining factors in the formation of business networks. Likewise, Lin Yutang (1998, 198) writes, "From the love of the family there grew a love for the clan, and from the love for the clan there developed an attachment for the land where one was born. Thus a sentiment arose which may be called 'provincialism,' in Chinese called *t'unghsiang kuannien* [*tongxiang guannian*], or 'the idea of being from the same native place.' . . . Fundamentally, they spring from the family psychology and do not depart from the family pattern. It is the family mind enlarged so as to make some measure of civic cooperation possible."[7]

As various historical studies demonstrate, native place in pre-twentieth-century China was the most often evoked organizational principle among migrants in need of assistance in new environments. These migrant communities' political affairs, work, residence, financial assistance, business cooperation, and leisure activities were organized along the lines of spatial kinship (Rowe 1984; Naquin and Rawski 1987, 47). Communities of fellow locals (*laoxiang*) tended to share occupational specializations. For instance, in Beijing, an urban center historically known for its large sojourning population of merchants and officials, northwestern merchants were central government bankers, while the "book-and-art" market was run by Southerners from the Lower Yangzi basin (Naquin and Rawski 1987, 142–43).[8] Further, those who ran stands selling steamed buns tended to be from Shandong (Shandong'er), while people from Shanxi (Laoxi'er) traded in salt and oils and worked in the funeral business making coffins. People from Zhejiang tended to operate shops with southern goods, while those from Dingxing in Hebei worked in public bathhouses (Liu Xiaochun 2003, 12).

Networks of fellow locals manifested institutionally first in the form of *huiguan* (guild hall, provincial guild), gatherings of rich merchants. From 1912 on, the more egalitarian associations of fellow locals (*tongxianghui*), sometimes also called common or collective place (*gongsuo*), emerged as an institutional representation of native-place bonds outside of familiar environments (Goodman 1992, 77). In addition to the main cities, guilds also densely covered rural regions of Jiangxi, Hubei, Hunan, and especially Sichuan (Ho 1966, 120–22). Most of the guilds in rural provinces were established by migrating farmers (*kemin*) and not by merchants, as they were in the cities.[9] Though place-based associations that promoted local sentiments could have evoked hostility from the central bureaucracy, this was not the case. Guilds were officially recognized and consulted on various community-related matters; in addition, tax collection and supervision of economic activities in the city were conducted in a mutually beneficial way by guild and city officials (Deglopper 1977, 647). With the rise of nationalism, guilds were conceived of not as a threat to the idea of a unitary nation but as entities that undergirded a new understanding of native place as synonymous with the state territory.

The outbreak of the civil war and the economic crisis it caused limited the field of activity of home-place guilds and associations (*huiguan* and *tongxianghui*), but some of them did survive into the Communist era. Their importance and number of members decreased greatly, though, as the new regime severed the flow of population between rural and urban areas by means of the household registration system (*hukou zhidu*). Additional restrictions on freedom of association and the accompanying governmental anxiety about informal associations effected further restrictions on the activities of associations of fellow locals. Eventually, the Cultural Revolution halted the existence of associations in mainland China, but in the reform era native-place networks again gained importance (Goodman 1995, 305–6).[10] Contemporary studies demonstrate that native-place identities, together with kinship, remain the foremost organizing principles for migrants in the cities. These identities manifest perhaps most clearly, but not exclusively, in so-called urban villages, communities that form through native-place networks in large migrant cities (Zhang 2001; Xiang 2005). Native place is not only a paradigm of spatial organization of fellow locals in China's modernizing cities; similarly to ethnicity, it also manifests in their business specialization. Elisabeth Perry (1995, 323–24) additionally highlights the importance of native-place identities in labor militancy and struggles for migrant workers' rights in post-1989 China. While the interests of permanent workers employed at state enterprises are officially represented by unions, contract and temporary laborers turn to native-place "gangs" for protection. Clearly, then, the increased labor mobility of the past few decades has again enhanced the role of presocialist forms of social organization alongside kin and native-place networks.

What's in a Term

Although popularly translated as "native place" in the literature cited above, *jiaxiang* and *guxiang* as used by contemporary Han have multiple meanings that cannot be fully rendered with the vocabulary of "nativity," that is, being born and originating in a place. *Jiaxiang* and *guxiang* refer namely to both nativity to a place by birth and to acquired nativity by residence. The terms also comprise ancestral nativity as relating to a place regarded as an ancestral home, even if the person has never actually visited that place. While some Han apply the terms *jiaxiang* and *guxiang* to places where they live (but where they were not born), others disagree with the flexible interpretation and insist that *jiaxiang* and *guxiang* are inborn or inherited and cannot be individually acquired. For some Han, then, the two Chinese terms are equivalent to the English "native place" (i.e., a place where you were born). For others, the terms also refer to a place in which you *become* a local by living there. Still other Han will say that *jiaxiang* and *guxiang* refer solely to the place where your ancestors originated. Within this last category, it is disputed whether only patrilineal *jiaxiang/guxiang* exists or if matrilineal *jiaxiang/guxiang* exists as well. The variety of ways in which these two Chinese terms are used demands a rendering in English that puts less emphasis on being "native" to a place yet is simultaneously broad enough to comprise this and other meanings. The English rendering should ideally convey this ambiguity and at the same time also convey the meaning of home inherent in the Chinese terminology.

A possible way to discuss *jiaxiang* and *guxiang* identities is to refer to them as place-based identities. However, this terminology seems too large and too generic. *Jiaxiang* and *guxiang* are merely one kind of possible place-based attachment. In the various contexts in which *jiaxiang/guxiang* are used, additional specification of the individualized meanings of place would be required. This would make it difficult to effectively apply these terms in a translation, as it would ultimately be the author's responsibility to determine which meaning(s) of place a Han individual might have had in mind when, for instance, she said that both Beijing and Zhejiang were her *jiaxiang*. Did she mean birthplace? Hometown? Native place? Place of residence? The place where patrilineal ancestors originate? More than one of these things? The author would necessarily be the one who "fixes" the ambiguity of the Chinese terms upon translation. Rather, "home place" emerges in the context of this study as a much more suitable rendering of *jiaxiang* and *guxiang*. This English phrasing is similarly open and unspecific and also connotes the notion of home that is implicit in the Chinese terms. It can render the meaning of an ancestral home place, a home place acquired by birth, and a place that one makes into a home by occupying it through residence. Home place is thus broad enough to comprise the idea of spatial kinship and primordiality associated with place bonds by some Han and also open enough to express the notion of individual agency in making a place into a home. Though "home place" may at first sound awkward to some native English speakers, *jiaxiang* and *guxiang* are thus rendered in this study. An attachment created through bonds with the home place is accordingly referred as home-place identity.[11]

Informants' Reflections on Home-Place Identity

More than half of research participants ascribed centrality to home place in their individual identity constellations, recognizing place as a central axis of identification and categorization processes. The analysis below thus sets out to understand how these individuals explain the importance of home-place attachment and how they relate this, in their personalized identity constellations, to being Han and Chinese.

In their answers, respondents tended to cycle through a few main narratives; indeed, these narratives were rather repetitious. What follows are selected statements representative of informant responses, including biographical data where needed to help make sense of the statements:

Hanzu are common; they live all over. Beijing People [Beijingren] make up an entity with boundaries. [Informant was born in Beijing.]

Hanzu are everywhere; one does not have to mention it. In my heart I am a Beijing Person. [Informant was born in Beijing. His parents were born elsewhere.]

Hanzu inhabit almost every region in China and thus the name Hanzu does not reflect regional differences.

There are too many Hanzu. Thus [Han-ness] is not very important when I want to highlight differences between myself and others.

Being Hanzu is the least important [identity] to me because there are many Han. What counts is my home place.

Minzu is not important; it is rather more significant that people from different regions have different characteristics.

All the people I meet are Hanzu. [On the other hand] I meet people who are not from Beijing and thus what I realize the most is that I am a Beijing Person. I am not a genuine Beijing Person though. [Informant was born in Shenyang, Liaoning, and came to Beijing as a child.] (Fieldwork interviews, Beijing and Shanghai, 2002–3)

The enormous size of the Han *minzu* and the perceived pervasiveness of this identity pose certain identification problems. Particularly in Han-dominated areas of China, being Han appears too obvious and too vague to be a significant identity. School education, state administration, and ID cards stating *minzu* membership play a crucial role in raising awareness of *minzu* categorization among the Hanzu (Gladney 1991, 310–12).[12] Obviously, however, this is not sufficient to make this identity meaningful in everyday interactions in communities where a *minzu* "other," which could reinforce this identity, is present only vaguely. Consequently, in mundane processes of identity in Han-dominated areas, a need to differentiate oneself from other Han is a much more pressing issue. It causes individuals to turn to identifications that are more concrete, that are spatially and numerically limited, and that are capable of marking individuals as unique amid more than a billion other Han. Home-place identities that preceded the Hanzu identity in the form conceived at the turn of the twentieth century respond most directly to this need for differentiation and specification. The modern Han identity apparently has not caught on enough to be able to compete with home-place identities in terms of their everyday and immediate meaningfulness.

While some informants drew attention to the identifying function of home-place identities, others ascribed primary importance to bonds with home place because of their emotionality. Here, home place is the imaginary space of familiarity, one's roots, a symbolic parent that "feeds" its children. These individuals stressed that home place had a determining influence on their lives; it determined what would become of them. The tangibility of home place via personal relations to it, whether actual or imagined, stands in a stark contrast with the generality of the *minzu*:

My home place is important to me because of the nostalgic feelings I have for it, because of the longing I have for relatives there.

All my strength comes from my roots, and my roots are in my hometown.

People always want to return home. I think I will never move to any other city. I am proud of being a Shanghainese [Shanghairen].

This soil gave birth to me and brought me up. This is my home.

One has the feeling of belonging and affiliation with the home place.

I love my home place. It is an honor for me to be a Zhejiang Person [Zhejiangren]. I do not care about the rest.

Native place counts more than Han race. [Interview in English.]

(Fieldwork interviews, Beijing and Shanghai, 2002–3)

These Han informants emphasized the emotionality of home place and its role as the locus of family networks, implicitly suggesting that *minzu* attachment is by contrast less emotional, less graspable, and more distant. In terms of sentimental appeal, the *minzu* identity obviously cannot compete with home-place attachments. These two lines of argumentation— the vagueness of Han-ness and the familiarity of home place—dominated conversations with these informants. The interview material further reveals how these informants negotiated their home-place identities and the strategies they employed to position themselves advantageously in relation to other Han with the help of these very identities. In the unfamiliar environments of large cities like Shanghai and Beijing, where Han migrants and ethnic-minority migrants gather from all across China, such strategies are arguably employed more frequently than elsewhere. The following statements of four interviewees, one born in Inner Mongolia, two in Subei (northern Jiangsu), and one in Henan, reflect some of the negotiation processes and strategies utilized.[13] Additionally, they reflect the dilemma many migrants must negotiate, namely, how to reconcile the feeling that home place is essential to one's identity with the fact that home place can be a burden in social interactions and a source of discrimination.

Beijing People have a dominant position in the whole country; they are in a position of advantage. Inner Mongolians are backward, and that is why I do not like to call myself Inner Mongolian [Neimengren]. I identify myself as a Beijing Person. [Informant was born in Inner Mongolia and currently lives in Beijing.].

I do not use the term Hanzu at all; everybody is Hanzu. I am also not a Beijing Person. I am from Subei but I do not feel like a Subei Person [Subeiren]. If someone asks me where I am from, I answer that I am a Jiangsu Person [Jiangsuren]. More specifically, I am Xuzhou de [from Xuzhou].

> I was born in Subei . . . but this is not important to me. I consider
> myself Shanghainese. [Informant was born in Subei and currently lives
> in Shanghai.]
>
> I am from Henan but I do not feel any special bonds with the name
> Henan Person [Henanren]. In terms of work, I would prefer to be a Beijing
> Person because it is easier for them to find a job. (Fieldwork interviews,
> Beijing and Shanghai, 2002–3)

Born in Inner Mongolia, the first informant above refers to himself
as an Inner Mongolian when asked directly for his self-denomination.
However, due to the negative associations that this label has in modernizing China, he conceals his Inner Mongolian identity in social interactions with other Han. Instead, he prefers to call himself a Beijing Person,
identifying with his current place of residence. His Inner Mongolian
identity becomes partially reactivated and performed upon his rare visits
to his hometown. This and other identity switches highlight the negotiated nature of home-place identities. Such switches also demonstrate that
although Han individuals prefer to discuss home-place identities in terms
of emotional attachments, these identities are also instrumentalized and
strategically employed; in real-life identity politics, these two dimensions
are virtually impossible to separate.

It is revealing that despite feeling uncomfortable about their home-
place identities, many of the interviewed Han still argued for the centrality
of home place in their individualized identity negotiations. In fact, numerous research participants identified this tension themselves, discussing
their idealization of home place as a space of familiarity alongside the
realization that public manifestations of attachments to these places may
be socially disadvantageous. Informants identified being a Beijing Person
or a Shanghai Person as socially most advantageous, particularly in terms
of employment or housing. At the same time, they were also aware that
especially being a Henan Person, Subei Person, or Inner Mongolian was
much less desired socially and could evoke discrimination. The Han informants from Henan, Subei, and Inner Mongolia all described experiencing
negative consequences of their spatial "roots" in their current lives. They
also discussed the various coping strategies they utilized to improve their
situations. Among these, one strategy was to maintain a belief that home-
place identities are central but to simultaneously conceal or blur one's own

place identity. Another popular strategy was to refer to one's home place with a different name. For instance, instead of Henan, an individual may use terms like Zhongyuan (Central Plains) or Jiangnan (South of the River, here meaning the Yellow River), which are geographically synonymous.[14] Instead of Subei, individuals may use the provincial designation Jiangsu or the regional designation Jiangbei (North of the River, here meaning the Yangzi River).[15] One informant who was born in Inner Mongolia—but in a region relatively close to the border of one of the northeastern provinces— referred to himself as a Northeasterner (Dongbeiren) instead of as Inner Mongolian. Some Han individuals also used a "counterattack" strategy, aggressively praising their own home place, despite its negative connotations in popular perception. Still other research participants employed a strategy of playing down the importance of place-based identities in general, instead emphasizing the centrality of being Han or Chinese. Each of these strategies reflects complex processes of hesitation, negotiation, and instrumentalization of identities. Although literature on place-based identities, particularly within mainland China, gives the impression that these identities are neat and well defined,[16] the interviews reveal that there is no clear definition of a home place, nor is there a set number of home-place identities that a person may maintain. Significantly, various locations can function as a home place. They can be emotionally adopted as a home and also be instrumentalized as such, particularly when it comes to highly desirable place-based identities like those relating to Beijing, Shanghai, and other major cities in eastern and southeastern China.

Interestingly, the research participants who identified themselves as Hakka/Kejia, ascribed equal centrality to their Hakka/Kejia and home-place identities.[17] A statement of one Hakka informant is representative of those I collected:

> I feel like a Kejia and Jiangxi Person [Jiangxiren] at the same time. We usually differentiate Hanzu according to the region of origin; it is related to our idea of home place. People care a lot about home place. Within such a huge mass of Han People, home place is the primary means of differentiation. (Fieldwork interview, Shanghai, 2002)

Hakka identity was originally anchored in migrant status, the status of not belonging locally (Leong 1997, 129). This was a social category of those listed in the population registers at their destinations as *keji* (registered as guests). While the guest status differentiated families of migrants from the "native" population in these registers, the families of "guests" shared neither a common ethnic nor cultural identity (Constable 1996, 12–15).[18] Still, the shared experience of migration, displacement, social exclusion, and discrimination from the "locals" resulted in the Hakka becoming a shared identity label in the nineteenth century. What is of particular interest to my later discussion is that the Hakka/Kejia identity is described here as equally central as home-place identities. This implies that Hakka/Kejia and even multiple home-place identities can coexist in a nonexclusive and intertwined way.

To summarize, then, a majority of research participants argued that home place mattered more to them than being Han in terms of how they identified themselves and other Han. The reasons for the primacy of this attachment can be roughly divided into two categories: first, the vagueness of the *minzu* identity and, second, the strong emotional bond to the spatial "roots" associated with home place. There is no regional pattern among the informants who ascribed primacy to home-place identities. Apart from Han individuals from Shanghai, Zhejiang, and Beijing (admittedly somewhat overrepresented here), the Han who ascribed centrality to identification with home place came from all possible locations, from geographically remote regions as well as central ones, from places referred to as economically backward as well as developed (*fada*), and from areas that evoked positive as well as negative associations. The research data show that Han individuals actively engage in the negotiation and formation of their identities; they carefully analyze their options and make decisions, however temporary. By implementing strategies of concealing or switching their home places, they also actively influence the ways in which they are perceived by other Han. Hence, although the inherited home place may sometimes be a difficult legacy to cope with, Han individuals creatively tackle this issue, shifting carefully between emotionality and instrumentalization.

Informants' Definitions of Home Place

Place-based identities are unquestionably relevant and important, including among younger generations of Hanzu. Still, few Han individuals have one home-place identity; the majority of Han move between multiple place identities they situationally refer to as home. Some of these identities are inherited, some consciously chosen, and some imposed by others. Clearly, home place is a concept defined by extreme flexibility. It appears to be used relatively rarely in its meaning of birthplace, an inherited home place, or a place identified with patrilineal ancestors. Indeed, home-place identities emerged during my research as much less long-term than originally expected, with some exceptions. Home-place identities were more individually determined, consciously negotiated, instrumentalized, flexibly and creatively interpreted, and as with most identities, impossible to systematize. The following informant responses illustrate these processes of home-place identity negotiation:

I feel 90 percent like a Beijing Person, but because my parents are from Shanxi, this is my home place [*jiaxiang*]. Owing to this, I am also a bit of a Shanxi Person [Shanxiren]. [Informant was born in Beijing.]

My own home place [*jiaxiang*] is not important to me, but my father's is. I have a feeling of belonging there. [Informant was born in Hainan, her father in Guangdong.]

My first home place [*guxiang*] is Shandong. . . . Beijing is my second home. [Informant was born in Shandong and currently lives in Beijing.]

I was born in Shandong, but now I live and plan to marry in Shanghai. Shanghai is my home place [*jiaxiang*] now.

Harbin is my home place [*guxiang*]. A person can live in different places but one cannot change one's home place.

Sichuan is my home place [*jiaxiang*] . . . this soil and culture nourished me. Beijing is a place where I pursue my studies. When I say "I am a Beijing Person" it is my individually determined decision (*renke*).

In fact, Shanghai is not my home place but I consider myself to be a Shanghainese. I refer to myself as Local Shanghainese [Shanghai Bendiren]. [Informant was born in Zhejiang.]

Being a Beijing Person is most important to me because I have studied here for four years. . . . The second most important is being a Zhejiang Person [Zhejiangren]. My home place [*jiaxiang*] is in Zhejiang. In a broader sense I am a Southerner, but I am also a Northerner, I grew up here. In the eyes of my relatives in the South, I am a Northerner. [Informant was born in Hebei; her parents are from Zhejiang.] (Fieldwork interviews, Beijing and Shanghai, 2002–3)

The places referred to as home place include, among others, the individual's own birthplace, location of household registration, father's or mother's home place, the place of living, the place of studying, and interestingly, in one case, the home place of the spouse. When it fits their identity imageries and individual positioning strategies, some Han emphasize their patrilineal "roots" and stress the primordiality and constancy of home-place attachments. Otherwise, other places can be adopted as home place and practiced as such in social interactions. One of the informants observed that the only occasion when the agency of an individual Han becomes restrained and the individually determined home-place choices do not matter is when a person confronts state institutions. These confrontations occur most often in matters of employment, housing, and education. When state institutions enter into individualized identity politics, the only place-related categories that matter for an individual's classification are the state-established household registration and the much older but still occasionally used notion of *jiguan*, the place of origin of one's patriline and family name.

While flexible, the attachment to home place is still extremely prevalent. It is to be expected, however, that personal mobility and the increasing pace of life will variously affect this attachment in the future. Individuals may, for example, increasingly favor more pragmatic or individually determined place-based identifications, for instance, those related to household registration or place of residence. At the same time, the experience of migration and the longing for the familiar may lead to assigning added importance to inherited home-place identities associated with one's spatial "origins" and "roots." However the meaning of home place develops, it will likely remain a complex and blurred concept that will allow for a great deal of negotiation and individual agency.

IDENTIFICATION WITH THE HAN *MINZU*

In contrast to the majority of informants who highlighted the centrality of home place in processes of identification, some research participants ascribed centrality to identification with the Han *minzu*. The following responses explain these interviewees' emphasis on their *minzu* identity and illustrate the role they ascribe to it:

Hanzu are one *minzu* and should not be subdivided. Most importantly, I am Hanzu. If it is necessary to differentiate regionally, I was born in the Northeast [Dongbei] and so I am a Northeasterner. A few years ago I came to Beijing, and Beijing became my second home place [*guxiang*].

I am in the first place Hanzu; this is because young Chinese people [*sic*] stress unity.

There is a feeling of belonging with other Han; this originates in the shared culture and *minzu* affiliation. That is why I feel primarily Hanzu.

I have life habits of a Xi'an Person [Xi'anren], but I am Hanzu. My home place is not important.

Hanzu make China different from all other countries and peoples. Only thanks to Hanzu, the numerous *minzu* of China can communicate with each other.

I am proud of being Hanzu.

Minzu affiliation marks the biggest and most important difference between me and other people; my home place [Chongqing] is secondary.

I do not have any home place. [Informant was born in Lanzhou, Gansu.]

My home place is not important to me. I have beautiful memories from my childhood but it has degenerated and become backward. [Informant was born in Subei.]

My home place is neither important nor unimportant to me. I do not mind the designation Subei Person, but I am not especially proud of it. I consider myself a Shanghainese. [Informant was born in Subei.] (Fieldwork interviews, Beijing and Shanghai, 2002–3)

These Han argue that Han-ness is a positive, unifying identity, unlike what they identify as the divisive and hierarchical attachments relating to home place. Other reasons they offered for the importance of *minzu* identity were the belief that all Han share a common "essence," a focus on the political centrality of Hanzu in China, an emphasis on their role as the nation's unifier, and pride in being Han.

The factor that must be considered here is how much these responses were influenced by what these Han thought their audience expected to hear, particularly when their audience was a foreign researcher. Indeed, conversations with some of these research participants hinted at an overt political position, one to be defended or protected. If not for these filters, the share of Han who primarily identify themselves through home-place attachments would likely have been even higher than my data indicate. Still, based on the content of conversations and my observations, it appears that the number of Han motivated solely by the obligation they felt as Hanzu and as loyal Chinese citizens conversing with a foreigner was rather small. Rather, a mutually dependent system of individual rationale and assumed political obligation fused to influence their identification. For instance, some Han who experienced discrimination because of their inherited home place emphasized the importance of the Hanzu identity by claiming pride in being Han. On the other hand, Beijing and Shanghai People who emphasized the centrality of the Han identity gave the impression that being a Beijing or Shanghai Person and a Hanzu was principally the same to them, for they assumed that these two powerful regional groups determined the overall definition of Han-ness. Moreover, my research shows that while some Hanzu imagine their identities as a hierarchical structure that situates the all-encompassing Han-ness on top and home-place identities below, others understand identity to be a cupboard with many drawers. When a scale of interaction and an "other" change, one drawer closes and another one opens, as for this informant: "Seen from the perspective of the whole country, I am Hanzu. At a smaller scale, I am Anhui Person [Anhuiren]."

Interestingly, the centrality of identification with the Han *minzu* was explained in a significant number of cases not so much by directly discussing Han-ness as by discussing the problems and difficulties encountered in relation to home-place identities. Identification with *minzu* was employed in these cases as something of an emergency exit from place-based differentiation, a differentiation these Han found troubling and uncomfortable and on which they were unable to capitalize. Their statements thus point to one of the presumably most important functions of the Han identity, which is to serve as a symbolic haven. The identity is a strategic resort for those Hanzu who feel uncomfortable in their home-place identities, those whose home-place identities are a cause of social discrimination, and those who through life circumstances (e.g., family conflicts) and personal choices do not feel like they belong in any particular place and thus have no home-place identity. Han-ness, similar to Chinese-ness, can function in such situations as an alternative to and refuge from discriminating, emotionally difficult, divisive, and shifting home-place identities.

IDENTIFICATION WITH THE CHINESE NATION AND STATE

In quite a contrast to home-place and *minzu* identities, research participants seldom discussed the centrality of the Chinese national identity. If they did, it was usually a deliberate attempt to decrease the importance of identity particulars when judging a person, to emphasize national unity in spite of the dividing boundaries of home place and *minzu*, or to express patriotic love for the country and pride in being Chinese:

> What matters most to me is that I am Chinese. Zhengzhou is my home-town, so it is quite important too. But being . . . Han or Henan Person does not matter to me at all. I look at the character of a person, not at the place where this person comes from. [Informant was born in Zhengzhou, Henan.]
>
> What matters is that I am Chinese; being a Jiangxi Person, a Shang-hainese or Hanzu are all equally less important. [Still], having a special feeling toward one's birthplace is an inherent attribute of Chinese people. [Informant was born in Shanghai; his mother's home place is in Jiangxi.]
>
> The country is my mother, it brought me up.
>
> I cherish feelings for my home place. [But] the only thing that matters is being Chinese.
>
> First of all, I am Chinese. I am proud of being Chinese. Second, I am a Hanzu Person (Hanzuren). Hanzu are the largest *minzu* of China . . . They have played a pivotal role in the history of China. Third, I am a Hunan Person (Hunanren). I love my home place.
>
> I begin from the broadest perspective: first of all, I am Chinese. Hanzu have common features. Being a Beijing Person [place of residence] is not at all important to me, apart from having some privileges related to the household registration here. [Informant was born in Chongqing.] (Field-work interviews, Beijing and Shanghai, 2002–3)

Chinese-ness is the most extensive and inclusive of all the identities discussed by my informants. It is an identity that ideally should embrace and protect all Chinese nationals in an equal way, independent of their *minzu*, home place, occupation, or access to wealth. While it is questionable that the Chinese identity indeed does this, the inclusive and egalitarian *potential* of Chinese-ness is, at least for some Han, the reason to emphasize its importance.[19] Interestingly, one of the quotations above stresses that it is a Chinese characteristic to have strong home-place identities, yet another example of nonexclusive, fuzzy, and nested identity processes. The final two quotes reflect deliberate switches between component nested identities—identities that are consciously considered, assumed, or concealed and identities that alter with changing scales of interaction.

Among all research participants, those who emphasized the centrality of being Chinese in their everyday processes of identity constituted a clear minority. This is somewhat surprising considering that the person who interviewed them was a foreigner and thus an international scale of interaction was, it would seem, explicit in the conversations. One reason for this small number of Han individuals who highlighted the importance of national identity could be the focus of the present study on identities that mattered in mundane identity processes. Perhaps being Chinese is not that crucial for such processes. Further, it may be that Chinese-ness gains significance when one crosses an international border, which very few research participants had done, or during international tensions that involve China, which was not the case during my fieldwork.

These results clearly contrast with a survey on national identity discussed by Wenfang Tang and Gaochao He in *Separate but Loyal* (2010). Among the three countries compared in the study, Chinese citizens scored the highest in the survey when it came to attachment to national identity (84 points out of 100), ahead of the United States and Russia. The significant difference between these survey results and the rather modestly expressed viability of Chinese identity in the present study may be a result of the methodology of data collection. The survey was conducted by state officials and thus implicitly enforced the importance of the state and national identity in the collected responses. Further, the survey singled out the Chinese identity by referencing it directly in the statements that respondents were expected to assess, such as, "I would rather be a citizen of China, than of any other country in the world" (Tang and He 2010, 40). Data generated through such a survey accordingly differ from data generated through semi-structured interviews and observations, where

Chinese-ness is merely one identity option discussed. When singled out, virtually any identity is likely to appear powerful—consider, for example, the way Han-ness is discussed in the previous chapter. When contextualized, however, it appears that Chinese-ness seems to have limited implications for the everyday identity negotiations of Han individuals in Han-dominated areas of eastern China.

IDENTIFICATION THROUGH NEGATION

A similarly small share of Han research participants identified themselves by negating each collective category of identity discussed in the interviews, including nation, *minzu*, and home place. Some individuals offered other forms of identification that mattered more to them than these well-established, and thus somewhat coercive and arguably worn-out, concepts.

> I am indifferent to being a Shandong Person [Shandongren; birthplace], Beijing Person [residence] and Hanzu. I have Beijing household registration. Differences caused by environment are diminishing now; none of the attachments are especially outstanding.
>
> Being a Hunan Person [birthplace], Beijing Person [residence], or Hanzu are all equally unimportant. If not for official papers, none of them would matter to me.
>
> All these things do not matter too much, whatever. Home place is a bit more important. I have a Beijing household registration, but I cannot say that I am a Beijing Person. Maybe later [I will be able to] when I have lived here for some time.
>
> They all do not matter to me. In terms of household registration I am a Beijing Person, but I am from Nanjing.
>
> Hanzu is a *minzu* attribute; Beijing is my birthplace. I cannot change either of them. I identify with people with broad horizons. (Fieldwork interviews, Beijing and Shanghai, 2002–3)

These Han individuals avoided accepting historically constructed identities and equally challenged the importance of *minzu*, home-place, and national attachments. One principal reason for a rejection of these well-established identities emerges in the final quotation above: all of these identities, as well as the associations they evoke, are beyond the influence of an individual. As such, they cannot convey any personal, individualized meanings, and they possess a coerciveness to which these Hanzu obviously object. An alternative that matters more to them is the state-established category of household registration. The location of household registration determines where one can legally work, buy an apartment at a preferential price, apply for a passport, or take a driving license exam. It may well be that with increasing migration and individualization, the "givens" of *minzu*, nation, and the primordially conceived home place may withdraw from dominant positions, while social classifiers such as household registration and individual identities will gain further importance.

CONCLUSION

When analyzed out of the social context of everyday identity politics, Han-ness appears as a powerful and tangible identity. When contextualized through its entanglement in identity processes, however, Han-ness turns out to be just one of many identity options that Hanzu individuals select from and switch between. Individual identity constellations often combine Han-ness with flexibly interpreted home-place identities as well as with the national Chinese identity. These three types of collective attachments—and many others—form individualized, complex, and intertwined topographies. Depending on the scale of interaction, any one of these identities may become activated and exposed. Although identity choices are situational, home-place identities seem to matter most to Han individuals in everyday encounters and in the ways they identify themselves and other Han. While the actual reasons they grant primacy to home-place identities are individual and fragmented, the narratives that inspire these Han can be summarized as follows:

- The Han *minzu* is too large, Han identity too obvious and omnipresent. This leaves some Han individuals feeling "undefined" and identity-less.
- Han-ness is not a meaningful identity in Han-dominated areas; home place is a more concrete attachment that matters in social interactions.
- Attachment to home place is something emotional. Home place is the locus of the familiar (although some interviewees have never

even briefly visited the places they refer to as home). Home place is an environment where family and friends are and where one belongs. It is made tangible through imagined or actual personal relations to it.

- Home place is imagined as the "roots" that determine one's life. In this imagery, the soil of the home place is a symbolic parent that feeds its children.

- Home place has an important influence on a person's social standing. Some places enjoy a particularly high social status. These places are more often than others claimed as home and emphasized in social interactions.

Home place is usually inquired about and revealed in the early stages of social interactions; stories associated with these places, the stereotypical characteristics of the people "originating" in them, and comments on local dialects are typically quick to follow.[20] Hanzu like to tease one another about their home places, and knowing the home place of their interlocutors makes individual Han assume certain roles in dealing with each other, roles based on stereotypical qualities ascribed to people "originating" in particular places.[21] In distant migrant locations, Han individuals who find they share a common home place (typically a province, often much larger than most European countries) are likely to celebrate their fellow locals' relations, toasting each other at the dinner table and offering examples of their languages and dialects.

The Han individuals who ascribed primary importance to home-place identities argued that Han-ness is a concept with minimal significance in their daily social interactions with other Han. Understandably, in Han-dominated regions where *minzu* "others" are missing, the omnipresent Han-ness can function as a meaningful identity only to a limited extent. Han individuals who wish to distinguish the Hanzu into smaller and more graspable categories rely primarily on the paradigm of home place. Still, although place is well recognized among the Hanzu as an important identity concept and a paradigm of differentiation, the definition of home place is very open. For one, different localities, not necessarily one's birthplace, can be adopted as a home place. Moreover, in the majority of cases, identification with home place involves referring to several localities as home, each pushed to the front line situationally. The landscape of home-place identities is thus a lively and chaotic field.

Although home-place identities are of great importance in Han-to-Han interactions, wealth, education, occupation, and other factors often dim the significance of place identities and reshuffle place hierarchies in social practice. If a distinguished guest at the dinner table turns out to be from rural Sichuan, the conversation will likely praise the beauty and tranquility of country life rather than discuss the millions of impoverished migrant workers who yearly leave Sichuan to find work elsewhere. Accordingly, then, home-place identities and the associations they elicit, while certainly present, should not be imagined as socially overwhelming. Whereas my research data highlight the importance of these identities, they also highlight the parallel agency of Han individuals in selecting, assuming, swapping, or rejecting home-place identities. Hence, this portion of research material offers four important conclusions: First, home place is a creative process of negotiation between the inherited, the given, the plausible, and the individually desired. Second, owing to this, Hanzu have multiple home-place identities that are situationally activated. Third, home-place identities are relational; they are especially important in situations when Han-ness and Chinese-ness are not meaningful as axes of identification. Fourth, like Han-ness, home-place identities must be analyzed in a relational context with other identities that may sometimes restrain their importance.

Whereas home-place attachments appear to stand in the center of everyday identity politics for the majority of research participants, Han-ness is central to significantly fewer of them. Still, depending on the context, Han-ness has important functions to fulfill and is also cherished as an encompassing and nondiscriminative identity. The Han who emphasized the importance of this identity were motivated by the pride of belonging to the dominant *minzu* and the pivotal role of the Hanzu in China; the desire to emphasize *minzu* unity beyond home place-related divisions; and the feeling of belonging together as Hanzu, sharing a "common essence" as a *minzu*. Some Han ascribed centrality to *minzu* identity because of the discrimination and discomfort they experienced through their inherited home-place identities. The Han from Subei and Henan seem to be most affected by this discrimination, as do some Inner Mongolians. Informants born in these regions tended to either conceal or swap their home places or to emphasize the importance of Han *minzu* identity. These practices offered them anonymity and shelter beyond the divisiveness of place-based categorizations.

Interestingly, although most research participants had no difficulty defining Han-ness and its boundaries, as demonstrated in chapter 2, when participants were confronted with home-place identities Han-ness appeared much less appealing and meaningful. Still, even if the majority perceived Han-ness as too common to be meaningful, strong place attachments do not necessarily call into question the sense and role of *minzu* identity. Rather, home-place and *minzu* identities coexist at different scales of reference. Home-place identities *tend to* matter primarily in Han-to-Han interactions, while *minzu* identity matters in inter-*minzu* interactions. Yet as identity processes in China's multiethnic regions demonstrate, identities are flexibly reformulated, and home-place identities can also be used to establish pan-*minzu* forms of solidarity. For example, while some Han identify themselves clearly vis-à-vis "the Uyghur" in Xinjiang, other Han establish a relationship of solidarity with some Uyghur based on a shared home-place identity, that is, being local to Xinjiang (Joniak-Lüthi 2014). Thus, as home-place identities do not deny the importance of *minzu* identities, *minzu* identities do not exclude non-*minzu* and cross-*minzu* forms of solidarity.

At yet another scale of interaction, the national identity as Chinese is evoked. This identity nominally plays down both *minzu*- and home place–drawn boundaries and draws attention instead to a larger, more encompassing national (or even transnational) community and the territorial state. Although the overwhelming majority of research participants were exposed for at least thirteen years to centralized state education and to the subject of patriotic education as taught from elementary level on, respondents relatively rarely emphasized attachment to the Chinese national identity. The efficacy of state education in influencing everyday identity choices and options in eastern China thus does not seem overwhelming. Further, my research data suggest that among the contemporary Han there is a small but not insignificant group of individuals who distance themselves from the coerciveness of "mandatory" attachments to soil, *minzu*, and nation. The instrumental category of household registration was put forth by some Han respondents as mattering most in practical, everyday terms. These Han rejected "participants' primordialism" (Brubaker 2004, 9) and refrained from "speaking continuities" (Anagnost 1997), sticking rather to the pragmatic household registration or individually determined attachments.

Identities are enacted across multiple axes (Carrico 2012, 25). Han-ness, as coherent and powerful as it appears in some situations, is merely one of these axes. It must therefore be contextualized in relation to other identities before we can understand its relational significance. The emphasis on the centrality of home place and not *minzu* indicates that Han-ness has powerful competitors on the "identity market," particularly in urban, Hanzu-dominated settings of eastern Chinese cities, where a reifying *minzu* "other" is largely missing in everyday interactions. There, Han-ness has to make space for home-place attachments believed to matter more in everyday social interactions because they establish and maintain distinctions from other Han. At the same time, home-place identities are situationally restrained by occupation, education, and many other factors that may be equally important as organizational and categorizing principles. Moreover, centrality ascribed to home place does not indicate that Han-ness is becoming a useless attachment—far from it. The universality and broadness of Han identity—in some contexts arguably its weaknesses—represent at the same time its great strength. Nominally, the category offers common space for all individuals officially identified as Hanzu, regardless of their origins and social status (both of which may be stigmatized) or their occupation (for which they may be discriminated against, underpaid, or made to feel inferior). The symbolic resources associated with "the Han" as the largest, most advanced, most modern, and most powerful *minzu* make Han-ness a situationally attractive identity. Attempts to increase the "visibility" of Han-ness for the Han themselves are being undertaken too. The reinvention of silk robes as "traditional" Han clothing is one fascinating example of reversed Orientalism that strives to make Han-ness more graspable (Leibold 2010). In this process, folklorization emerges as a way to "domesticate" the Han *minzu* by ascribing to it a set of easily definable characteristics.

Despite the relative coerciveness of home-place, *minzu*, and national identities, many options remain open to an individual who negotiates between them. In a conflict-free situation where none of the identities is mobilized more than others, the most common paradigm seems to be the one in which multiple identities are activated situationally. This process of flexible identity swapping and identity negotiation is obviously not unique to China; indeed, it is arguably present in all identity negotiations in all societies. And yet, the data analyzed above demonstrate that despite Han-ness being promoted for many decades as a unitary identity, it still cannot compete with home-place attachments in terms of meaningfulness and familiarity. "The Han" remain a deeply divided category. Home place–related divisions are only one aspect of the fragmentation and boundaries that crisscross the Han *minzu* in contemporary China.

CHAPTER 4

OTHERING, EXCLUSION, AND DISCRIMINATION

The Communist government has attempted to shape and steer Chinese citizens' processes of identity formation via large-scale biopolitical projects, such as the Minzu Classification Project, which have created new categories of classification and new ways of differentiating the population. The government has also utilized education, language policies, and mass media to shape identity formation. Yet because processes formative to ethnic, national, and other social identities cannot be entirely planned and controlled, the outcomes of government campaigns remain to a certain degree unintended and spontaneous. Furthermore, because processes of identity negotiation are ongoing, their effects are temporary and nondefinite. The form, role, and functions of the Han *minzu* identity, along with the ways in which Han-ness is defined, are thus transitory effects of both the government's controlling attempts and the identity negotiations of Han individuals. Han-ness is one of a number of collective identities, one that is relationally entangled in complex identity networks. Home-place identities are an important component of these networks but they are not the only axis of distinction. At closer range, "the Han" disintegrate into a myriad of identity categories whose members struggle to position themselves favorably in social hierarchies and to influence the positioning of others.

To trace the identifications that matter to Han individuals in mundane identity processes, I asked them to provide examples of socionyms, or collective identity labels, that they use to refer to themselves when encountering other Han. I was also interested in what labels they use to identify their Han counterparts. The great majority of the research participants were visibly comfortable with this task and seemed to especially enjoy labeling others. I collected more than four hundred socionyms in this way. Next, I asked informants to discuss these labels and characterize the people they supposedly represent. This query generated more than five hundred characteristics (*tedian*) and associations. In order to highlight the stereotypical, repetitive content and the automatic, mechanical reproduction of most of these characteristics, I refer to them as "stereotypes" or "stereotypical characterizations."[1]

The collected socionyms and stereotypes offer a glimpse into the major differentiation paradigms among contemporary Hanzu. There appear to be five. Four are broadly place-based. First, Han individuals think of themselves and other Han in terms of regional differentiation. This is related to the aforementioned "home-place-determined mind-set," a belief that place imbues the people who originate there—the constructed nature of origin is blended out in this belief—with an "essence" that makes them similar to one another. The second paradigm of differentiation is between urbanity and rurality as two very different modes of being. Third is the distinction between Locals and Outsiders or Natives and Strangers. And fourth is the differentiation between Mainlanders, on one hand, and Taiwanese and Hongkongese, on the other. Admittedly, this last contrast was rather rare. In a few cases, a boundary was additionally drawn between the Hakka/Kejia and all other Han.[2] Besides introducing major identification paradigms, socionyms and stereotypes offer crucial insights into how Han individuals position themselves and other Han in social hierarchies of power. Accordingly, the focus of this chapter's analysis is on categorization, fragmentation, boundaries, and social hierarchies reflected and objectified through the acts of labeling and stereotyping.

SOCIONYMS, STEREOTYPES, AND PROCESSES OF CATEGORIZATION

Socionyms and stereotypes are both the instruments and the effects of categorization processes. Stereotypes and ethnonyms, nationyms, and other forms of socionyms emerge during identification and differentiation processes. In this sense, they are a universal part of any boundary-making project. Naming, or labeling, and stereotyping "us" and "them" is also intimately bound to the negotiation of social hierarchies and power distribution. Self-ascribed names as well as names ascribed by others and to others "record a particular stage of struggles and negotiations over the official designations and the material and symbolic advantages associated with them" (Bourdieu 1991, 240). In these negotiations, agents "resort to practical and symbolic strategies aimed at maximizing the symbolic profit of naming" (Bourdieu 1991, 240). My research demonstrates that similar struggles occur between social actors who compete over symbolic resources related to naming on a scale not directly related to the state politics of categorization and designation. For instance, labels such as Beijing People or Shanghai People are proudly enacted and highly desired because they connote political centrality and economic advancement. At the same time, designations such as Sichuan Rats or Henan Vagabonds are used by Beijing and Shanghai People to establish an asymmetric relationship of power with those migrant laborers who arrive from Sichuan and Henan to the two megacities to seek wage labor. Hence, socionyms reflect and naturalize social hierarchies. They are also used to negotiate and objectify specific power relations.

Like naming, the aim of stereotyping is to construct and naturalize certain categorizations, social orders, and social relations. This aim is achieved when actors begin to recognize vague differences as significant and crucial or when they believe differences exist where there are in fact none (Tajfel 1969, 82; compare the notion of ethnicity in Barth 1996). For instance, though differences between Northern Han and Southern Han may not be apparent to an outsider, the stereotypes collected reveal a powerful belief that these two categories do exist and are diametrically and thoroughly distinct. Through ascription and active use of labels and stereotypes, the Han reify and naturalize these social constructs in discourse and enact them in social practice.

Stereotypes are based on the belief that all members of a given category are alike, that they are homogeneous and predictable on the basis of their membership in that category (Oakes, Haslam, and Turner 1994, 102). Yet stereotypes are not fixed, final images: when the sociopolitical frame changes, new stereotypes gradually arise. Competition-focused theories argue that stereotypes are strategic devices employed in certain contexts by individuals and by social, ethnic, or national actors to achieve certain ends. Stereotypes should thus be understood as products of competition between social groups over material as well as symbolic resources (Sherif 1967, 152; Tajfel et al. 1971, 172). Studies from social psychology especially reveal that, often, "status, self-esteem and beliefs override objective benefits in importance" (Leyens, Yzerbyt, and Schadron 1994, 52–53). Still, although notions of status and self-esteem are crucial to stereotyping, they fail to explain the not uncommon occasions in which members of a category hold negative stereotypes of themselves while maintaining positive stereotypes of others. Among my research participants, Subei People and Inner Mongolians frequently demonstrated this phenomenon. In response to the inability of competition-focused theories to explain such negative self-stereotyping, another function of stereotyping was formulated, describing stereotypes as devices that maintain the social status quo even at the expense of individual or group interests (Jost and Banaji 1994).

Stereotypes are thus employed to naturalize and reify. Stereotypes also "justify" existing relationships within ethnic, national, and other social systems, providing subjectively meaningful explanations for the processes and events that affect individual actors (Tajfel 1981; Hoffman and Hurst 1990, 206; Jost and Banaji 1994, 20). In their justificative function, specific stereotypes are thus ascribed to a group to validate certain behaviors and attitudes toward its members. Accordingly, Shanghai employers are said to avoid hiring Subei People because the latter are reportedly "backward" and "dishonest." Likewise, rural migrants in urban areas are patronized by Urbanites as supposedly "dumb" and "unsophisticated."[3] Moreover, stereotypes function as "causal explanators": a subjectively meaningful understanding of events emerges through the stereotype-based identification of those actors responsible. Accordingly, a Henan Person unable to find work in Beijing will likely explain this event as rooted, at least in part, in the negative stereotyping of Henan People in today's China. Hence, stereotypes and socionyms function as *subjectively* accurate and *subjectively* meaningful representations of social, ethnic, and national categories and the relations between them (Oakes and Reynolds 1997, 64, 70; Spears et al. 1997, 5). Stereotypes and socionyms reflect and order the worldview of the people and groups that reproduce them, shrouding their logics of action and argumentation in an aura of seemingly obvious, universal conclusions.

LABELING, STEREOTYPING, AND SOCIAL BOUNDARIES

Although recent mass education and professional migration theoretically could have weakened place-based differentiation and the attachment to the "soil," the socionyms I collected during my research confirm that spatial categorization remains central to identification processes among the Hanzu. With visible pleasure, my Han informants provided numerous examples of socionyms they use to label other Han and themselves. Table 4.1 provides a representative sample of these socionyms elicited from my interviews (right-hand column) and the main paradigms of categorization on which they build (left-hand column).

These labels obviously do not represent tangible, clearly distinct groups. Like "the Han," all of these socionyms should be placed in quotation marks; they are identity labels creatively conceived by some Han to describe other Han (or themselves) and as such are flexibly and strategically interpreted and applied. These socionyms are capitalized throughout this book as a reminder that they are to be read as identity labels and not as analytical terms. For example, the designation Local Shanghainese (Shanghai Bendiren) nominally denotes a person whose ancestors lived in Shanghai for generations and who is thus "genuinely" local. In practice, however, the act of claiming this label, the grounds on which this claim is based, the reasons for which it is claimed, and the context in which it is used are all flexible and strategically motivated. In spite of this flexibility, the collected socionyms are helpful in tracing the identifications that matter to Han individuals, even if they are transitory and nonexclusive. They also help identify the boundary-making processes with which Han individuals engage.

Stereotypical characterizations are another important component of the mundane processes of boundary making. Gauging from the ease with which the overwhelming majority of research participants suggested these characterizations, it is apparent that stereotyping, like naming, constitutes a familiar element of everyday social interactions. During the interviews, stereotyping occurred without any great deliberation or hesitation. After identifying a number of socionyms (on average, between eight and ten), each interviewee typically introduced and discussed between twenty and thirty "characteristics." While some Han participants only briefly commented on these characterizations, others engaged in more lengthy explanations as to why, for instance, the Shanghainese are "shrewd" or

TABLE 4.1. Categorization paradigms and examples of socionyms collected

Categorization paradigm (total socionyms collected)[a]	Selected examples of socionyms
Socionyms that differentiate the Han spatially (279)	*Regional:* Beifangren (Northerners) Kuazi (Clumsy Fellows, used by Southern Han to denote Northerners) Huo Lei Feng[b] (Living Lei Feng, referring to Northeasterners) Nan Manzi (Southern Barbarians, used by Northern Han to describe Southern Han) Zhongyuan ([Person from] Central Plains) Dongbei Dahan (lit., "Big Burly Fellows from the Northeast") Tufei (Bandits, Brigands, referring to Northeasterners) Xilairen (People from Western China, referring to Han from the Northwest) *Provincial:* Gansu Yangyudan (Potato Heads from Gansu) Shaanxi Lengwa (Simple Folks from Shaanxi) Hubeilao (Fellows from Hubei) Jiumaojiu (Ninety-Nine Cents, referring to Shanxi People and meaning parsimonious) Luren (People of Lu; Lu is the historical name for Shandong) Xinjiangren (Xinjiang People) Xiao Sichuan (Little Sichuanese) Shandong Dahan (Burly Fellows from Shandong) Jiutouniao (Nine-Head Birds, referring to Hubei People as supposedly shrewd and cunning) Yunnan Daduxiao (Drug Smugglers from Yunnan)

(continued)

[a] I include the total number of related socionyms collected to demonstrate which categories were more and which less popular among research participants.

[b] Lei Feng (1940–62) was reportedly a selfless young soldier who was devoted to helping people, working for the fatherland, and studying the works of Mao. After his death in an accident, Lei Feng was transformed through a nationwide campaign into a model hero, portrayed as hardworking, helpful, cheerful, obedient, and wholeheartedly devoted to Communism.

TABLE 4.1. *continued*

Categorization paradigm (total socionyms collected)[a]	Selected examples of socionyms
	City-based:
	Beijingren (Beijing People)
	Ala (We, in Shanghai dialect; designation used by Shanghai Locals)
	Shanghai Yazi (Shanghai Ducks, referring to Shanghai People whose language reportedly sounds like the quacking of a duck)
	Bazuizi (Bigmouth, referring to Beijing People)
	Wuxiren (People of Wuxi)[c]
	Xuzhou de ([Person] from Xuzhou)
	Wenzhou Xiao Laoban (Little Bosses from Wenzhou)
	County-based:
	Jiashanren (Jiashan People, county in Zhejiang)
	Taiheren (Taihe People, county in Jiangxi)
Socionyms that differentiate between urban and rural Han (60)	Xiao Shimin (Petty Townsfolk, used by rural migrants in Shanghai to describe Shanghainese)
	Shamao (Silly-Billies, used by Beijing People to identify rural migrants)
	Guazi (Dummies, used by Xi'an People to denote rural migrants)
	Xiangxiaren (Provincialists, Rustics; used in cities to denote rural migrants)
	Xiangbalao (Country Hicks, used by Shanghainese to identify rural migrants)
Socionyms that reflect the differentiation into Locals/ Natives and Outsiders/ Strangers[d] (80)	Lao Beijing (Genuine Beijing Natives, indicating people whose families have lived in Beijing for generations and who are thus "genuinely local")
	Shanghai Bendiren (Local Shanghainese)

[c] Through associations with the sweet local cuisine, the Wuxiren designation gained a broader meaning and is now understood to mean a sugary person.

[d] Because I conducted research in Beijing and Shanghai, my informants from these locations interchanged the labels Local and Urban.

Categorization paradigm (total socionyms collected)[a]	Selected examples of socionyms
	Waidiren (Outsiders, Strangers; used by Shanghai and Beijing People to denote immigrants)
	Lata (Local, from here; endonym used by an informant from Subei who lives in Shanghai)[e]
	Xiaochilao (Barefoot Bumpkins, used by Shanghainese to denote rural migrants and Outsiders in general)
	Shabi (Fools, Dummies; used by Beijing People to denote Outsiders living in the city)
	Zhongguo de Jipusairen (Chinese Gypsies,[f] referring to labor migrants from Henan and Sichuan, emphasizing their spatial detachment)
	Jiangbeiren (People from North of the Yangzi River, used by Shanghai People to denote immigrants from Subei)
Socionyms that reflect a distinction between Mainlanders (Han in mainland China) and Taiwanese/Hongkongese (19)	Daluren (Mainlanders, used in Hong Kong to describe Han from mainland China)
	Daomin (Islanders, referring to Taiwanese, used in Shanghai)
	Taibazi (Taiwan Hicks, used in Shanghai)
	Biaoshu (Maternal Uncles; used in Hong Kong for Mainlanders, indicates a person from a different descent group)
	Beigu (Northern Sisters, used by Hongkongese to describe young women from northern mainland China who work in Hong Kong)
	Gangba (Hicks from Hong Kong, used in mainland China)
	Gangpian (Hong Kong Movies, used in mainland China)[g]

(continued)

[e] For a detailed description of how the idea of Subei as a distinct region was constructed, see Honig 1996.
[f] The Gypsy label has pejorative connotations, as in English.
[g] An informant explained that the Gangpian socionym indicates that Hongkongese "are not very sophisticated, just like the movies they produce."

TABLE 4.1. *continued*

Categorization paradigm (total socionyms collected)[a]	Selected examples of socionyms
Socionyms referencing the category of Hakka/Kejia (4)	Kejiaren (Kejia Person, in the standard Chinese pronunciation) Hakka (in the Hakka- and Yue-language pronunciation)

Source: Fieldwork interviews in Beijing and Shanghai, 2002–3.

Beijing People have a high "cultural quality." The hundreds of stereotypical characterizations collected comprise an enormous body of data that is impossible to analyze comprehensively in this study. Regional groups like Northerners, Southerners, Beijing People, Shanghai People, Cantonese, Sichuanese, Northeasterners, Subei People (among informants in Shanghai), Henan People, and Rural Han/Peasants were commented on with considerable frequency. These identifiers yielded characterizations from an overwhelming majority of my informants. Other identity labels yielded characterizations from a smaller number of informants, typically four to ten informants per term. These labels included Wenzhou People, Zhejiang People, Tianjin People, Shandong People, Hubei People, Hakka/Kejia, Dalian People, Hongkongese, and Xinjiang People. Still other identifiers were characterized by one or two informants each, including Sunan People (People from Southern Jiangsu), People from the Northwest, Jiangxi People, People from Shenzhen, Hangzhou People, and many others.

My research data clearly demonstrate that Han individuals tend to have multiple home-place identities and that they extensively utilize their agency to negotiate the question of spatial belonging. Yet these very same Han engaged in the act of stereotyping as if both socionyms and stereotypes referred to coherent groups of people and as if place-based identities were always a given. This contradiction, between the agency manifested in everyday identity negotiations and the primordial "home-place-determined mind-set" that informs how many Han imagine and discuss identity processes, permeates the material discussed here. Table 4.2 shows the major narratives that surfaced repeatedly in many stereotypical characterizations, along with selected representative examples of stereotypes quoted from the interviews.

TABLE 4.2. Major narratives and examples of associations
and stereotypical characteristics

Major narratives	Selected examples of associations and stereotypical characteristics
Work, money, and economy	Zhejiang People have brains for business. Hubei People are cunning. Henanese are lazy. Shanxi People are the "traders of the North." Rural Han have low income. Beijing People prefer to become officials rather than businessmen. Xinjiang People are oil-field workers. Wenzhou People are daring. Many Kejia work abroad.
Culture, cultural level (*wenhua shuiping*), and cultural quality (*wenhua suzhi*)	Sichuanese are unsophisticated. Northeasterners are wild and uncivilized. Beijing People possess high "cultural quality." Peasants have a low cultural level. Zhejiang People have a weak cultural basis. Rural Han are dumb. Subei People have a low cultural level.
Openness, flexibility, and modernity	Shanghainese like changes. Tianjin People are conservative. Cantonese are flexible. Hakka are feudal. Mainlanders are badly educated and conservative.
Tradition and traditional values	Family lineages are very powerful in Fujian. Taiwanese care for tradition. Hakka follow etiquette and show filial obedience. Rural Han are traditional.
Social skills and interpersonal relations	Northeasterners are very loyal and ready to help friends. Hongkongese are cold and unconcerned. Sichuanese are warmhearted and honest.
Relationships with other identity categories	Shandong People are similar to Northeasterners. Beijing People do not like Shanghainese. Zhejiang People are similar to Cantonese. Hakka are like Fujianese.
Languages and dialects	Beijing People speak standard Chinese. Fujianese do not speak proper Putonghua. Tianjin People speak with a strong local dialect. Men from Nanjing talk gently, "like silk."

(continued)

TABLE 4.2. *continued*

Major narratives	Selected examples of associations and stereotypical characteristics
Character traits and mentality	Hangzhou People are romantic. Cantonese are deceptive. Shanghainese are shrewd. Subei People are boorish. Taiwanese are good natured. Han from the countryside are feudal. Henan People are dishonest and evil. Yunnanese seek a carefree life. Chengdu People are at ease. People from the Central Plains are honest and simple.
Food	Sichuanese love eating spicy foods. Cantonese are gourmands. Tianjin People like crunchy foods. Hunanese like eating spicy foods. Fujianese like seafood.
Physical differentiation	Shandong People are tall and robust. Northerners are stockier than Southerners. Cantonese have a darker complexion.

Source: Fieldwork interviews in Beijing and Shanghai, 2002–3.

Stereotypical characterizations and associations further confirm the importance of regional and rural/urban distinctions. A more thorough analysis of stereotyping mechanisms and the contents of stereotypes also confirms the third paradigm of differentiation signaled through naming, namely that between Locals and Outsiders. In my research, due to research location, Locals are represented by Beijing People and Shanghai People. Outsiders are most saliently personified by the Subei People in Shanghai and by the Henan People in Shanghai and Beijing, but also more generally by migrant workers excluded in both cities. Furthermore, like socionyms, stereotypes demonstrate that there is some "othering" along the mainland versus Hong Kong/Taiwan boundary, though this type of "othering" was mentioned by only a few interviewees. Moreover, few informants discussed the political context of this relationship. Rather, they focused on how they believed Hong Kong and Taiwan Han differed from or were similar to themselves. This way of thinking is, of course, a "mainland thing." Had my research been conducted in Taiwan or Hong

Kong, the results would have been very different with regard to this axis of differentiation. In Beijing and Shanghai, however, very few informants discussed Taiwanese and Hongkongese in terms of distinct political categories. Rather, Hong Kong and Taiwan Han were both included in the category of Southerners, along with the Han of Shanghai, Zhejiang, Fujian, and Guangdong. Because the "othering" along the mainland versus Taiwan/Hong Kong axis was only marginally popular with my interviewees, like the categorization of Hakka/Kejia, in the analysis below I prioritize the three dominant axes of distinction: regional, based on the rural/urban distinction, and based on the distinction between those who claim local belonging (Locals) and those who are spatially excluded (Strangers, Outsiders).

My approach to exploring these three modes of categorization, alongside the identifiers and stereotypes that manifest them, differs from the method of analysis proposed by many Chinese scholars (e.g., Xu 1999; Yang 1994; Yi 2002). Primordial and ecologically determined framing dominates these scholars' discussions of characteristics that people who "originate" in specific places reportedly inherit. The notion that home place—its soil, water, climate, and *qi*—determine character and human physiology focuses such analyses of socionyms and stereotypes on racialized notions of inheritance, evolutionary development of regional communities, racial predispositions, inborn qualities, and ecologically determined cultural differences (see Chen 2012).[4] Quite differently, of interest to my analysis is instead the *politics* of naming and stereotyping among the contemporary Han. Not that history does not matter, especially its backward reading and teleological reinventions. Yet if we focus on the present day, we see acutely how stereotypes and socionyms are used to produce and naturalize social constructs (e.g., feudal Ruralites) and social hierarchies (e.g. Beijing People as having a higher "cultural quality"). Accordingly, attention must be paid to how these social constructs and hierarchies are objectified, to the language in which these naturalizations are framed (e.g., as "regional"), to boundaries they maintain and enforce, and to their historical contingency. Socionyms and characterizations are strategic devices employed to achieve certain aims, for instance, to influence negotiations over the positioning of "us" and "them." Hence, the discussion below focuses on how these labels are used in identity politics, boundary making, and power negotiations in contemporary China.

CATEGORIZATION AND THE MAKING
OF SOCIAL HIERARCHIES

Regional or Place-Based Categorization

Much like the Chinese scholars referred to above, the overwhelming majority of my informants believed that people who share a home-place (region, province, city, or county) also share a set of historically and ecologically determined characteristics that supposedly predestine people of a common spatial origin for things like specific careers and occupations. Beijing People are thus thought to be destined for employment as officials and bureaucrats, Shanghainese and Cantonese as businesspeople, Anhui People as household helpers, and Sichuanese as small-scale traders. These place-based stereotypes also convey that different localities and the people who "belong" in them differ in terms of "culture." Informants often mentioned notions of "cultural level" and "cultural quality." While the former typically refers to education and the level of schooling, the latter is more complex. Interviewees' understanding of cultural quality reflects the notion of culture in the Confucian sense, along with more contemporary issues pertaining to economic success and modernity (*xianjin*).[5] The closest identification with culture in the sense of rituals, courtesy, good manners, etiquette, and classical education was ascribed to Beijing People both by the Beijing People themselves and by others. However, while Beijing People tended to brag about this, others remarked that this characteristic made Beijing People lazy and arrogant, conservative big talkers but "small doers." The Southern Han—a collective label including Shanghainese, Taiwanese, Cantonese, and Fujian and Zhejiang People—were rarely associated with the same notion of culture as Beijing People. Instead, the Southern Han were described as having "respect for tradition" and as maintaining lineage-oriented family organization and the practices of ancestral worship. Somewhat paradoxically, these very same Southerners were simultaneously associated with development, advancement, flexibility, and modernity to a much greater and more explicit degree than the Northern Hanzu, including Beijing People.

The rapid development of commerce, industry, and the service sector since 1978 significantly increased individual wealth, particularly in urban areas. An accompanying effect of this development has been growing wariness and disgust toward agrarian lifeways. Informants most commonly associated such lifeways with the Han from Hebei, Shanxi, and Henan in northern China, popularly stereotyping them as "uneducated" (*wenhua shuiping di*), "backward," and "feudal" Country Rustics.[6] By contrast, occupations in the business sector associated explicitly with southern China received more respect.[7] Though these jobs were despised under Mao, the social regard for them has changed dramatically since the launching of economic reforms. Accordingly, research participants from both northern and southern China equally praised the Southerners as being "skilled businesspeople," "good with business," and "modern," even though they simultaneously described them as "lacking culture" (*meiyou wenhua*). This set of stereotypes was used to depict the Han of Fujian, Guangdong, and Shanghai as well as Taiwanese and Hongkongese. In contrast, the Northerners—including Han from Beijing, the Northeast, and sometimes also from Hebei—were ascribed a "lack of economic spirit" and "laziness" but were at the same time imagined as "immersed in traditional culture."

Somewhat surprisingly, the stereotypes reported rarely reflected the linguistic diversity of the Han. This likely corresponds with research participants being fluent in standard Chinese and could suggest that for the younger, educated generation of migrating Han, linguistic differences may be of lesser importance than for other social groups. Yet this seems somewhat unlikely. Linguistic differences are usually among the first to be observed and commented on during first-time meetings of Han from different locations. Moreover, in those sections of interviews focused specifically on languages and dialects, or when Northern and Southern Han were contrasted, research participants counted spoken language as one of the most significant dimensions of regional distinction. The relatively low number of language-related regional stereotypes is thus difficult to explain.

The differences in character (*xingge*) that reportedly exist between Han from specific regions, provinces, and cities were yet another axis of differentiation. It appears that almost any locality beyond the county and town level is associated with character traits that are broadly known. Accordingly, the Shanghainese are labeled "shrewd," Sichuanese women "hot tempered," and Hubei People "cunning" and "clever." In the interviews, the discussions of these traits seemed almost like a game: as soon as a socionym popped up, the interviewee rapidly composed a list of the traits reportedly characteristic of people from the specific area. It was a game played seriously and with much engagement, and the impossibility of such clear-cut classifications and generalizations was rarely discussed or considered.[8]

The final areas of comparison were regional food differences and physical differentiation. Regional cuisines and a fondness for certain foods were said to differentiate Han according to larger regions and provinces as well as to major cities. In terms of physical differentiation and body build, stereotypes generally implied that Han from the North are taller and more robust, while those from the South and from Sichuan are smaller and thinner. The majority of my informants connected these physical differences to distinct regional diets: flour products were believed to make people in the North robust; rice, a staple food in the South, reportedly made Southern Han small and slender.

The active and vivid contrasting of the North (Beifang) and the South (Nanfang) constitutes one of the most pervasive themes in the place-based characterizations. The overwhelming majority of research participants argued that Northern and Southern Hanzu differ, primarily in terms of character and temper, food, spoken languages, life habits, and mentality. The relationship between the two was typically constructed through oppositions: Northerners were believed to be "frank" and "lazy," while Southerners were "sly" and "industrious." Northerners eat noodles; Southerners live on rice. While in the North one speaks standard Chinese, in the South one speaks Wu, Yue, Minnan, and other languages that "are difficult to understand." The South was associated with linguistic diversity, while the North was depicted as a linguistically unified space. The pace of life (*shenghuo jiezou*) was reported as fast in the South and slow in the North. The North was culture, the South commerce. As one informant stated, and many others echoed, "The South stands in the opposition to the North." Yet unlike the relationships between rurality and urbanity, or between locality and outsideness discussed below, the relationship between Northerners and Southerners appears to be symmetrical. The divide between the two is clear, oppositions are readily built, and differences are quickly emphasized. But the popular saying, "In the South they are barbarian and in the North they are clumsy" (Nan man bei kua), depicts a symmetry in which both sides are equally equipped to ridicule the other. North-South divergences are obviously no modern invention, and overcoming them has been a national priority since the turn of the twentieth century.[9] At that time, the nationalism-motivated revolutionaries hoped to divert the attention of the Han/Chinese from inter-Han divisions to an external "other," the Manchu. The strategy was somewhat successful: it did mobilize some Han and contributed greatly to the promotion of this unitary identity label. The Minzu Classification Project furthered this process, placing both Northern and Southern Han/ Chinese in one *minzu*. Yet, that so many Han individuals continue to perceive Northerners and Southerners as significantly distinct proves that the Nationalist and Communist efforts have only partially achieved their unifying objective to create an understanding of "the Han" that would bridge this distinction.

Differentiation into Urbanites and Ruralites

The next important distinction was the one drawn between urbanity and rurality. Significantly, the majority of the socionyms and stereotypes that relate to this distinction were classified by the informants as abusive or pejorative. While the socionyms used to refer to Rural Han (lit., "Han from the countryside") or Peasants (Nongmin) are particularly unpleasant, the designations that Rural Han used to describe Urbanites also reflect neither fondness nor even indifference.[10] In addition to the socionyms listed in table 4.1, these include Biesan (Wretched Tramps Who Live from Stealing), referring to Shanghainese; Jing Youzi (Sly Old Dogs), used to denote Beijing Urbanites by interviewees from rural Shandong and Inner Mongolia;[11] and Xiaobie (Beggars), used by Beijing and Shanghai Urbanites to denote rural migrants in both cities. All the collected socionyms, as well as stereotypes, suggest that the boundary between Urban Han and Rural Han (the latter personified in urban settings by peasant migrant workers) is dense and distinct. Interactions across this boundary are strongly asymmetrical and limited. Though decisively a much more recent phenomenon, the relationship between Urban and Rural Han arguably comprises many elements of the Confucian civilization-wildness discourse developed in imperial China,[12] with Rural Han ascribed the role of "barbarian other" by Han Urbanities in their social identification and stratification projects. As one informant claimed, unlike Rural Han, "Urban Han are civilized."

The boundary between urbanity and rurality emerges from the research data as equally important for self-identification and identification of others as the paradigms of home place and *minzu*. An overwhelming majority of research participants claimed that Rural Han and Urban Han form two distinct categories. Among the significant dimensions of difference were economy, mentality, occupation, living standards, and material conditions. Rural Hanzu were referred to as "poor" and having a "hard life," "low income," and "limited job opportunities." Every third research participant associated the countryside with a lack of economic development and low living standards. A statement by an interviewee from Shanghai is representative: "In the cities people have TV, and in the countryside there is not even running water." The next most common marker of difference was "mentality" and "thinking" (*sixiang, guannian*). Informants framed Rural Hanzu as feudal and backward, saying that "in the countryside, leftovers of feudal thinking are still alive" and that Rural Hanzu are "conservative" and "less open." Further, Rural Han were believed to show "unhealthy behaviors." For instance, "They marry too early and prefer sons over daughters"; they are "traditional"; they "treat men and women differently" and "have narrow horizons." Also, interviewees reported that in the countryside, "there is no marital freedom and children must obey their parents." Informants also posited that Rural Han are "poorly educated" or "have only basic education." In China's cities, on the other hand, "children receive nine years of compulsory schooling." Rural Han were further described as "dumb," "stubborn," and "unsophisticated." They were identified as having strong bonds with tradition and as resistant to change. In contrast to the majority of research participants, a few associated the countryside with "tranquility" and "pureness."

Overall, as Urbanites themselves, the majority of my informants connected rural Han-ness with economic backwardness, narrow-mindedness, feudal thinking, a lack of sophistication and education, low living standards, and a lack of material resources. In addition to being socially discriminating and exclusionary, the stereotypical markers that the urban informants used to differentiate themselves from Rural Hanzu felt almost hostile. The many denigrating designations, as well as the high frequency of adjectives like "feudal," "dumb," and "uneducated," call to mind the notion of peasants as the "inappropriate other" in discourses of propriety, civility, and modernity (Anagnost 1997, 77). Rural Hanzu have been constructed into a salient "other" by the class of educated and relatively well-off Han Urbanites, Hanzu who through this relationship reinvent their own economic, cultural, and social superiority.

Until the mid-nineteenth century, the rural/urban dichotomy was much less significant. Numerous scholars emphasize that urban and rural places constituted a well-integrated and interpenetrating system. Though differences between urban and rural populations were noticed and ridiculed by both sides, no clearly asymmetric power relationship existed between them in social and cultural terms (Cohen 1993; Lu 2010). In significant contrast to today's notions of the countryside, the majority of elite families in late imperial China had rural residences, even if some of their members lived part-time in cities. More than half of Shandong, Anhui, Henan, and Shanxi candidates for the highest *jinshi* imperial examinations in late nineteenth and early twentieth century were in fact from rural settlements (Skinner 1977, 266–67).[13] Literati, philosophers, and painters likewise did not shun residence in the countryside.

In the twentieth century, China's rural/urban divide grew. This process occurred in part through the reframing of the countryside with Marxist vocabulary during the first half of the twentieth century. In the development of the Communist revolution, the countryside was constructed as a locus of feudalism, superstition, old culture, and old society, obstacles to national development to be overcome through socialist transformation. The "informed" and "rational" leaders were to demonstrate their efficacy by reforming the "inert" peasants (Cohen 1993, 154–55).[14] The growing separation of the city and country was also encouraged institutionally. Increased through industrialization, the disparity between China's rural and urban populations climaxed with the introduction of the household registration system by the Communist regime in the late 1950s (Chan and Zhang 1999; Chan and Buckingham 2008). Household registration bound people to the location of their household and categorized them into rural and urban populations. These categories determined accessibility to state-provided benefits. Household registration as a system of social control also made spontaneous migration very difficult, particularly from the countryside to cities.[15] Viewed as sites of potential bourgeois decadence and, accordingly, as threats to socialism, cities were intended by the Communists to remain small; they were to be divided into secluded and controllable working unit (*danwei*) compounds (Bjorklund 1986; Lü and Perry 1997; Bray 2005). As a result, the system of household registration not only incarcerated peasants in multiple ways, but also enhanced a general disgust toward rurality among the urban population and a view that spontaneous mobility threatened the social order (Siu 2007, 330).

Though the early Communist state invested little in the countryside, the urban population has received a variety of benefits from the government, including secure employment, housing, food rations, and health care (Chan and Zhang 1999, 821). The countryside as a place of banishment has been further enhanced with the practice of punishing political enemies by stripping these individuals of their nonagricultural urban household registration (Wang 2010, 221).[16] In the fifty years since the implementation of the household registration system, Chinese citizens have come to form two caste-like categories: the agricultural population (which is, significantly, *not* entirely engaged in farming) and the nonagricultural population. Even today, these two "castes" have very different rights and opportunities (Whyte 2010).

Hence, though a major force in Mao's revolution, rural Han became marginalized through the apartheid-like division of city and country implemented during the High Communist Period. In post-1978 China, the marginalization of farmers further increased as Deng Xiaoping's reforms reinforced economic and social inequalities between China's cities—particularly municipalities and provincial capitals with high accumulations of investment and employment—and the countryside, from which millions of peasant workers (*nongmingong*) migrated in search of wage labor (Lu 2008). In the late 1990s, the government identified the countryside as the source and locus of most serious social and economic problems subsumed under the slogan "Sannong Wenti" (Three Problems of Rural China) (Day 2008).

Despite the growing phenomena of rural urbanization and industrialization and a general de-agriculturization of the countryside, the folk view that contrasts the rural/poor/farmer/agricultural with the urban/rich/worker/industrial has not yet been seriously challenged (Guldin 1996). With the relaxation of the household registration regime in the 1980s and 1990s, millions of rural Han have migrated to urban areas, thereby bringing rural and urban populations into large-scale, immediate contact for the first time in decades. Yet this process does not seem to have weakened the urban/rural distinction. Although in some areas of China, "townization" of village life and de-agriculturization of the village population

(Guldin 1996) may be creating a new rural/urban continuum, my research suggests that increasing flows between large cities and the countryside have instead reinforced the rural/urban boundary. Along with a disdain toward rurality and "blind flows" (*mangliu*)—a term for nongovernment-initiated migration—the directly related fear of losing privileged positions in rural/urban hierarchies feeds the exclusionary discourses of ruralness that urban Han maintain and perpetuate (Lei 2003, 637).

Differentiation into Natives and Outsiders

The distinction between Natives or Locals versus Strangers, Outsiders, or Migrants constituted yet another major axis of categorization. Among the numerous collected identifiers that refer to the concept of locality, some related to specific places, like Lao Beijing (Genuine Beijing Person) or Lao Shanghai (Genuine Shanghainese). Others were detached from a concrete location and were more broadly applicable, such as Bendiren (Locals, Natives) and Waidiren (Outsiders, Strangers).

Places and individuals' experience of them are always socially constructed.[17] Because of this, it is necessary to explore how spatial meanings are established, what is at stake, and who has the power to make places and ascribe them with meaning, in this instance as "outer place" versus "home place" (Gupta and Ferguson 1992, 11). Bargaining over nativity and belonging is, obviously, an inherent component of many localized power struggles.[18] Like those who claim urbanity, those who claim nativity are not necessarily more urban and native than the individuals they intend to exclude from this category. A great variety of actors make claims to these labels for both instrumental and emotional reasons, and with varying degrees of success. One person may claim local status after having lived in, for example, Beijing for a couple of years, while another person will argue that only a third-generation native of Beijing is worthy of that categorization. These identity labels are open to negotiation, interpretation, and social bargaining over who is more "native" and who "belongs"; they are likewise fragmented and personalized in their meanings and applications. Thus, although identity labels relating to nativity or urbanity do not refer to any consistent group of people, they do stand for important categories of belonging as well as exclusion.

Differentiation between Natives/Locals and Strangers/Outsiders or, put differently, the attempt to reinforce the boundaries of nativity via the construction of strangeness, is a vividly present theme in identity negotiations of the contemporary Han. In urban, metropolitan settings, such as the primary settings of this study, this differentiation is often further entangled with the rural/urban paradigm to produce the socially and politically discriminated category of rural strangeness or migrant ruralness. In every larger city, different and locally significant Strangers/Outsiders are constructed. In my two fieldwork locations, this process manifests in the active assigning of the Stranger label to Subei People in Shanghai and to Henan People in both Shanghai and Beijing. These two identity categories—Subei People and Henan People— are used below to discuss the boundary of nativity and the competition that motivates the social exclusion of Outsiders as practiced in contemporary Chinese cities.

Today, the label Subei People is popularly used by Han individuals who claim nativity in Shanghai to identify Migrants/Outsiders from the northern part of Jiangsu who work and reside in Shanghai. Since the mid-nineteenth century, immigrants from this region have come in large numbers to Shanghai to escape war, famine, or floods in their home districts. Emily Honig (1996) reports that upon their arrival, these migrants often took over the lowest-paid and least desirable jobs, such as rickshaw pullers, dockworkers, construction workers, garbage collectors, night-soil haulers, barbers, and bathhouse attendants. These occupations have since become identified as "Subei jobs." The development of Shanghai and southern Jiangsu in the nineteenth century, and the economic decline of northern Jiangsu, spawned the idea of "Subei."[19] Through this label, "natives" of Shanghai and southern Jiangsu were able to distinguish themselves from the impoverished immigrants of northern Jiangsu, with whom they shared not only the Chinese and Han identities but also provincial affiliation (Honig 1996, 149–51).

Although the category of Outsiders in contemporary Shanghai includes immigrants, especially rural immigrants, from all over China, Subei People still constitute the principal, most familiar "other" for those who wish to imagine themselves as Local Shanghainese. Shanghai People among my informants depicted Subei People as having "low cultural quality" and "narrow horizons" and as "conservative," "backward," "boorish," "unkind," "poor," "selfish," and "dirty." Subei People were also referred to as "cheats," "misers," and "savages." Socionyms used to label Subei People were extremely pejorative and included Subeiren (Subei Person), "a label pejorative in itself and used as a curse word," according to a number of interviewees; and Jiangbeiren (People from North of the Yangzi River), similarly classified by the informants as derogatory. Further, the socionyms Beiman (Northern Barbarians) and Jiangbei Zhulou (Swine from North of the Yangzi River) were mentioned. The Outsiders from Subei were described by my informants in particularly harsh, negative terms.[20] Some informants nevertheless did recognize that the construct of Subei People as lowness and meanness personified was directly related to how Shanghainese wanted to imagine themselves. As one individual perceptively pointed out, "It is in the eyes of the Shanghai People that [Subei People] are backward." In Shanghai, a city that has grown by absorbing millions of migrants, struggles over nativity status are not only vivid and harsh but also particularly entangled. The verticalization of the relationship constructed between Shanghai and *waidi* (outside, outer place), with Subei as the most familiar personification of this "outside-ness," is a crucial component of social bargaining over belonging and nativity in the city (Gu 2002; Wan 2002; Yang 2002).

While the categories of Shanghai Locals and Subei Outsiders are products of the boundary-making processes that accompanied the rise of modern Shanghai, the stigmatization of another identity category associated with outside-ness, namely the Henan People, seems a matter of the last two decades (Ma 2002). Despite the overall economic development of eastern and southeastern China, Henan has somewhat lagged behind economically and in terms of educational and employment opportunities. This resulted in a massive outmigration of Henanese seeking employment in the cities. Among the most populous provinces in China, Henan thus became associated with millions of impoverished migrant workers, migrants who soon represented Outsiders, Strangers, and Country Rustics within the modernizing spaces of urban China (Ma 2002, 196–97). The category of Henan People is, next to Subei People, perhaps the most discriminated against category in both Beijing and Shanghai. Designations referring to Henanese include Henanren (Henan People), with informants saying repeatedly that "this name is, in itself, already derogatory"; Henan Bangzi (Henan Fools); Jiangnan Pianzi (Cheats from South of the Yellow River), and Zhongguo de Jipusairen (lit., "Chinese Gypsies"). Henan People were further referred to as "demons" and "bandits" and described as "evil," "dishonest," "lazy," "feudal," and "conservative."

In contemporary eastern and southeastern Chinese cities, Henan People often encounter employment discrimination—with some companies and shops openly refusing to hire Henanese[21]—as well as problems finding housing. Because of this, some Henan People conceal their home-place identity, instead presenting themselves as Shandong People, that is, as originating in the neighboring province. Also, by using different-sounding self-designations, such as People from Central Plains, Henan People try to blur their home-place identity. At the same time, because they find work and accommodation in urban destinations almost exclusively through their home-place networks (*laoxiang guanxi*), solidarity between fellow Henanese is maintained and even strengthened. The Subei People at the regional scale of Jiangsu and the Henan People—and to a lesser degree Sichuan People—at the scale of the whole country function as the embodiment of the discriminated and patronized category of migrant strangeness, not rarely combined with the equally despised rurality.[22] Obviously, these labels are instrumentalized by those who claim the status of urban nativity to determine the social hierarchization and the distribution of symbolic and material resources. Although Subei, Henan, and Sichuan People, as well as Rural Han and Outsiders in general, also engage in negative stereotyping and naming of Locals and Urbanites, the influence of this collective voice is much weaker, with little impact on existing geographies of exclusion and discrimination.

CONCLUSION

Regional, rurality/urbanity, and nativity/strangeness differentiations were the three most significant paradigms of identification among my research participants.[23] The intensity with which informants discussed these paradigms, and the hundreds of related socionyms and stereotypical characterizations collected make the common Hanzu identifier and the idea of shared Han-ness appear extremely remote at this scale of identity negotiations. The identity processes occurring around the oppositions of Ruralites/Urbanites, Locals/Outsiders, and Southerners/Northerners clearly demonstrate dependence on "them" in the making of "us," a key point of inquiry in studies of ethnicity. Accordingly, the North needs the South to become the North, Natives need to construct the category of Outsiders to become native, and Urbanites need Ruralites in order to be urban. These categorizations and differentiations draw attention to their historical and institutional contingency and to the ambiguous role the state has played in their making.

The regional and, particularly, the North/South distinctions are clearly historical. Their obviousness to nearly all informants indicates that the unifying efforts of the twentieth-century governments have done little to erase such divisions. On the other hand, the asymmetric relationship of urbanness and ruralness as well as the discriminatory differentiation between Locals and Outsiders seem to have even increased in the second half of the twentieth and early twenty-first centuries due to specific state policies. Although these two distinctions are universal and also at work elsewhere in the world, the discriminatory and abusive ways they are employed by the contemporary Han are particular. The introduction of the household registration regime that divided the Han into agricultural and nonagricultural populations had incalculable effects on identity politics of the Hanzu. In the post-Mao era, the accumulation of capital in China's cities further contributed to the marginalization of the rural population and gave rise to new classes of Outsiders (compare Chan and Zhang 1999, 843). Combined, these two processes effectively enforced deep social divides. Although arguably unintended, these policy outcomes nonetheless demonstrate how the state powerfully intervenes in collective and individual identity processes. The sheer number and the humiliating contents of socionyms and stereotypes ascribed to Outsiders and Ruralites illustrate that these paradigms of differentiation assume critical roles in identification and stratification processes occurring in eastern China's urban settings where *minzu* "others" are not easily found.

The fragmentation of Hanzu occurs along multiple axes. The large-scale categorizations and pairs of oppositions discussed above do not exhaust the possible processes by which Hanzu differentiate and "other" among themselves. In particular, studies from southern China introduce many existing distinctions, such as between Han land dwellers and boat dwellers, between "sea people" and "land people," and between Hakka, Punti, Hokkien, and Boat People.[24] Language, home place, legends of ancestral origin, spatial distribution, and occupation are all significant differentiating variables in localized identity politics.

Socionyms and stereotypes reflect boundaries that fragment contemporary Han in everyday social interactions. These boundaries powerfully influence life opportunities of Han individuals and affect their social standing. While Subei People report experiencing job discrimination in Shanghai, Zhejiang People are commonly identified as excellent business-people solely because of their origin in this southern province. Further, Han from Beijing construct their cultural superiority over other Hanzu by referencing the imperial history of the city and the fact of "living at the emperor's feet." With something of a symbolic revenge, Southern Han ridicule the clumsiness of the Northerners, including Beijing People, and their rusticity. Urbanites ridicule the Country Hicks, and Natives look down on the Outsiders. Through this complicated game of difference and discrimination, Han individuals attempt to position themselves and others in intra-Han hierarchies of power that have practical effects on every-day life. They affect job and educational opportunities as well as one's chances on the marital "market." That individuals who engage in these fragmented identity politics remain classified as Hanzu does not dimin-ish the relevance of these "otherings." The common Han denominator, as salient as it may appear vis-à-vis other *minzu*, does not have the power to erase or overshadow the power struggles, competition, and discrim-ination that persist among the Hanzu. Indeed, it appears that the Han identity has little potential for enforcing social solidarity. At this scale of interaction, identity as Han, shared nominally by all those involved and affected by these processes, feels like a distant concept. The Minzu Clas-sification Project that officially established the unitary Han *minzu* did not terminate the intensive discourse of distinction among those it classified. In their daily, mundane social interactions, the so-called Hanzu disinte-grate into a cohort of competing collective actors.

CHAPTER 5

FRAGMENTED IDENTITIES, THE HAN *MINZU*, AND ETHNICITY

The fragmentation of the Hanzu is substantial and all permeating. In mundane social interactions, "the Han" disintegrate into multiple identity groups that engage in relationships of competition, exclusion, and discrimination. Despite this fragmentation, many Han simultaneously understand Han-ness as a powerful identity, and they imagine "the Han" as sharing a set of common markers—the "essence"—and unitary feelings. The notion of relationality that understands Han-ness as entangled with other collective identities allows us to see Han-ness but also home place, national, rural, urban, native, outsider, and other identities as transient and situational. This helps us develop a clearer understanding of an apparent paradox: the extreme fragmentation of the Hanzu through a variety of spatial, social, and linguistic boundaries, on the one hand, and their parallel "unity in Han-ness" exhibited at other times, on the other. The integrity of the Han *minzu* depends on a complex set of relationships—relationships between the multiple identity categories into which "the Han" disintegrate in everyday life, and between these fragmented identities and Han-ness. In some contexts Han-ness is a tangible identity, one that most of my research informants talked about extensively and felt strongly related to. However, when contrasted with other collective attachments, particularly those relating to home place, Han-ness becomes vague and situationally invisible. Thus, Han-ness can, paradoxically, be at once meaningful and invisible, immediate and distant. Ethnicity may offer a framework to analytically grasp these multiple identities of the Hanzu, the ways they are constructed and practiced, and their mutual relationships. First, however, Chinese-language terms must be explored, revealing the contextuality of collective identities assumed by Han individuals and the intertwined networks of relationships that link them. The question of ethnicity proves to be directly related to the scales at which identities are enacted, their degree of "density," and their transitory nature.

FRAGMENTATION AND HAN-NESS

Social exclusions, discrimination, and othering among Hanzu in eastern China are likely as strong as they are between the Hanzu and other *minzu* elsewhere. Apparently, the Han identity does not have the potential to create the social solidarity necessary to mediate these asymmetric exclusions. At the same time, when directly asked to discuss Han-ness, most Han research participants had no trouble composing a favorable unitary image of the Han *minzu*, one to which they declare attachment and are proud to belong. This appears somewhat contradictory. To better grasp how Han individuals understand Han-ness and the simultaneous fragmentation of those classified as Hanzu, I concluded every interview with the three questions below, bringing the attention of informants back to this relationship.

"Do Hanzu all over the Country Share the Same Culture [Wenhua]?"

A clear majority of my research participants answered this question in the negative. These individuals believed that Hanzu are culturally distinct according to their place of "origin." One informant argued, "Hanzu are like the Slavs; they divide into many branches." Others expressed the view that Han are *generally* the same but with many *local* differences. This suggests that the feeling of sharing something with other Hanzu is situated elsewhere than in the notion of shared culture, and that this feeling refers to things other than the social fragmentation manifest in place-based, urban/rural, native/outsider, and North/South modes of distinction. Yet another informant suggested, "As there are different countries, so there are different Hanzu." In contrast to these opinions, a clear minority of research participants argued that Han do share the same culture, defined as the main-stream culture (*zhuliu wenhua*), which, they said, "is the same everywhere."

The research participants who conceived of the Hanzu as culturally fragmented discussed the many local or regional cultures (*diqu wenhua, diyu wenhua, quyu wenhua*) into which Han divide. A number of inter-viewees focused on differentiating between the "culture of the North" and "culture of the South"—a distinction discussed in the previous chapter. More spatially restricted regional cultures were also mentioned. Infor-mants referred to the Shanghai area as "the culture of the Wu language" (*Wuyu wenhua*) or "the small family of Wu" (*Wu xiaojia*). Guangdong was referred to as "the culture of the Yue language" (*Yueyu wenhua*). Infor-mants also differentiated between "the coastal culture" (*haipai wenhua*) of Jiangsu, Zhejiang, and Shanghai; "the *hutong* culture" of Beijing; the culture of the Sichuan basin; the cultures of the Yellow River, Yangzi, and Pearl River basins; and the culture of the Central Plains. In the percep-tion of these research participants, these "regional cultures" differ to a considerable degree.

My informants imagined the so-called regional cultures as neat, traceable spatial-human formations comprising both places and people who "originate" in them. Linguistic differences were among the prin-cipal dimensions of distinction between these regional cultures. Infor-mants argued that "in Sichuan, language is soft and gentle" or that "in the South, there are many local dialects and thus people there are not as integrated as in the North." Another informant stated, "Although in the South they are also Hanzu, language differences make contact difficult." Character (*xingge*) was also a popular theme in discussing regional cul-tures. For instance, several research participants described Hanzu from western China as "conservative," "hospitable," as those who like "singing and dancing in front of others and sharing things," but also as "lacking a sense of competition." Conversely, Hanzu from coastal areas reportedly "hate when others touch their belongings" and "have brains for business." My informants also posited that each regional culture has specific habits and customs (*shenghuo xiguan, fengsu xiguan*), like different ways of cel-ebrating festivals. Regional cultures were further detailed as having spe-cific, traditional cuisines; as characterized by different modes of thinking (*siwei*); as having distinct paces of life, traditional opera styles, climate, architecture, education, and economies.

How informants framed "regional cultures" is similar to the stereo-types ascribed to place-based identity categories discussed earlier. Yet when compared with markers of Han-ness, the ways in which informants described regional cultures is indeed strikingly distinct. As already revealed, Han-ness was framed by research participants in terms of shared history and ancestors, powerful culture, and a dominant position in relation to "the minorities." Han-ness also emerged through language (as an instrument of national unification), Confucianism, the notion of "the Han" as an omnipresent and encompassing population, and through links to state power. In quite a contrast, the way that regional cultures are narrated focuses distinctly on diversities in speech, character, regional customs, diet, and mode of thinking. Han-ness and, on the other hand, the regional differentiation are thus clearly located at two different registers, registers that only partly and situationally overlap.

"Are All Hanzu Inherently Alike [Tongzhi]?"

Informants responded to this primordial query differently than to the first one. A small majority professed that Han do share a "common essence," or that they are "inherently" alike. These Han argued that Hanzu "have mixed to such a degree that one cannot see any significant regional dif-ferences." Interestingly, just a few minutes earlier in our interviews, a majority of the very same informants posited that Han were culturally diversified and formed distinct "regional cultures." One reason for this inconsistency might be semantic: the Chinese term *tongzhi* translates lit-erally as "sharing a common quality," "being inherently alike." It is thus likely that some research participants imagined the Han as sharing a common "essence" (*zhi*) but simultaneously as distinct in terms of "local cultures." For instance, one informant observed, "The Han are *tongzhi*, but there are also many local differences." This seemingly paradoxical perspective offers further clues for understanding the simultaneity of identity processes relating to Hanzu identity, and processes of fragmenta-tion linked to other social and ethnic identities to which Han individu-als relate. My research data suggest that the two processes are thought to operate on two different, rarely intersecting scales. These parallel scales allow processes related to the making, performing, and imagining of the Han *minzu* identity and processes related to the making and performing of non-*minzu* identities to continue largely undisturbed and independent of one another.

"Do All People Classified as Hanzu Have 'Enough' in Common to Form One Minzu?"

I posed this provocative question at the end of each interview, allowing informants to reflect once again on what they had shared about Han-ness and the boundaries crisscrossing it. In answering it, an overwhelming majority of research participants maintained that, indeed, all people classified as Hanzu shared "enough" in common to be classified together as one *minzu*. They found this classification well grounded.

Though this question was similar to the first two, its reference to the politicized category of *minzu* made it distinct; accordingly, it evoked very different responses. In its simplistic formulation, it was meant to incite research participants to confront the abundance of identity categories that surfaced in our talks and to consider them in light of the official state classification that lumps all these identity categories together into one *minzu*. Informants reacted by closing ranks to defend an apparently important stake. Their arguments included the following:

The important things—history and culture—are the same; regional differences are secondary.

What is important are ancestors and history; regional differences are secondary.

There are, of course, differences, but the character of the *minzu* is unitary [*tongyi*].

Even if local customs are not the same, the spirit remains the same for all: diligent, patriotic, and simple.

They all share common territory and Confucian thinking; the central government supports harmonious development.

It is just like this, it is something you cannot change; you simply are Han. (Fieldwork interviews, Beijing and Shanghai, 2002–3)

These individuals argued that history, blood, ancestors, culture, land, and *minzu* character or *minzu* spirit—generally, the primordial "givens"— were the binding elements of the Hanzu. When considering these "givens," the overwhelming majority of informants identified the boundaries and exclusions performed in everyday social interactions as secondary in importance. A few of them emphasized the "given-ness" of Han-ness as an imposed identity out of their control. Others stressed the centrality of the Han *minzu* in the Chinese state and its leading role in maintaining Chinese statehood:

> The Han form the center, they do not change. It is others who assimilate and adopt.
>
> Hanzu are the center, they are most numerous. The country needs this strong center to be strong itself.
>
> We [Hanzu] believe that we are the masters of China. (Fieldwork interviews, Beijing and Shanghai, 2002–3)

These responses further reinforce the link between the Chinese state and the Han *minzu*. They reveal the success of Han-making projects to date in the sense that individual Han appear to have internalized the centrality of the Han *minzu* in the Chinese national narrative and in Chinese nation- and state-making projects. The political awareness of how much depends on "the Han" is well established. The responsibility for the mission that "the Han" have to play in the Chinese state, also in relation to "the minorities," is also well established. So too is the responsibility for protecting this classification when it is challenged, as I did in our interviews. The responses to this query show that, although perhaps not overwhelmingly important in mundane identity processes in eastern China, Han-ness as an overarching identity is something Hanzu individuals are willing to defend. Whether they do so because they internalized the identity during patriotic education lessons, because they feel emotionally attached to it, and/or because Han-ness is a resource to draw upon in negotiating their social standing vis-à-vis other *minzu* is impossible to distinguish. Several of these motivations likely merge together.

Although *minzu* categories were rather arbitrarily conceived in the Minzu Classification Project, since then they have assumed a life of their own (Harrell 2001). Han *minzu*, conceived primarily for nation-making purposes, has become an identity and a way of thinking that many Hanzu voluntarily identify with today and internalize in their interactions with other *minzu*. It is an identity that they assume at this scale of interaction. Informants' observations of the political status quo appeared to only strengthen their opinion that "the Han" must have "enough in common" because the *minzu* has indeed so far succeeded in accommodating all fragmentation and power asymmetries existing between the various Han. Because *minzu* are state-conceived and enforced categories, fragmentation and power struggles among their members have no impact on group cohesion, which is institutionally established and maintained. It is likely that the majority of my informants have never considered whether it makes sense to pack 1.2 billion very different people into one Han *minzu*. Accordingly, the interview question elicited quick, almost rote recitation of the familiar rhetoric of *minzu* unity.

Still, while an overwhelming number of informants responded in this manner, some did express serious doubts about this classification. They argued that the boundaries dividing Hanzu were too significant to unequivocally classify all Han as members of one *minzu*. Others believed that while Hanzu shared some things ("history," "tradition"), other and no less important differences existed ("languages," "cultures"). Similar to discourses transmitted through national language, questioning a social institution from within—in this case the *minzu* classification—is obviously a difficult task for those who had grown up with it. Still, more than one-tenth of my informants challenged the official classification and questioned its sense.

SIMULTANEITY OF HAN-NESS AND FRAGMENTATION

The majority of my research participants stressed that Hanzu are culturally heterogeneous and fragmented by boundaries of "regional cultures." Socionyms and stereotypes analyzed earlier highlighted numerous other salient boundaries and forms of differentiation. Yet an overwhelming majority of informants supported the official classification, in which these fragmented identity categories are packed together into one Han *minzu*. Despite differences and divisions, they argued, all the Hanzu still have something important in common. These responses suggest that regional and social fragmentation is perceived by many Han as detached from the political mission that the Han *minzu* has to fulfill, and from the politicized understanding of *minzu* identity. That "ancestors," "history," "tradition," and "spirit" are framed as the Han "essence" (*zhi*), whereas "mentality," "culture," and "language" are framed as regional and secondary differ-ences—differences with no significant impact on that "essence"—is argu-ably not accidental. Behind these constructions of "the essential" and "the secondary" exist substantial efforts by imperial and postimperial govern-ments to develop an identity framework that would unify the Han despite the many boundaries that divide them.

Unlike scholars in the Herderian tradition, who assumed a "natural" equation of culture = people = nation (see Denby 2005), Edmund Leach (1970, 40) critically argues that "uniformity of . . . culture is correlated with a uniformity of . . . political organization," in the sense that politi-cal organization determines the "cultural dress" it assumes. On the other hand, differences in cultural practices do not necessarily imply belong-ing to different social systems (Leach 1970, 17; see also Bentley 1987, 25). My research data engage with this debate in several ways. Basically, the data show that culture, language, and the idea of community do not have to coincide, not even in participants' primordialism. Rather, communal identity is constructed flexibly out of what is available and feasible (Wall-man 1979, 2–3). The distinction into the aforementioned "essentials" and "secondaries" shows the effects of the Han-making process in China. Interestingly, and contrary to Herderian understanding, culture is per-ceived by some members of the Han *minzu* as an uneasy subject that can augment unitary feelings as much as it exposes uncertainties and discon-tinuities. The challenge in the making of "the Han" has thus been to create an understanding of elements that have a unifying potential as essential and of those with a divisive potential as secondary. The government and a majority of the Han *minzu* closely collaborate in this process.

Although Han individuals "domesticate" the *minzu* identity by invest-ing it with personalized meanings in their identity negotiations, Han-ness has a crucial political dimension, one that Han individuals become aware of through socialization in and beyond the educational system. The notion of historical responsibility becomes enmeshed with individualized iden-tity politics, where the role of "the Han" as the core and leader of the nation can be utilized to establish specific, asymmetric relationships with *minzu* "others." The categorical togetherness of the Hanzu coexists with the actual social fragmentation. This is illustrated by the informants who argued that Hanzu are "all the same" in the sense of "mainstream cul-ture" but who also spoke extensively about significant differences between "regional cultures." The scale of regional cultures and the other social differentiations is where boundaries are registered, admitted, and permitted to exist.[1] These boundaries only in minor ways affect the *minzu* unity imperative that is located elsewhere and sensed differently. Due to this, and to the relationality and situationality of these identities, it is perfectly possible for the Hanzu to be fragmented and unified at the same time.

The "Secondary Cultural Differentiation" Paradigm

The interest and enthusiasm with which research participants discussed "regional cultures" and "regional differences" proves that place-based diversity of the Hanzu is not a taboo topic in China; on the contrary, it is to a certain degree celebrated, gauging from the number of scientific and popular publications that address the subject. Still, while the state admits to differences among the Hanzu, political considerations determine how this "regional diversity" is represented in the literature. I refer to this form of narration as the "secondary cultural differentiation" paradigm (Joniak-Lüthi 2009).

This paradigm identifies the territory of China, including the Hanzu who are imagined as anchored in it, as divided into "place-bound cultures" much the same as my informants did. The core of the paradigm lies in four interrelated assumptions, assumptions that are present in many Chinese-language publications and that underpin this permissible discourse of Han diversity. The first assumption is that the non-*minzu* identities of the Hanzu are local and have a minor to nonexistent political significance. The second assumption is that "regional cultures" are secondary in the sense that they all originated from a "common source" (*tongyuan*) in northern China. Alternatively, they have distinct regional origins but have blended with and been powerfully influenced by the northern "culture of the Central Plains." In this process of evolutionary melting and historical progression, it is argued that cultural "diversity" has merged into a "unity." In the first variation, regional identities are secondary in relation to the core "essence" (*zhi*) that is Han and believed to be inherited from earlier peoples of Xia, Shang, and Zhou (Weng 2001). In the second variation, regional, ecologically determined differences blend into the Chinese "snowball," which they enrich as they melt with the "core" (Fei 1989; Xu 1999). The third assumption is that "regional cultures" each have unique characteristics that distinguish them from one another. These unique qualities, however, do not challenge the regional cultures' broader shared "essence," which is Han/Chinese (see, e.g., Xiong 1996, 100–104; and Zhang 2000). The fourth assumption is that, unlike the ancient "culture of the Central Plains"—which is narrated as the trunk line in the development of the Chinese nation and state—the ancient "regional cultures" are considered minor contributors to this predominant line of national unfolding. Significantly, regional histories are not used to weave distinct national narratives of regional cultures or to advance federalist ideas (compare Liu 2002, 2–13).

Although these four assumptions are popular, the parallel revalorization of southern cultures—like that of Chu (state of Chu, eleventh to third century BCE)—as important components of the Chinese national narration does occur. Among the Southern Han, the notion that the South developed culturally independent of the North, even in racial terms, is also gaining popularity (Friedman 1994). For instance, it is questioned whether the culture of Chu indeed had northern origins, as long represented in the Chinese historiography. Instead, Chu is increasingly regarded as an indigenous culture of the South, one that perhaps even influenced the North (Friedman 1994; Gladney 1995). There is also significant resistance to prioritizing the North in the framing of Han/Chinese origins and in the Chinese national narration, for instance among Sichuan People proud of the ancient Shu culture. Moreover, Cantonese and Hakka ridicule the Northerners, considering them barbarized Han tainted by Mongol and Manchu influences, unlike themselves—Southerners who retained Han-ness/Chinese-ness in its "pure" form.

Nevertheless, my research results demonstrate that the North, and in particular the basin of the Yellow River, is still popularly understood as the geographical source of Han culture. A great majority of my informants located this source in the Yellow River basin, in the Central Plains, or in the North more generally. This occurred even though informants who called themselves Southerners were actually a majority among my research participants. At the same time, however, every fifth informant also posited that the basin of the Yangzi River and southern China in general are the "source of Han culture." Some said that as the Yellow River basin is the place of origin of the Northern Han, so is the Yangzi River basin the place of origin of the Southern Han. Still, no matter how revalorized, southern and other "regional cultures" are not imagined in ways that would challenge the notion of them all being Han. The geographically dispersed origins of "the Hanzu" also do not challenge the paradigm of evolutionarily developed national coherence and national unity, which developed out of the diversity that had once existed but long since been bridged (compare Fei 1989). Hence, although the national narration has evolved from a focus on the North to also include influences of southern "regional cultures," the framework within which this diversity is discussed remains unchallenged and backwardly determined by the current political imperative, that is, the need to strengthen both the idea of a unitary Han *minzu* and a unitary, peacefully developed Chinese nation.

"Regional cultures" are imagined as stable, objectively definable units with distinct, ecologically determined characteristics. Despite this "secondary diversity," these cultures reportedly share a certain homogeneity that highlights either their cultural consanguinity or, in the other narrative, the successful blending with the core of the "snowball." As an extremely elaborate example of this narrative, Xu Jieshun (1999) argues that the Han *minzu* is a conglomerate of many *minzu* (Hanzu and "minority" *minzu*) that became assimilated by "the Han" in the course of history (compare also Xiong 1996; and Huang 1998). In his discussion of "the culture of the Guangdong Hanzu," Huang Shuping (1998, 386) offers another example of an attempt to reconcile regional fragmentation with the political imperative of cultural and historical continuity of the unitary Han *minzu*. Guangdong Hanzu, he posits, are divided into three main branches (*minxi*): Guangfu (People of Guangzhou Prefecture), Chao-Shan (People from Chaozhou and Shantou), and Hakka. Cultures of Guangfu, Chao-Shan, and Hakka, Huang suggests, "all originate in Han culture; [at the same time], each of them has also local characteristics [*difang tedian*]" (Huang 1998, 386). The Han culture, he argues, was introduced in the South by migrants from the North carrying with them "excellent technologies of production," "advanced material culture," "brilliant culture of the Central Plains" (*canlan de Zhongyuan wenhua*), and "lineage organization" (Huang 1998, 388–91).

These attempts to discuss the history of "the Han" revolve around an inherent tension. One side of this tension is created by sensed attachments to home place and the perceived importance of "regional cultures" in everyday identity performances. The other side of this tension is created by the assumed necessity of streamlining the histories of "regional cultures" and independent kingdoms that existed within the territory occupied by China today to construct a unitary national narrative and a progressive national history. This tension is negotiated in daily lives by both academics and nonacademic Hanzu like my research participants.

The zealous, nationalist search for historicity is integral to the Chinese-language literature on "regional cultures." However, while historicity with regard to regional cultures is claimed, it is largely done without questioning or challenging the three other assumptions of the "secondary cultural differentiation" paradigm. Constructing the historical narratives of regional cultures in this way is similar to how "minority" histories are constructed in China: these are namely featured as long established but also as an integral part of China's *national* history from its earlier stages onward (Xu 1999, 44; Weng 2001, 4).[2] Just as "minority cultures" are narrated as having contributed to the splendor of the Chinese nation, so "regional cultures" are framed as contributing to the splendor of the Han *minzu*.[3]

The "secondary cultural differentiation" paradigm frames much of what has been written about social, and arguably also ethnic, differentiation among the Hanzu. That the majority of my research participants admitted and even celebrated cultural diversity is as much a manifestation of this narrative as is the parallel claim (by the very same majority) that the Han *minzu* is a proper vessel for accommodating this fragmentation. As long as the politicized Han *minzu* category remains unchallenged, multifarious cultural, linguistic, or even racial differentiations, categorizations, and forms of discrimination and competition are visible, admitted, and extensively discussed. As soon as *minzu* enters the conversation, the optics of fragmentation is replaced by primordial references to the Han "essence" and narratives of common history, ancestors, and political centrality. This suggests that political awareness of the critical role of the Hanzu in the making of China and the Chinese nation is a well-established dimension in individual topographies of identity.

TERMINOLOGICAL DELIBERATIONS

How to grasp in analytical terms the multitude of non-*minzu* identity categories that remain in competition with one another and simultaneously exist alongside the common Hanzu identity was a central question that informed this study. There exist many different analytical approaches to this issue. In Chinese-language publications, the predominantly place-based fragmentation of the Hanzu is framed in terms of distinct "communities of Han People" (*Hanren shequ*), "subgroups of Hanzu" (*Hanzu cisheng jituan* or *Hanzu yaqunti*), "human groups" (*renqun*), and "groups" (*qunti*) or "branches within the *minzu*" (*minxi*). Also, the term *lineage group* or *ethnic group* (*zuqun*) is sometimes used. In Western scholarship, Shanghai People, Sichuan People, Hakka, Hokkien, Cantonese, Chaozhou, and other non-*minzu* identity categories are sometimes discussed as *subethnic* distinctions, divisions, and groups, implying that the Han *minzu* identity is the ethnic one.[4] Countering this approach, other scholars argue that conceiving of these categories in *sub*-ethnic terms is unwarranted and misleading, as they are ethnic in their own right (Crossley 1990b, 15; Brown 2004, 7). Much in the same way, it is argued that the southern Hakka, Hokkien, Swatow, Cantonese, and Boat People are each an exclusive ethnic identity (Blake 1981; Gladney 1998, 70; Skinner 2001). The argument that "conventional definitions of ethnicity cannot contain the variables—dialect, native place, economic status, immigration history, among others—that divide and unite groups of people in China" (Lipman 1996, 97–98) succinctly summarizes these approaches.

This ethnic framework turned out to be difficult to meaningfully apply in the early stages of my analysis. Though differences between the *minzu* and non-*minzu* identities of the Hanzu are apparent in my research material, the ethnic approach subsumes them all as ethnic. Other scholars suggest that *minzu* are too different from ethnic groups to be analyzed with the concept of ethnicity. Putting aside the term *ethnic group* to explore locally used identity labels became the first step to address this tension and establish a more differentiated understanding of these attachments. Only after that can the concept of ethnicity be reintroduced and its usefulness probed to grasp the quality of the relationships that bind these fragmented identity categories to one another and to the Han *minzu*.

Minzu, Ren, Min, and Jia

In this study, I have so far refrained from employing the term *ethnic group* when discussing the identity categories identified in the research material, the relationships they create, and their intertwinings, because the term would reify and conceal data in troubling ways. *Ethnic group*, "a term brought in from western sociological discourse, is a poor translation of indigenous categories . . . and hinders the analysis of their subtleties and ambiguities" (Tapper 1988, 31). From my research material, especially the hundreds of socionyms collected, and the secondary literature, four Chinese-language terms for the collective identities assumed and performed by Han individuals emerged: *minzu*, translated as "nationality," "ethnic group," or "nation"—but also comprising the meaning of racial lineage (*zu*) inscribed in it at the turn of the twentieth century—and *ren*, *min*, and *jia*, all of which can be generally translated as "person" or "people."[5]

Although more than four hundred groups applied for recognition as *minzu* in the 1950s, only fifty-six (some of them combinations of several ethnic groups) were officially recognized by the state following the Minzu Classification Project. These groups were officially designated as *minzu*, "nationalities" in the terminology of the 1950s and 1960s.[6] Because of this, *minzu* are often considered stiff categories, conceived of and imposed by the state onto a fluid ethnic reality. "What ultimately makes a group a *minzu* is that the government, more precisely the *Minzu* Commission . . . says it is one" (Harrell 1989, 181). While this is true in regard to ethnic groups with limited access to power, the Han *minzu*, representing a powerful majority, appears to require a different conceptual approach. The question thus becomes, who were the actors who narrated the fragmented Han/Chinese into a *minzu*? It is particularly crucial to emphasize that "formations which appear as ethnic groups, as cultures, or as nations . . . should be interpreted as the products of history, therefore as resulting from concrete acts that are motivated by people's interests. Such formations are constructions naturalized by social actors in the interest of their own social standing" (Wicker 1997, 1).

Han-ness is not a modern invention, even though the usage and reference group of the Han identifier has historically been unstable (Elliott 2012). In a complex interplay of local and empirewide processes, those who identified with Han-ness constructed and maintained boundaries between themselves and "uncultured others" by, among other things, cultivating specific rituals or emphasizing the importance of Han family names and genealogies. Alongside transformations in the political arena at the turn of the twentieth century, political and intellectual Han/ Chinese elites dramatically redefined the role and meaning of Han-ness in an effort to reimagine the Han as a national community with common ancestors and a linear national history. This national imagery was later adopted by Han Communists, who additionally glorified the Han/ Chinese as leaders of the proletarian revolution. Parallel to this development, individuals who thought of themselves as Han/Chinese narrated Han-ness and reproduced the meaning of *minzu* belonging in terms that were understandable and meaningful in their daily social interactions and identity negotiations. Hence, Han *minzu* is not a category produced by distant state institutions. Rather, it is a collective actor that has emerged from a complex interplay of local and statewide processes. These processes were initiated by Han/Chinese revolutionaries who tried to generate a national majority that would act as the core of the Chinese nation and fulfill the role of the Stalinist "unifier of nationalities." The Han *minzu* (as synonymous with the Chinese nation but also as one of the fifty-six "nationalities") thus emerged from processes that were driven by those who identified themselves as Han/Chinese in pursuit of localized but also large-scale political agendas.[7]

When it comes to other identity categories, three popular Chinese-language terms can be identified from my research material and from secondary literature. These are *ren*, *min*, and *jia*, all of which can be translated as "people" or "person" but each of which also has its own distinct connotations. Most of the identifiers collected in my research comprised the term *ren*, which additionally indicates "person from," referencing the home-place identity. The locality aspect of the term is clear, as in identifiers such as Beijing People (Beijingren) and Sichuanese (Sichuanren). The spatial aspect is also manifest in some identifiers related to rurality and urbanity, such as Xiangxiaren (Ruralites, or People from the Countryside) or Nongren (Peasants), the latter common in Taiwan and formerly in mainland China. The spatial aspect is also indicated in identifiers such as Pingdiren (Flatland People) and Shandiren (Mountain People), which are locally used as substitutes for Han and non-Han, respectively.[8]

While *ren* is indisputably the most common term, some of the non-*minzu* identity categories are referred to as *jia*, for instance in the socionym Kejia. The term *jia* can be translated as "people" but it also can mean a "family," "household," "members of one family name group," or a "family engaged in a certain occupation," which implies a stronger kin-ship relationship.[9] The third term, *min*, which is present in the secondary literature in terms like Boat People (Danmin) or Fallen People (Duomin), translates as "people" or indicates a person of a certain occupation or a civilian.[10] The term emphasizes occupational identity. Now classified as Hanzu, Fallen People of Zhejiang and Boat People of Guangdong once belonged to the category of the demeaned people, who engaged in occupa-tions of low social status that were often hereditary (see Eberhard 1962).

Thus, in addition to their common meaning as "people," *ren*, *jia*, and *min* each has other connotations. *Ren* is spatial and refers to home-place identity; *jia* is kinship related, connoting a household or a family; and *min* refers broadly to occupation and civilian status. These terms and their associations are critical in understanding the historical background of non-*minzu* identities of the Hanzu and the paradigms in which they were constructed. The terms confirm that home place, occupational specializa-tion, kinship, and family bonds were important identity coordinates in premodern China. As they are used today, these identity labels connote multiple memberships and nonexclusivity. It is possible for one person to simultaneously be, for instance, a Kejia, a Fujian Person, and a Hanzu. Understanding the connotations and intertwined nature of these identi-ties is crucial to the following discussion of ethnicity.

That most, though not all, of my research participants did not object to home place–, occupation-, and kinship-based identity categories being lumped together under one Han *minzu* suggests that Han-ness has been established as a meaningful, overarching identity. It thus seems legitimate to venture that only very few people classified as Hanzu today would insist on being recognized as members of the distinct Hakka *minzu*, Shanghai *minzu*, or Cantonese *minzu*.[11] It seems unlikely that any of my informants would voluntarily give up Hanzu membership entirely to become exclu-sively Cantonese, exclusively Hakka, or exclusively Shanghainese, despite the importance they may attach to these identities. As "the core of the nation," the Han *minzu* is ascribed extreme political and social relevance, as well as historical and cultural greatness. Accordingly, membership in this category offers access to symbolic resources that most individu-als seem unwilling to give up.[12] This was clearly evidenced during the interviews when I challenged the sense of the Han *minzu* classification or referred to non-Han *minzu*; the majority of the research participants promptly abandoned their discussion of intra-Han fragmentation and boundaries and turned instead to reiterating "the Han" as a powerful national majority and the big brother of other "nationalities."

Is This Ethnicity?

The focus on local categories of identity such as *minzu, ren, min,* and *jia* has been essential in the early stages of my analysis. At the same time, it is equally important to go beyond the local specificity of the Chinese context and consider more universal queries, namely: Are both *minzu* and non-*minzu* identities, like those that relate to home place or kinship, *ethnic*? Are the relationships they form relationships of ethnicity? What are the limits to the concept of ethnicity?

Ethnicity is most often referred to as an ongoing process of identification between two collective actors, "us" and "them" (with possible multiple "thems"). As Sandra Wallman (1979, 3) argues, "Ethnicity is the process by which 'their' difference is used to enhance the sense of 'us' for purposes of organization or identification"; hence ethnicity can only exist at the boundary of "us" as it is in contact or is contrasted with "them" (Barth 1996; see also Jenkins 1997, 53). While the interactive relationship between "us" and "them" is certainly critical to ethnicity, the state is a third crucial component in processes of ethnicity (Barth 1994, 19–20; Harrell 1996b; Gladney 1998). Ethnic identity arises namely "in a three-way interplay between a group that considers itself distinctive, neighboring groups from which the group distinguishes itself, and the state, which establishes categories . . . and distributes benefits" (Harrell 1996b, 274). Accordingly, local processes of boundary making can only be understood in light of the workings of the state and the global-scale developments with which they remain in a relationship of mutual dependence (Cole and Wolf 1999). Ethnicity thus lives in the "us"/"them" paradigm but is also entangled in the politics of the state and in local-global interfaces.

Students of ethnicity further draw attention to the imaginative component of ethnicity and to the agency of those who do the imagining. Although "all communities are imagined," the ways in which they are imagined differ (Anderson 1983, 15). Ethnicity is one form of imagining. Hence, whereas processes of identification and categorization are universal, they are not always ethnic (see Martiniello 1995; Brubaker 2004).

What is it, then, that makes ethnicity different from other social categorizations? Unlike many forms of social organization, ethnicity is not always voluntary. Nor is it necessarily instrumental. Moreover, ethnicity, particularly in times of confrontation, tends to employ essentialist discourses of shared culture, shared blood, common origin, and common history (Roosens 1989; Jenkins 1997; Eriksen 2002). The *belief* in common descent, history, and shared culture as well as the *sense* of shared destiny are essential to ethnicity. Ethnicity builds on continuity in time, both imagined and actual. Reliance on ideologies of common ancestry, history, and culture, all of which project the present onto the past, constitutes the core strategy of ethnic boundary making and maintenance (Barth 1996). Ethnicity can manifest in various ways but typically combines culture (the so-called ethnic markers that make "us" similar to one another but different from "them"), kinship (imagined and actual), and history (the invented continuity within "us" and a history of conflict with "them") (Harrell 2001). When not in situations of confrontation and conflict, ethnicity seems quite flexible; it does not need to be framed in essentialist terms and can be practiced as a nontotal, nonexclusive, instrumental, and situational paradigm. This flexibility is however restricted by the *relational* quality of ethnicity, which necessitates recognition of the identity switches and negotiations performed not only by other "us" but also by "them." Nevertheless, until the moment of confrontation such as an "ethnic" conflict beyond which switches in ethnic identity are made more difficult by exclusivist and essentialist narratives, distinguishing between social and ethnic identities in daily practice is a difficult task.

Still, the underlying premise here is that it makes sense to draw boundaries around the concept of ethnicity. If we label every form of categorization processes "ethnic," the concept will quickly lose its meaning and relevance. To keep it useful, ethnic, national, and other social categorizations should be kept analytically distinct to the extent permitted by a fluid, changing reality. This will allow for an understanding of each categorization process in its own right, for a thorough recognition of its specificities and a discussion of its effects. To meaningfully apply the concept of ethnicity to my research material, the *minzu* and non-*minzu* identities that mattered to my informants are below contrasted in terms of four criteria: exclusivity, flexibility, the scales at which identities matter, and their place in the regulatory workings of the Chinese state.

Minzu and *ren, min* and *jia* identities have much in common. They are all imagined, if not always practiced, as primordial and given identities relating to descent, inborn qualities, origins, and shared history. As such, they can each be classified as ethnic. Even rurality as constructed in opposition to urbanity, and nativity as constructed in opposition to outsideness, can be argued to be ethnic, as they are based in discourses of descent, shared inborn predispositions, and shared destiny. At the same time, these identities, as well as *ren, min* and *jia* identities, differ in important ways from how Han *minzu* identity is imagined and practiced. I suggest here that the concepts of scales, density, degree of ethnicity, and transitory ethnicity are helpful in grasping these differences.

Exclusivity

The first difference between the *minzu*, home place–based, and other non-*minzu* modes of distinction my informants referenced is related to the concept of exclusivity. As I have demonstrated above, the different connotations of *ren, jia,* and *min* identities allow, and indeed almost necessitate, membership in multiple identity groups. As they are conceptualized and used, these categories are thus nonexclusive. Hence, the home-place identity and other collective non-*minzu* identities as they are practiced by my research participants are much more mutually inclusive and overlapping than *minzu*.

The relationship between the *ren, min,* and *jia* identities and Hanness has undergone significant changes since the late nineteenth century, particularly as the mobilizing power of home-place, kinship, and occupational identities has been challenged by the increasingly powerful notion of *minzu*. Throughout the twentieth century, China's central governments—assisted by scientists, as in the Minzu Classification Project—invested great effort into narrating the *ren, min,* and *jia* identities as secondary to Han-ness. Likely because of this, the overwhelming majority of my research participants perceived the boundaries between the Han *minzu* and other *minzu* as obvious, clear-cut, and impassable, a markedly different understanding than that pertaining to the non-*minzu* modes of differentiation through which they moved more fluidly. Hence, in terms of exclusivity, or in terms of the mode in which *minzu* and non-*minzu* identities are narrated and practiced, these attachments are quite distinct. Obviously, the fact that the interviews were conducted in Han-dominated cities significantly shapes this observation. In multi-ethnic areas, other paradigms of identification may be practiced as more exclusive than *minzu*. In Zuosuo, for example, *minzu* identities co-exist with ethnic identities from the pre-Communist period that are no less important in regulating mundane interactions. Though classified as one *minzu*, some ethnic groups still today do not intermarry (e.g., Prmi and Bo, both of which are classified as Tibetans). At the same time, others that are classified as two different *minzu* do intermarry (e.g., Prmi classified as Tibetan and Na classified as Mongol). In southern China, where long-standing distinctions between different *ren, min*, and *jia* categories exist, *minzu* boundaries are not necessarily narrated in the most exclusive terms or practiced as the least negotiable. In eastern Chinese cities, however, and also for instance in Xinjiang, this seems to be the case.

Flexibility

The second point of difference refers to flexibility, a notion closely linked to exclusivity. My research material demonstrates that there is a great deal of individual agency involved in the negotiation of home-place and other non-*minzu* identities. These identities are much easier to assume and easier to switch between than the *minzu* identities. Because they are not state regulated, shifts between these identity categories are widespread and individual agency in negotiating these ascriptions is more explicit. While my research data show multiple *ren* identity switches and negotiations, *minzu* tend to be discussed and practiced as flexible and negotiable to a significantly lesser degree. With one exception, none of my research participants in Shanghai, Beijing, Zuosuo, and Xinjiang practiced situational *minzu* switches as they did, for instance, in regard to home-place identities.

The Han-dominated state agencies of the twentieth century have clearly enhanced an understanding of Han-ness as a stable identity, one not subject to negotiation but to maintenance. In relational terms, the home-place, rural/urban, local/outsider, and other *ren* and *jia* identities of my Hanzu informants were much more negotiable, flexible, and dependent on the individual than the *minzu* identity.[13] For example, although most research participants emphasized that home place was crucial to how they identified themselves and other Han, what they actually defined as home place was extremely situational. Moreover, Han individuals shifted between multiple such individually negotiated home-place attachments. For instance, if a person from rural Sichuan has lived for some years in Xi'an, she may refer to herself as a Xi'an Person and an Urbanite when confronted with more recent migrants. When confronted with Han from her birthplace, Han with whom she wishes to establish a friendly relationship, she is likely to "return" to her birthplace identity and call herself a Sichuan Person. On yet other occasions, she may try to ascribe to herself *ren* identities located higher on the social hierarchy, such as Beijing Person.

Although Han-ness and other *minzu* identities are also instrumentalized and negotiated in terms that make sense in local, individualized contexts, the same sort of flexibility can hardly occur at the scale of *minzu* categorization. Unlike *ren*, *min*, and *jia* categories, *minzu* are imagined and to a great extent also lived by Han individuals as stable, given, and mutually exclusive categories of identity. This representation of *minzu* identities is obviously enforced by a powerful state apparatus, which contributes significantly to the prevalence of such imagery.

Scales and the State

Scales of interaction and the role of state policies in regulating the categorizations is a third crucial point of consideration. As I have observed in non-Han-dominated areas, particularly in Xinjiang, divisions between Rural and Urban Han, Shanghai People, Henan People or Cantonese, and Northern and Southern Han are quickly downgraded when Han are exposed to a *minzu* "other." Otherwise fragmented by numerous boundaries, Hanzu on such occasions tend to promptly disregard this fragmentation and identify with their Han-ness. When a Sichuan Person comes across a Uyghur in Xinjiang, she tends to de-emphasize her Sichuan home-place identity. Rather, she typically highlights being Han. This is because the Han *minzu* and the Uyghur *minzu* exist in Xinjiang in a mutually reifying relationship that has a clear ethnic quality as discussed above. While important in other situations, the home place–, occupation-, and kinship-related fragmentation of the Han has little bearing on this relationship and has a limited power to negotiate *minzu* boundaries. These identities relate to and exist at different scales of interaction. With regard to the Han, the scale of *minzu*-to-*minzu* interactions appears more ethnic than the scale of home place, North, South, urban, native, and other categorizations.

In order to fulfill its purpose, ethnic identity must be performed in relation to one or more "thems" or "others." The Han *minzu* has obvious "others," namely China's fifty-five "minorities." In contrast, the *ren*, *min*, and *jia* identities assumed by Hanzu do not have clear "others"; rather, they coexist in a relational system of identification *with* some and *against* others. As an example, many informants posited that Northerners were distinct from Southerners but that Shandong People were similar to Northeasterners, or that Zhejiang People and Shanghainese were very much alike. These "alliances" and their "others" shift based on selected and situationally specific criteria. Thus, while clearly constructed vis-à-vis one another in one process of othering, Northern and Southern Han jointly form a category of Mainlanders when contrasted with Taiwanese Islanders in another form of othering. Further, the identity categories regarded as similar to "us" change depending on whether one is utilizing the criterion of language, "cultural quality," "rurality," or, for example, "mentality" for categorization. The processes of othering at the non-*minzu* scale of distinction are extremely fragmented and fluid. The aim of these differentiations and distinctions is not so much to draw excluding boundaries between a specific "us" in relation to specific "them." Rather, the goal involves locating and positioning oneself in a relational system formed by multiple "us" and multiple "them" that fluctuate in relationships of othering depending on selected reference points.

To summarize, then, when compared with *minzu*, the home-place, occupational, and kinship identities of the Hanzu do not possess a similar degree of "density" and exclusivity. Moreover, they rarely travel across different scales of interaction. For example, would the boundary between Uyghur and Han become insignificant if they met outside of China? Would the international scale of this encounter render Han-ness and Uyghur-ness insignificant? From my observations, it would not, even if situationally and in individualized contexts the boundary is renegotiated and does become less salient. Still, the national Chinese identity does not have the power to render boundaries between the Han and Uyghur *minzu* irrelevant. Likely driven by similar observations, calls for increasing the importance of the Chinese identity and decreasing the role of divisive *minzu* identities have been formulated by some Chinese scholars concerned about the integrity of the Chinese nation and state (Ma 2014). Arguably, the Uyghur and Tibetans are the most politicized and most othered non-Han *minzu* in China. These identities are further strength-ened by their involvement in international and transnational politics. It is possible that some *minzu* boundaries may disappear in Chinese-ness at the changing of scales.[14] More focused studies of such relationships would need to be conducted to provide insights into why, how, and when some *minzu* boundaries become invisible with changing scales and why, how, and when other *minzu* boundaries travel globally.

In the case of the Han/Uyghur *minzu* othering discussed here, the international scale of interaction that would favor mobilization of the Chinese identity does not have the power to make Han and Uyghur *minzu* identities insignificant in social interactions. The same cannot be said *in a similar degree* about the home-place, rural/urban, local/outsider identities when these "meet" outside of China. Although differences in language, occupation, or home place may be registered, their influence on social practice is *in relative terms* less significant than *minzu* identities today, more than a hundred years since the launching of the nation-making proj-ect by Sun Yat-sen and fellow revolutionaries.

Before the modern period when Han-ness became institutionalized, home-place identities did have determining influence on mundane inter-actions among Han/Chinese who settled abroad. The role of the state, the third actor in processes of ethnicity, is explicitly manifest in how this rela-tionship changed over time. Because home-place, kinship, and occupa-tional identities are not systematically promoted as collective identities by the state, they are not capable of achieving the same degree of "density" as the institutionalized *minzu*; they thus do not travel across different scales in the same way, or at all. In China, where the government presence is so pervasive, the state component in processes of ethnicity should be given even more weight than elsewhere.

CONCLUSION

The notions of relationality, density, degree of ethnicity, and scales of interactions are of great importance to any discussion of ethnicity. The *minzu* and non-*minzu* identities of the Hanzu could both be potentially rendered as ethnic with regard to the notion of shared descent, history, and some of the cultural markers that many of the non-*minzu* identities comprise. Yet *minzu* and non-*minzu* identities also differ significantly.

Hence, I suggest that while Han *minzu* identity is more ethnic in relation to other *minzu* identities in China, the multiple home place–, kinship–, and occupation-related identities of the Han are less ethnic in relation to one another and to the *minzu* identity. They obviously overlap and they do not claim exclusivity. Their importance fades when their Han-ness is challenged or when scales of interaction change. Lacking the institutional support of the state and not being part of its biopolitical classification attempts, these identities are formulated less in either-or terms than in terms of networks and relations. Access to them is not guarded by state institutions; accordingly, switching between them is a more fluid process.

At the same time, in regions where a salient *minzu* "other" is not present in daily interactions, the *ren, min,* and *jia* attachments become ethnic, albeit in a transitory way. Likewise, the relationships of Urbanites and Ruralites or Locals and Strangers may become ethnic, especially in Han-dominated environments of eastern Chinese cities. In such settings, these identities are felt to be more meaningful and emotional than Han-ness; they assume the cloak of primordiality and have clear organizational functions. From my observations, however, whenever Han-ness of these identities is perceived to be challenged, their ethnicity diminishes. Accordingly, the great success of Han-making projects is manifest in the fact that most home place–, kinship–, occupation–, and language-based identities of Han/Chinese have become to a significant degree naturalized *as* Han.[15] As my informants demonstrated, these identities are currently conceived of as parts of the same symbolic entity, the Han *minzu*. In this sense, these identities have since the early twentieth century become successfully "nested" in the Han *minzu* identity.[16] Although not critically important in mundane identification processes in eastern Chinese cities, Han-ness is an overarching identity that few Hanzu permit to be questioned or deconstructed. Consequently, it is discursively essentialized and practiced as a given, primordial identity to a much greater degree than non-*minzu* identities. The apparatus of state-constructed myths of national unfolding in which "the Han" play a central role effectively enforces such an understanding of this identity. As a significant contrast, switches between non-*minzu* identities are rather fluid and to a great degree individually determined. This extent of individual agency and voluntary flexibility is not practiced with *minzu* identities. There, not only "us" and "them" but also the state guards the classification. Therefore, I suggest here that home-place, occupational, and kinship identities are *relatively* less ethnic than *minzu* and more transitory in their ethnicity. The role of the state, a crucial component of ethnicity processes, cannot be overestimated in establishing and regulating this relationship.

EPILOGUE

The exploration of Han-ness and of the parallel fragmentation of the Hanzu through multiple boundaries form the focus of this study. Though at first glance the argument here may appear similar to earlier studies on "plurality in unity" (*duo yuan yi ti*) (Fei 1989) or on the "Han snowball" (Xu 1999), the present exploration is crucially distinct from these conceptualizations. Importantly, it does not utilize "diversity" and "unity" as paradigms to characterize "the Han." It has even less to do with the idea of organic, evolutionary merging from plurality/diversity to unity that these scholars propose. Rather, the focus here is on the study of the *politics* of fragmentation and the *politics* of unity.

This book contributes to the small but growing field of critical Han studies (see Mullaney et al. 2012). Scholars in this field grapple with the immense category of "the Han" from multiple perspectives in an attempt to demystify and de-teleologize its making and maintenance. This is done by critically discussing the processes through which the category of "the Han" has become what it is today, by focusing on its historical contingency, by drawing attention to its imagined nature, and by analyzing its practices and discourses in their social and political contexts. The present book contributes to this field of study in several ways. First, it explores how the Han *minzu* identity that originated in the nationalist symbolic order of the late nineteenth and early twentieth century fit itself in between other collective identities of the Han/Chinese that originated in the prenationalist period. Although Han-ness was meant to ultimately cover or even replace them, these home place–, kinship/lineage- and occupation-based identities have not disappeared but continue to exist alongside Han-ness today. While most scholars emphasize the importance of "minorities" in the making of the modern Han *minzu*, the Han *minzu* was as much constructed vis-à-vis these place-, kinship-, and occupation-based identities. During the twentieth century, new collective, non-*minzu* identities of the Hanzu emerged. These newer identities, most significantly constructed along a rural/urban axis, as well as inside/outside or native/stranger differentiations, developed through the substantial "contribution" of the state. Through the household registration regime, the state institutionally reinforced the categories of urbanity, rurality, locality, and outside-ness. These identities, together with home-place identities, significantly influence othering processes among Hanzu in eastern Chinese cities.

As we have seen, at first glance Han-ness appears to be a powerful, unifying identity. Yet by adjusting our perspective, the limits of Han-ness—as evidenced in the fragmentation, discontinuities, and power struggles among Hanzu—become apparent. As it functions today, the *minzu* identity is unable to mediate the power struggles and exclusions dividing contemporary Hanzu. In eastern Chinese cities, Han-ness is perceived by many Hanzu as meaningless in mundane identity negotiations. Instead, home place and a "home-place-determined mind-set" emerge as critically important to how Hanzu identify themselves and other Han. While Han individuals tend to discuss home-place identities in terms of ascribed and emotional attachments, these identities are also instrumentalized and strategically employed. At the same time, though home place is important in identification processes, it is, like *minzu*, not a socially overwhelming identity. As home-place identities restrain Han-ness, so they are in turn restrained by other collective identities—being Chinese, urban, migrant, a graduate of a specific university, a government employee, a Communist Party member, and more. These multiple identities maintained by Hanzu are situationally activated depending on the corresponding "other."

This deconstructive analysis highlights the Han *minzu* as a deeply divided category. However, my research data compel us to simultaneously recognize that despite the existing fragmentation, the Han-making projects of the twentieth and twenty-first centuries have been at least partially successful. The non-*minzu* identities of the Hanzu, both those originating in the premodern period and those reinforced in the twentieth century, have become to a significant degree nested *within* the Han *minzu* identity. Even though Han-ness is marginally important in everyday identity processes in eastern Chinese cities, the Han *minzu* has been successfully promoted as an overarching denominator. This hierarchization of identities in which Han-ness prevails over the fragmented non-*minzu* attachments is clearly in the interest of the Chinese state and is reinforced by it.

One of the central questions of this book has been which identities are performed in which situations, and why some of them appear as more ethnic than others. My research material demonstrates that in mundane identification processes in eastern Chinese urban settings, Han-ness is unable to mediate social exclusions. In these settings, many Hanzu turn to home-place and other non-*minzu* identities to find a feeling of belonging as well as social solidarity and crucial support networks beyond immediate kin. The identities on which these solidarity and assistance networks are established are framed in these situations as given, primordial, and exclusive attachments. Networks established along these attachments may behave like ethnic groups, for example forming occupational niches where the employment of fellow locals is prioritized. Further, there are the privileged identities as Locals and Urbanites, which are established and assumed to protect the symbolic and material resources these identities offer access to, such as preferential employment, lower housing prices, higher wages, and so on. In these processes of establishing boundaries, these identities are also constructed as primordial and inaccessible to Outsiders. They are ethnicized to create networks of solidarity and to erect barriers to maintain specific power asymmetries and resource control. The state does little to diminish this existing hierarchization among the Hanzu. The state-promoted *minzu* identity seems unable to create social cohesion and everyday ethnic solidarity among fellow Han in eastern Chinese cities. Han-ness, formulated in terms of political mission, power, history, and ancestors, although certainly an appreciated alternative is nonetheless perceived as too distant; lacking the familiarity of home-place attachments, it is rarely an everyday identity choice.

The Han *minzu* was constructed at the turn of the twentieth century with a clear political goal in mind. In the early twentieth century the meaning of Han-ness was reformulated through a new nomenclature inspired by discourses of race, nation, and state. This way of imagining Han-ness prevails today. Yet its framing, as well as its *minzu* form, will likely change again in the future, particularly as we consider the growing transnationalization of identity politics, the individualization and fragmentation of identity expression made possible by the Internet, and increasing national and international mobility. In the era of global flows, discourses of ancestral land and cultural ancestry are likely to gain even greater importance in the articulation of Han-ness. At the same time, othering vis-à-vis "minorities"—or discourses of modernity and advancement constructed in relation to "minorities"—will potentially lose their validity. Perhaps institutional frames will also change again, as *minzu* categorizations are difficult to export globally.[1]

This book is a series of photographs. At a single moment in time and space, it captures fluid identity positions that reveal instances of the complexity of identity negotiations.[2] This study proposes possible approaches to—and analytical terminology for—a discussion of the processes of inclusion, exclusion, merging, and distinction that occur among the contemporary Hanzu. Of course, this analysis is restricted by the locations of fieldwork and the selection of research participants. Further research in different regions and communities is needed to elaborate on and possibly deconstruct some of the assumptions made here. There is still much to be done to create even a basic understanding of how Han-ness functions, what it does, what its limits are, and where it remains insignificant. Though some processes of Han identity negotiation and identity performances are discussed here, scholarship that traces categorization and identification paradigms in multiethnic and rural areas is needed to further complicate our current understandings. In Qinghai, for example, religion rather than language or *minzu* appears to affect the formation of social alliances between Buddhist Han and Tibetans in opposition to the Muslim Hui (Vasantkumar 2012). In Xinjiang, some Xinjiang Han (e.g., early Han settlers and their descendants) side with some Uyghur to contest the influx of new Han migrants, thereby investing the paradigm of shared home place with more weight than the paradigm of *minzu*.

Further studies in multiethnic and rural areas are needed to help understand the practices of being Han in non-Han-dominated and rural locations and also the identities these Han activate in their daily interactions. Such studies would allow for a nonhegemonic, transitory, and pluralistic understanding of the Han identity, just as this identity is lived by Han individuals. Exploration of identity switches to and away from Han-ness, between various *ren*, *min*, and *jia* identities, and between still other modes of classification are necessary to contest the monolithic representations of "the Han." Still other forms of differentiation, such as the Cantonese distinction between *yan* (humans), *lau* (semihumans), and *kuai* (ghosts) must be explored too.[3] These will take the analysis of categorization processes into an entirely new dimension. Ultimately, microlevel studies are necessary to help understand the processes that divide and unite contemporary Han, the making of identities, their simultaneous porosity and primordiality, the complex dynamics of identity politics, the fluctuations and the fragmentation of Han ethnonationalism, and the challenges Han individuals face in negotiating between them.

NOTES

ABBREVIATIONS

DNC   *Documents of the 16th National Congress of the Communist Party of China*
ZRTN   Guojia Tongjiju Renkou he Shehui Keji Tongjisi, ed., *Zhongguo renkou tongji nianjian 2002 / China Population Statistics Yearbook*
ZZWY   Zhonggong Zhongyang Wenxian Yanjiushi and Zhonggong Xinjiang Weiwu'er Zizhiqu Weiyuanhui, ed., *Xinjiang gongzuo wenxian xuanbian, 1949–2010*

INTRODUCTION

1   Hanzu are the members of the Han *minzu*.

2   See Anderson 1972; Blake 1981; J. Watson 1988; R. Watson 1988; Honig 1992a; Choi 1995; Constable 1996; Chen 1999; Hansen 2005; and Vasantkumar 2012.

3   See Eberhard 1962; Fei 1992; Duara 1995; Dikötter 1996; Ebrey 1996; Xu 1999; Harrison 2000; Leibold 2007; Elliott 2012; and Joniak-Lüthi 2014.

4   These socionyms are collective identity labels conceived by some Han to describe other Han. They are capitalized as a reminder that they are to be read as emic identity labels and not as analytical terms.

5   I would like to thank Ellen Hertz for her insightful comments on the question of relationality.

6   In localized contexts, Han-ness/Chinese-ness was likely intertwined with other identities, such as "the cultured ones"; "farmers, not herders"; or "having bound feet." In late nineteenth-century (and also twentieth-century) Guangdong, bargaining over who was more and who was less Han/Chinese could be as fierce a debate among Han/Chinese as the differentiation between Chinese and "barbarians" (Blake 1981; Constable 1996; Leong 1997).

7   I use *biopolitical* in the meaning discussed by Foucault, for instance in *Discipline and Punish* (1991).

8   For a discussion of the anti-Manchu rhetoric, see Crossley 1997 (189–201).

9   For detailed analyses of this process, see Duara 1995; Chow 2001; Harrison 2001; and Leibold 2006. See also Rhoads 2000 for an analysis that draws on the perspective of Manchu-Han relations.

10   See Elliott 2012.

11   Minzu is not an indigenous category of identity sensu stricto but rather was imported from Japan in the late nineteenth century.

12   The Han *minzu* is to a certain degree a new form conceived to regulate a much older and fragmented attachment that has been perpetuated in a complex interplay between imperial and local identity processes.

13   An individual can only have one *minzu* (even if her or his parents are of two different *minzu*) and one nationality (as Chinese). Double citizenship is not permitted in China.

14   In overseas communities, Chinese-ness has different associations that tend to focus on common ancestry and shared cultural identity. Political and scholarly elites in mainland China, however, present the overseas Chinese as a transnational extension of the Chinese nation (Barabantseva 2010).

15   Putonghua (lit., "common speech") is the sole national language in the People's Republic of China. It is based on the vocabulary of the northern Han languages, Beijing pronunciation, and grammar as used in literary works written in *baihua*, a colloquial script. Putonghua is the standard language; it is what is referred to in English as Mandarin Chinese.

1. NARRATING "THE HAN"

1   See Gladney 1991 (72–73) for some illustrative quotes from Fei's book. Xu Jieshun and the Han Studies Center he established at the Guangxi University for Nationalities played a crucial role in relaunching Han studies as a discipline in mainland China during the late 1980s.

2   Compare James Leibold's 2010 study of Han supremacism on the Chinese Internet and his contribution in *Critical Han Studies* (Leibold 2012).

3   References to earlier dynastic periods in this book are offered to demonstrate that some processes in late imperial China clearly originate in much earlier periods.

4   I would like to thank Jonathan Lipman for his helpful comments on the meaning of Semuren and Semuguan (Officials of Various Categories). Although some scholars in China argue that *semu* means "colored eyes"—for example, Weng 2001— Lipman follows Frederick W. Mote, convincingly arguing that the usage of *semu* in Yuan-period sources indicates no such meaning. See also Lipman 1997 (33).

5   Among others, see Eberhard 1962 (18–30); Ebrey 1996 (23); and Harrison 2001 (30–31).

6   Sun, n.d. (1–6).

7   In Sun's lectures, *Han* and *Chinese* often appear as interchangeable terms.

8   See Ramsey 1987 (8–11); Dikötter 1996 (250–51); Harrison 2000; Chow 2001; and Leibold 2006.

9   For examples, see Faure and Siu 1995; Zhang 2001; Hansen 2005; Whyte 2010; Carrico 2012; Joniak-Lüthi 2013.

10   However, Duara (1993) argues that the spatial idea of the Han community inhabiting a concrete country was not an invention of twentieth-century nationalism but had already been proposed by part of the scholarly elite during the Jin invasion in the twelfth century CE. Furthermore, the classification of Han subjects by the Yuan dynasty was spatial too. Northern Han/Chinese, together with Khitans, Jurchens, and other former subjects of the Jin dynasty, became classified as Han People. This was a category distinct from the Southern People, which included both Han/Chinese and other subjects of the defeated Song dynasty (see Elliott 2012). One can also argue that there was a spatial link between Han-ness and a sedentary lifestyle. Han were "fixed" spatially by cities, fields, towns, and markets, in contrast to the fluidity of the pasturelands. I am grateful to James Leibold for pointing out that association.

11   Compare Weng 2001 for examples of these terms used in historical records.

12   Yet there were certain limits to this openness. See Dikötter 1992 (10–17) and 1997 (20–21) for a discussion of the racial discourse of exclusion with regard to "African slaves" in China. Kang Youwei, on the other hand, argued that even "African slaves" could be "improved" through change of dietary habits, intermarriage, and migration (Dikötter 1992, 89).

13   It is necessary to pay attention to the agency of non-Han/Chinese in assuming or rejecting the Han identity, a point ignored in earlier acculturation and sinicization theses that presented Chinese culture as an overwhelming power that assimilated everything in its way (compare Crossley 1990).

14   For examples, see Blake 1981 (7–16, 87); Choi 1995 (104–22); Hayes 1995 (90–92); and Ching 1996 (58).

15   Until the seventeenth century CE, access to imperial power structures was largely restricted to the Han/Chinese through the system of imperial examinations. Wolfram Eberhard (1962, 18–30) emphasizes that non-Han were permitted a certain quota for the imperial examinations only from the seventeenth century onward, under the Manchu. Drawing on the reality of imperial examinations, he argues that upward social mobility was not as easy in China as many authors maintain. Indeed, large groups were excluded. While gentry and farmers were admitted, merchants were admitted only much later, and even then they were limited to 0.3 percent of the total quota. Sons of criminals (even if they came from the two top classes), monks, or non-Han were also excluded. Moreover, until the seventh century CE no free competition was possible, as candidates had to be recommended by local authorities according to a quota system. At certain times, however, a degree could be purchased. Periods of war also opened paths for upward social mobility.

16   See Blake 1981; Ching 1996; M. Cohen 1996 (1962); Segawa 1996; Leong 1997; and Harrison 2001.

17   For examples, see Fei 1980 on Chuanqing who "lost" the memory of being Han; Rhoads 2000 (278–79) on Han who joined Manchu banners and later registered as Manchu; Tapp 1995 and 2002 on complex identity constellations in mixed Han-Miao families; and Hansen 2005 on *minzu* switches of the Hanzu in present-day Xishuangbanna/Sipsongpanna.

18   Weng Dujian (2001, 61) quotes *Discourses of the States* (Guoyu), compiled probably in the fifth and fourth centuries BCE, which reports that "Rong and Di . . . are like beasts [*ruo qinshou ye*]."

19   However, Tamara Chin (2012, 133–34) emphasizes that there was no single "Chinese" worldview. Although the classical philosophers of the fifth to third centuries BCE generally distinguished between those within and outside of the Central States according to their adherence to Zhou ritual code, the cultural superiority of the Zhou was not always assumed.

20   On Han culture, see Leibold 2007 (23). Leibold demonstrates that even among Han-dynasty officials, the belief in the transforming power of Han culture and the emperor's way (*dao*) was not shared by all. Some officials believed that some barbarians (such as the Xiongnu) could never be transformed into cultural beings; the only option was to keep them at distance and tame them by appeasement.

21   There are also some double-syllabic Han names such as Sima or Zhuge. They are, however, very rare.

22   For more details and examples of names, see Eberhard 1942; Fan 1961; and Müller 1980.

23   *Xing* originally meant a kin group of blood-relatives, a lineage. Another similar term, *shi*, referred to patriarchal clans of the nobles. During the Qin and Han dynasties, the two terms fused into one: *xingshi*, a surname group (Yuan and Zhang 2002, 3).

24   Among the Han, children inherit ancestral home place, or a place of origin along the patriline (*jiguan*), after their fathers. The idea of *jiguan* is very similar to the Swiss concept of *Heimatort* (patrilineal ancestral home place). People with the same family name, or branches within large family-name groups, share the same *Heimatort* (which is in most cases different from birthplace). For a detailed discussion of the concept of home place, see chapter 3.

25   James Watson (1993) isolates nine stages: ritual wailing to announce death, wearing hempen garb and other symbols of mourning, the ritualized bathing of the corpse, the transfer of goods (through the medium of fire) to the deceased, the preparation of a soul tablet with the name written in characters, the use of copper and silver coins in ritualized contexts, high-pitched piping and percussion to mark transitions in rites accompanied by a procession, sealing the corpse in a wooden coffin, and expelling the corpse from the community.

26   A Chinese expression that refers to times of great social disorder reads, "Fathers do not act like fathers, and sons do not act like sons" (Fu bu fu, zi bu zi) (Fei 1992, 128).

27   It is believed that Confucius taught that a correct mind follows from proper behavior: "When funerals are conducted in accordance with the rites, and sacrifices to remote ancestors are given devoutly, the morality of the people will naturally reach its peak" (*Lunyu* 1994, 6).

28   The oldest characters found on oracle bones date from the Shang dynasty (sixteenth to eleventh century BCE).

29   From the sixteenth century CE onward, bureaucrats and merchants also shared a common spoken language, the Officials' Speech (Guanhua) (Yuan 1983; Ramsey 1987). Even if not a standard language—pronunciation differed depending on the speakers; and southern speakers were proud of their southern accents, which retained older distinctions from the Tang period lost in the North—Guanhua likely functioned as an important marker of belonging to these social classes (Ramsey 1987, 5).

30 Although the category of Boat People is organized to a considerable degree around the occupational distinction to agriculturalists, not all Boat People have actually engaged in fishing. Some have also been bamboo-basket weavers and farmers (Ye 1995, 83–84).

31 The Hakka (Kejia in standard Chinese, lit., "Guest People") believe themselves to be—and historians partly confirm their self-representation—descendants of Han/ Chinese who migrated from north-central China before the fourth century CE and settled in southeast China by the fourteenth century (Constable 1996, 7–15). The Hokkien (or Fujian People) are descendants of migrants from Fujian; they speak southern Min languages (dialects of Quanzhou, Xiamen/Amoy, or Chaozhou). Punti (Bendi in standard Chinese, lit., "local," "native") claim the status of "nativity" in Guangdong.

32 Cole (1982) reports that the Fallen People (Duomin) from Shaoxing Prefecture in Zhejiang, also referred to as "beggar households" (gaihu), were, like the Boat People, emancipated in 1723 from legal discrimination. Still, they were barred from engaging in farming and commerce in some parts of Shaoxing as late as 1945. Naquin and Rawski (1987, 148), as well as Eberhard (1962, 18), argue that the low status of the Fallen People is not only related to their occupations (hairdressers, bridal attendants, matchmakers, prostitutes, opera singers, banquet attendants, and fortune tellers, among others) but also perhaps to their origin among non-Han people, who, in the course of Han expansion, lost their livelihoods and came to specialize in these hereditary professions.

33 Interestingly, the imperial Qing understanding of China and the Chinese is similar to what these terms nominally represent today. In 1755 the emperor Qianlong pronounced, "There exists a view of China (Zhongxia), according to which non-Han people cannot become China's subjects and their land cannot be integrated into the territory of China. This does not represent our dynasty's understanding of China, but is instead that of the earlier Han, Tang, Song, and Ming dynasties" (Zhao 2006, 4).

34 Pamela Crossley (personal communication, 2014) emphasizes that while genealogies were an important part of Nurgaci's (1559–1626) state building, they were first used in an ethnicized way to demonstrate Manchu identity in the mid-eighteenth century. Part of Nurgaci's state building consisted of forcing subjects to write down their genealogies—which were earlier mostly committed to memory by designated members of the lineage, as paper was rare and expensive—for purposes of organizing companies within the Eight Banners. However, although committing genealogies to writing is an important historical threshold, genealogization as such does not begin with Nurgaci's rule. Likewise, ethnicization of Manchu identity does not automatically begin with genealogization. For instance, imperial genealogies (yudie) were already being compiled in the mid-seventeenth century. Yet, the yudie were the exclusive preserve of the Aisin Gioro zongshi (clan) and thus not particularly relevant to Manchu identity generally. The yudie trace ancestry back to the time of Giocangga (in the case of the central line, back to Mongke Temur). This was important in establishing rights within the banners and the stipendiary bureaucracy of the Qing but had little to do with emphasizing ethnic boundaries. See also Crossley 1990a, 1999.

35 For an excellent study of Manchu-Han relations in late premodern and early modern China, see Rhoads 2000.

36 Sun, n.d. (1–6). Others, like Wang Jingwei or Liang Qichao, added a shared habitat, national spirit, and writing system (Harrell 2001, 29; Harrison 2001, 104).

37 Sun, n.d. (31).

38 Tracing ancestry back to mythical ancestors like Shennong (also called Yandi) and the Yellow Emperor (Huangdi) was already established by Sima Qian's time and was still present in the genealogies from the Tang and Song periods (Ebrey 1996, 26–28). Revolutionaries reinvented the Yellow Emperor as the ancestor of all Han rather than of individual lineages. For Peking Man, see Sautman 2001.

39 Chinese revolutionaries and reformists tried to avoid making European history "the standard reference in temporality" by adopting the birthdays of either Confucius or the Yellow Emperor as the beginnings of Chinese chronology (Chow 2001, 63–65). However, judged by today's awareness of these temporalities among the Han in the mainland China and among the overseas Chinese, the revolutionaries' efforts did not have a lasting success. See also Ramsey 1987 (8–11); Dikötter 1992, 1996 (250–51); Duara 1995; Harrison 2000; Chow 2001; and Leibold 2006.

40 Although the Han used the same written language throughout the empire, spoken languages differed greatly. Some of the northern and southern languages were and remain mutually unintelligible.

41 Harrison 2001 (115).

42 On the Minzu Classification Project, see Wong 1979; Fei 1980; Heberer 1984; Harrell 1995; Huang 1995b; Gladney 1998; Wang, Zhang and Hu 1998; Joniak and Lüthi 2001; and Mullaney 2011.

43 The last of the currently fifty-six *minzu*, the Jinuo, was officially recognized in 1979. Since then, no new *minzu* have been officially recognized, but some groups have been given semiofficial status as distinct *ren* (people) within a larger *minzu*.

44 Stalin's definition of *nation* echoes Marx and Engels: modern nations are ethnocultural and linguistic communities with their own states, while nationalities are ethnocultural and linguistic groups that did not develop into full nations because they lacked their own state. Marx and Engels also argued that "national communities incapable of forming national states are hindering the development of the progressive centralization and uniformation of humanity, and must therefore assimilate to more 'vital' and 'energetic' nations capable of forming national states with democracy 'as compensation'" (Nimni 1995, 72). Inspired by both Marx and Stalin, Mao envisaged the new Chinese nation as a composite of the Han, constituting its core, and the nationalities located at the margins of the national imagery.

45 Stalin chose a dual path of citizenship and nationality: one was Soviet (citizenship) and at the same time, for instance, Ukrainian or Russian (nationality). Stalin's solution to the "national question" was also implemented by Mao in China: one is simultaneously Chinese (citizenship) and Han (*minzu*), or Chinese and Tibetan, and so on. Although Mao imported many Soviet political ideas, he never copied the Soviet state model as a union of republics. China was to become a multiethnic but unitary state.

46 Although this model was adopted as Marxist in China, for Asia (especially for India and China) Marx and Engels originally conceived a distinct "Asiatic mode of production" that posited Asian societies as doomed to stagnation and lacking the driving power that would push their development forward. Marx and Engels interpreted the activity of colonial powers in China as modern capitalist institutions

making the country develop the "proper" way (Wicker 1974, 3). Understandably, the Asiatic mode was a cause of consternation in the East, and it was eventually deposed from Marxist theory at a conference in Leningrad in 1931 (Wicker 1974, 127). Still, Marx was not consistent on this point, and in the introduction to *A Critique of Political Economy* he wrote. "Asiatic, ancient, feudal, and modern bourgeois modes of production can be designated as progressive epochs in the economic formation of society" (quoted in Tong 1989, 196).

47   Morgan's model reached the Chinese Communists through Engels's interpretation of his ideas in *Der Ursprung der Familie, des Privateigenthums und des Staats* (http://marxwirklichstudieren.files.wordpress.com/2012/11/engels-ursprung-der-familie-usw.pdf). Engels also based his analysis on Marx's notes on Morgan.

48   Morgan linked savagery with a "Punalua family" (group marriage). The early stage of barbarism was connected with matriarchal family structure, the middle period with both matriarchal and patriarchal structures, and the late with patriarchal family structure. The final stage of civilization was marked by monogamous marriage (Morgan 1976, 33–34).

49   In the 1990s, the label "living fossil" was successfully promoted as a slogan to attract Han tourists searching for exotic marital customs.

50   Similar to the early twentieth-century revolutionaries, Mao conceptualized the Han as a community that had existed uninterrupted since time immemorial and that had developed in an evolutionary way from a primitive classless society to a feudal class society and, later, to a semicolonial one. In Mao's version of history, after thousands of years of classless society China evolved four thousand years ago into a phase of slavery, and during the Zhou and Qin dynasties (eleventh through third century BCE) into feudalism. Afterward, it developed only slowly, with the period of feudalism lasting almost three thousand years. After the Opium Wars, China transformed gradually into a semicolony and then into a semifeudal society (Mao 1968–69, 354–88).

51   For popular contemporary markers of Han-ness, see chapter 2.

52   In one case, Han *minzu* belonging is a matter of choice and not descent only, namely when a child of mixed non-Han and Han parents decides at the age of eighteen which *minzu* she wants to belong to, her mother's or her father's.

53   In fact, there is still a substantial population with an "unidentified *minzu* status" (*wei shibie de minzu*); most of them live in Guizhou. This population without a *minzu* status numbered 734,438 in the year 2000 (ZRTN 2002, 106) and 640,101 in 2010 (National Bureau of Statistics of China, www.stats.gov.cn).

54   However, signifiers like "mixed blood" (*hunxue*; indicating a person of a mixed-*minzu* descent) or "half Yi, half Han" (Stevan Harrell, personal communication, 2014) are also used as self-denominations in contexts where the information may be important. Mixed descent may be deliberately concealed in other contexts. Significantly, these individual negotiations have no impact on the official classification of the persons who use them.

55   Compare Ann Anagnost's (1997) "nation as narration" and Homi Bhabha's (1990) notion of nation as a narrative of historical progress.

56   Duara (1995) brilliantly calls for "rescuing history from the nation" by attending to the appropriation of history by nationalisms.

57   Compare Harrell's (1996a) argument about the role of ethnic leaders in creating teleological narratives of national and ethnic unfolding.

2. CONTEMPORARY NARRATIVES OF HAN-NESS

1   For analysis of these processes in contemporary China, see Gladney 1994; Schein 2000; and Blum 2001. For the pre-1949 period, see Duara 1995; Dikötter 1996; Harrison 2001; Chow 2001; Leibold 2006, 2012; Elliott 2012; and Giersch 2012.

2   Some markers could also be called *stereotypes*, but this term does not as clearly convey the act of marking, which is the focus here.

3   Chu (n.d.) demonstrates that Tibetan, Uyghur, but also Mongol *minzu* are the most often represented "minorities" in elementary-level textbooks.

4   But see Blum 2001 (57–59) for how Han-ness also differs from whiteness in several important respects.

5   Kaiser (1997, 11) compellingly argues that a nation is a "mass based community of belonging and interest, whose members share a backward looking sense of common genealogical and geographic roots, as well as a forward-looking sense of destiny."

6   By "High Communist Period," I am referring to James Scott's (1998) definition of Authoritarian High Modernism.

7   Stevan Harrell (personal communication, 2014) points out that, in quite a contrast, non-Han such as the Yi stereotype "the Han" as having no family feelings or family loyalty. Similarly, Uyghur individuals often contrast their complex system of family obligations and filial piety with "the Han." Especially the fact that Han children often live away from their parents in cities and thus do not fulfill the filial obligation to take care of parents has been popularly discussed.

8   The three terms Hanyu (Han language), Zhongwen (Chinese language), and Putonghua (Common Speech) are customarily rendered in English as "standard Chinese." I use them interchangeably in this book. Interestingly, parallel to the tension between Han-ness and Chinese-ness, a tension in linguistic nomenclature exists in the overlapping use of the terms "Han language" and "Chinese language."

9   Hansen (2005, 22) observes that apart from being a lingua franca, Chinese is also a "language of success."

10   Since the Central Committee of the Communist Party endorsed the popularization of the new national language (Putonghua) in 1954, it has been promoted as the only official language. This despite the fact that about 30 percent of the Hanzu speak languages that are mutually unintelligible with Putonghua, and almost all non-Han *minzu* have distinct languages. Although the difficulty of mastering the Han language makes the idea of multiple national languages attractive, the dominant position that the Han language and education in the Han language grant the Hanzu leaves little space to entertain such ideas in the current political constellation. On how the national language standard was negotiated, see Yuan 1983 and Ramsey 1987.

11   Although the markers about clothing were collected between 2002 and 2003, they relate directly to the later Han clothing movement (*Hanfu yundong*) (Leibold 2010; Carrico 2012). The goal of the Han clothing movement, which had momentum in the late 2000s, was to "revive" the "traditional" Han silk robes in contrast to the "foreign" Qing robes. It was also intended to equip the Han with some attributes of ethnic uniqueness and particularity, qualities most popularly associated with Chinese "minorities."

12   Lin Yutang in *My Country and My People* offers a prominent example of how Han-

ness/Chinese-ness can be biologized: "[The] cultural homogeneity [of the Han/ Chinese] sometimes makes us forget that racial differences, differences of blood, do exist within the country. At close range the abstract notion of a Chinaman disappears and breaks up into a picture of a variety of races, different in their stature, temperament and mental make-up" (Lin 1998, 17–18).

13   Non-Han, particularly those from rural areas and autonomous regions, receive for instance extra points at the university entry exams.

14   This argument does not relate to non-Han peoples, such as the Manchu or Mongols, who have assumed Han identity in the 1950s as a protection against discrimination and persecution. When the Maoist era concluded, these people and their descendants began to openly manifest their previously concealed identities, often changing their *minzu* status.

15   At the time of research, Han female fashions in the Lugu Lake region included self-embroidered shoes, blouses, and trousers. Some of these items were also exhibited for sale on the village streets.

16   It is possible that some of these markers and associations reached villagers during political education meetings, particularly the long public meetings of the Cultural Revolution, which many villagers remembered. It is difficult to assess what influence newspapers or migration had on transmission of these markers. Newspapers may have had some influence on the literate Han. Migration and word of mouth may have had some influence as well, but they do not explain why younger generations of school attendees who had not yet left the village were so articulate about these markers.

17   This is particularly visible in the control of private educational institutions. For instance, private kindergartens or language schools run by Uyghur individuals in Xinjiang are subject to much more control and institutional discrimination than other Uyghur-run enterprises.

18   Because Zuosuo is located within the Liangshan Yi Autonomous Prefecture, the junior high offers Yi (Nuosu) language classes. These were mandatory for all non-Han students in 1999 and voluntary for the Han, a Yi-language instructor reported.

19   Some Nuosu settled on the Zuosuo plain in a government program that provided them with land and timber for house construction. At the time of research, some of those who had originally moved had already returned to the mountain hamlets where they had lived before.

20   The Chinese state message is somewhat ambiguous on this point. "Minority" languages are constitutionally guaranteed the right to be used as a means of communication and education. At the same time, in practice they are rarely the languages of instruction beyond the third elementary grade. But there are exceptions. For instance, in southern Xinjiang in 2011–12, Uyghur was the language of instruction in the majority of primary Uyghur schools and in some secondary schools. Following the pressure to switch to "bilingual education" (*shuangyu jiaoyu*), circa 2010 Uyghur schools began turning to a "bilingual" curriculum where standard Chinese would be the language of instruction from third grade on. Given the lack of qualified teachers, however, this transformation has been occurring very slowly. There are also different models for the transition from a native language to standard Chinese as the language of instruction in non-Han-dominated regions, even if standard Chinese usually begins to replace other ethnic languages beginning in the third grade. While in some schools the change of language is abrupt, in others

it occurs gradually. In yet other schools, some subjects are taught in Chinese while others remain taught in Uyghur far beyond the third grade, for instance due to the lack of Chinese-speaking teachers.

21 Compare Gladney 1991, 2004; Schein 2000; and Harrell 2001.

3. TOPOGRAPHIES OF IDENTITY

1   In chapter 4, I discuss other boundaries and attachments that emerged in my research data.

2   Ho 1966; Naquin and Rawski 1987; Watson 1988; Fei 1992; Honig 1992a; Goodman 1995; Leong 1997; Gladney 1998; Zhang 2001; Yi 2002; and Liu Xiaochun 2003, among others.

3   *Jia* translates as "family," "household," "home," "people who share the same surname," or simply "surname"; *gu* refers to services in which sacrifices are offered and also means the "old," "former," or "ancient." *Xiang* indicates a "village," "native place," or "hometown." Another popular term is *laojia* (old home), which tends to refer to birthplace or ancestral home place. Goodman (1995, 2, 4) also mentions other related terms such as *sangzi* (native place) or *yuanji* (ancestral home, native place).

4   *Zuji*, where *zu* means "ancestors" and *ji* means "record" or "registry," is a term similar to *jiguan*.

5   *Jiguan* has to be registered, for instance, when checking in at a hotel.

6   This seems to indicate that Fei Xiaotong conceives of Han-ness as a kind of shared, racial descent.

7   Territorial bonds, like kinship bonds, come into play in economic life (Fei 1980, 95). Ho Ping-ti (1966, 120) also points out that common native place, together with kinship ties, used to be the most fundamental basis for voluntary association.

8   Contemporarily, clear specialization appears to exist too. For instance, Yi (2002, 111) discusses specialization among food sellers in Shanghai where Cantonese sell fish porridge, Shaoxing People specialize in fermented dried vegetables, Subei People market dough twists fried in sesame oil, and Ningbo People sell dumplings made of glutinous rice.

9   In late Qing, there were also guilds (*hang*) in Guangzhou, which gathered local merchants and were organized on the basis of specific services or products. However, unlike the Shanghai guilds, they did not have a strong influence on public life in Guangzhou (Rhoads 1974, 103). As merchants were not granted any political voice, the guilds were traditionally not involved in politics. This changed as the Qing weakened and the revolution neared.

10 That people are today migrating around the country does not mean that the household registration system has been abandoned. The transfer of registration from rural to urban areas is as difficult for rural migrants as it was under Mao. Migrant workers' vulnerability continues in the cities. Although the need for changes in household registration has been recognized, including by central authorities, changes have so far been limited (Chan and Buckingham 2008).

11 Other possible terms with which to discuss Han place-based attachments are *tautotopic identity* (place-based identity) or *topocentric koinosis*, that is, a sense of commonality based around a place. I would like to thank Jonathan Lipman and

Stevan Harrell for brainstorming about this terminology. Ultimately, however, the final choice of *home-place identity* was mine. I bear the responsibility for any conceptual slippages and inconsistencies.

12 I discuss the importance of state education in establishing *minzu* labels as viable categories of identification in my master's thesis, "'Since they have never been to school, they do not know who they are'" (University of Bern). The title is a quote from a government official in Zuosuo, Sichuan, who reflected on some villagers' lack of awareness about the officially endorsed *minzu* classification.

13 Honig (1992a) thoroughly studies the processes through which Subei identity was created and stigmatized.

14 Jiangnan refers literally to the region south of the Yangzi River. South of the Yellow River would be *henan* in Chinese, but this is precisely the term that the interviewee wanted to bend.

15 Self-denominations put forth by the respondents from Subei included the following: Person from South of the River, here meaning the Yangzi River (Jiangnan-ren); from Xuzhou (Xuzhou de); Hanzu; Shali Person (Shaliren); Local (Lata); Huai'an Person (Huai'anren); Qihai Person (Qihairen); Person from North of the Yangzi River (Jiangbeiren); Taizhou Person (Taizhouren); and Shanghainese. No respondents referred directly to the term Subei in their self-denominations. Self-identifiers used by respondents from Henan included the following: (Person from) Central Plains (Zhongyuan), Zhengzhou Person (Zhengzhouren), Chinese (Zhongguoren); and Henan Person (Henanren).

16 For examples, see Chen 1999; Lin 2001; Ding 2002; Ma 2002; Liu 2002; and Liu Xiaochun 2003.

17 Hakka and *Kejia* are two different pronunciations of the same socionym, Guest People. *Hakka* is its pronunciation in the Hakka and Yue (Cantonese) languages, while Kejia is the standard Chinese pronunciation. Although these two pronunciations are most commonly used in China and abroad, other pronunciations include *Khe-ka* in the Minnan language (as used in Fujian) and in Taiwan, *Khe-lang*. Hakka from Sichuan are locally called Guangdong People (Guangdongren) (Stevan Harrell, personal communication, 2014).

18 Blake (1981) and M. Cohen (1996) argue that it was language and not migrant-native discourse that played a central role in the delineation of "us" and "them" in Guangdong and Guangxi where the Hakka settled.

19 This also seems to be one of the motivations of Ma Rong's idea to "depoliticize" *minzu* categorizations in China (Ma 2014). He suggests that "the minorities" should stop imagining themselves as political collectives and instead focus on a self-understanding based on cultural differences among Chinese citizens. These citizens, Ma argues, should enjoy equal protection from the state and equal rights on the basis of being Chinese. In light of the Chinese government's inability to guarantee equal rights today (e.g., in terms of language use or forms of representation in school textbooks), and the rather difficult task of convincing "the minorities" to abandon "emotionality" and focus instead on culture and socioeconomics, it is difficult to grasp who Ma's call addresses, how it should be implemented, and by whom.

20 "Origin" must here be in quotation marks, as it is as likely to be invented as inherited.

21 A similar phenomenon was observed by Siegel (1989) in the Central African Copperbelt.

4. OTHERING, EXCLUSION, AND DISCRIMINATION

1   In chapter 2, to emphasize their marking function in processes of identity, I referred to *tedian* as markers. Here I wish to emphasize their stereotypical quality and collective reproduction.

2   In localized communities, other paradigms may be important. Compare for instance localized markers of distinction in Zuosuo in chapter 2.

3   These adjectives are quoted directly from my research interviews.

4   See also Hanson's (1998) historical analysis of the discourse of difference between the North and South based on the notion of *qi*.

5   On the historical notions of culture (*wenhua*), see Fairbank 1968; Bauer 1980; and Watson and Rawski 1988.

6   Though southern provinces also have large agricultural outputs, in the perception of my informants they did not function as "agricultural provinces." Instead, southern China was unanimously associated with developed industry and commerce.

7   Though southern provinces also have large rural populations, many of the informants nonetheless seemed to link agriculture with backwardness and the North.

8   For historical and linguistic explorations of regional distinctions and regional characteristics, see Moser 1985.

9   See Elliott 2012 for a description of how this influenced the idea of Han-ness and Chinese-ness.

10   On the idea of peasants as the embodiment of the premodern, and city people (*shimin*) as synonymous with modern, self-determining citizens, see Day 2013.

11   The Jing Youzi socionym was used by some Beijing People too. They argued that it positively connotes being experienced and having a broad knowledge of the world. The immigrants from Shandong and Inner Mongolia said instead that it reflected the slippery and cunning character of Beijing People.

12   See Müller 1980; Heberer 1989; and Thierry 1989.

13   In some of the southern provinces, however, the gentry were more urbanized. The southern gentry began shifting their residence to market towns and cities in the sixteenth century CE. However, at the same time wealthy city dwellers began to invest in agricultural land (Elvin 1977, 459–60).

14   See Cohen 1993 for a discussion of the politics of peasant categorization. However, Cohen (1993, 154) points out that the notion of countryside as a locus of feudalism and superstition was not shared by all. In particular, social anthropologists and sociologists with fieldwork experience in rural China did not subscribe to this reading of the countryside.

15   But Chan and Zhang (1999, 830) point out that long-term undocumented rural migrants, the so-called black households, did exist in cities prior to 1978.

16   For an excellent account of rural/urban inequality, see Whyte 2010.

17   See Malkki 1992; Feld and Basso 1996; Paasi 1996; Lovell 1998; and Navaro-Yashin 2012.

18   In China's multiethnic borderlands, the issue of who is "native" to an area (are Han settlers "native" to Yunnan, for instance?) is overtly political (Hansen 2005). On the role of "nativity" in ethnic tourism in China, see Swain 2001. Zhang (2001) explores the construction of migrant "strangeness" in Beijing. I discuss the question of belonging to a place and the making of Han places in Xinjiang in Joniak-Lüthi 2014.

19   Southern Jiangsu was referred to briefly as Jiangnan (Region South of the Yangzi River) and Sunan (Southern Jiangsu). Together with immigrants from Guangdong and Subei, Jiangnan natives have comprised some of the largest migrant communities in Shanghai from the mid-nineteenth century on. As Honig (1992b, 239) argues, "Which of these areas one hailed from was critical in shaping work opportunities, residential patterns, cultural activities, and social status. Hierarchy was structured largely according to local origins: the elite was composed primarily of people from Guangdong and Jiangnan, the unskilled service sector staffed mostly by migrants from Subei."

20   In contrast to this prevailing view, some interviewees from Subei argued that Subei People are "industrious," "nimble," "quick," "hardworking," "reliable," and "earnest." Further, they believed that they have "willpower" and "perseverance" and that they are "kind" and "good-hearted."

21   Ma (2002, 54–58) reports having seen notices posted in shops and restaurants warning, "Henanese are forbidden to enter" (Henanren bude ru nei) or "We do not employ Henan People" ("Bu zhao Henanren" or "Bu yao Henande").

22   Anhui People were also associated in Shanghai with the category of rural strangeness, but only by a couple of my informants. Additionally, the terms used to characterize Anhui People were much milder than those used for Subei People.

23   Other identifications, for instance with work unit, once of a critical importance, were not mentioned.

24   See Blake 1981; Choi 1995; Hayes 1995; Liu 1995; Ching 1996; Constable 1996; and Leong 1997.

5. FRAGMENTED IDENTITIES, THE HAN *MINZU*, AND ETHNICITY

1   I do not imply here that the *minzu* scale is located *above* the "regional differentiation" scale or that it encompasses it; on the contrary. Because most of my informants claimed that identification with home place is more central to them than identification with the Han *minzu*, one could argue that these scales are parallel or that the *minzu* scale is actually secondary, including historically so, to that based on the notion of home place.

2   Compare for instance this quote from Weng 2001 (3): "At the times of Xia, Shang, and Zhou [twenty-first century BCE–256 BCE], each *minzu* of our country [*woguo ge minzu*] and their mutual relations experienced great progress and development."

3   My thanks to Stevan Harrell for suggesting this parallel.

4   See Rowe 1984 (247); Moser 1985; Watson 1988 (133); and Cole 1996 (161).

5   The term *zu*, a component of *minzu*, connotes territorial lineage. This makes it related to *ren* or home-place identities. As a term that relates to kinship, it is also somewhat similar to *jia*. However, it is virtually never used as a suffix in contemporary Chinese in ways similar to *ren* and *jia*. For instance, while it would be possible to say *women Zhangjia* (lit., "we people of the Zhang family"), it is not possible to say *women Zhangzu*. This is because *zu* as a suffix was politicized as a corruption of *minzu*.

6   For a detailed analysis of this process, see Mullaney 2011.

7   Yet we should not forget that the label was arbitrarily imposed onto some local

groups and denied to others during the process of *minzu* classification. For examples, see Fei 1980.

8 I would like to thank Steve Harrell for his insightful comments on the spatiality of *ren*.

9 Before the Minzu Classification Project, some non-Han in the Southwest were also referred to in the Chinese language as *jia*, as in Minjia or Yijia.

10 On the Danmin, see Anderson 1972; on the Duomin, see Cole 1982. As "people," the term *min* is used, for instance, in combination with some *minzu* identifiers like Huimin (Hui People) and in designations like Nongmin (Peasants).

11 But see Carrico's (2012) study in Guangdong, where he found people calling for the independence of Guangdong from the North. Still, I understand this to be a call for the revision of power relationships with Northerners rather than for independence from Han-ness.

12 But compare Hansen (2005, 40), who reports on Han cadres in Sipsongpanna registering their children as "minorities." Also, children of mixed couples (Han and non-Han) have the right to choose between the *minzu* affiliations of their parents. Often, these youth decide to identify as a "minority," as this status has certain advantages (e.g., permission to legally have more children, priority access to positions in local government, and extra points on university entrance exams).

13 This may be different in other cases. For example, the Mosuoren of the Lugu Lake region were granted recognition as a distinct people (*ren*) within the Naxi *minzu* (in Yunnan) and Mongol *minzu* (in Sichuan) to which they were assigned during the Minzu Classification Project. This *ren* identity is likely less negotiable and individual-dependent than the *ren* identities of Han in eastern China.

14 But see Barabantseva 2012, which analyzes the discourse of overseas Chinese minorities and the ways in which the Chinese government reinvents the Chinese *minzu* categorizations in overseas Chinese communities.

15 A similar project of nesting *minzu* identities within the Chinese national identity has been less successful in relational terms. When the Chinese national identity is challenged, or when the scale of interaction becomes international, a similar "disappearance" of *minzu* identities in Chinese-ness does not occur, with the exception of Han-ness, which is Chinese-ness itself. The nesting efforts of the Chinese state have been the least effective with transnational *minzu* such as the Tibetans, Uyghur, or Dai. While Han-ness merges into Chinese-ness at the international scale of interaction, these *minzu* identities do not disappear in Chinese-ness but remain to a significant degree distinct. Hence, while most *ren*, *min*, and *jia* identities of the Hanzu have been successfully nested in the Han *minzu*, the parallel nesting of *minzu* identities in the Chinese identity has been much less effective and is still very much in progress.

16 The notion of nested identities (Brewer 1993, 1999; Calhoun 1994; Medrano and Gutiérrez 2001) is similar to how the functioning of multiple *minzu* and non-*minzu* identities is conceptualized in this book, namely as compatible because each fulfills a different function. However, I argue here that it is crucial to pay close attention to how identities become "nested." Further, my research data do not support discussing nested identities in terms of higher- and lower-order identities or higher- and lower-level identifications. Instead, identities appear more parallel. They may be verticalized and hierarchized for certain purposes and by specific actors, but not in analytical terms.

EPILOGUE

1   Barabantseva 2012 describes Chinese attempts to export these categorizations.
2   I am grateful to James Leibold for this metaphor.
3   This distinction was formulated by the late Karl Lo, University of Washington librarian (Stevan Harrell, personal communication, 2014).

GLOSSARY OF CHINESE CHARACTERS

aiguo 爱国

Ala 阿拉

baihua 白话

Bazuizi 巴嘴子

Beifang 北方

Beifangren 北方人

Beigu 北姑

Beijingren 北京人

Beiman 北蛮

Bendiren 本地人

Biaoshu 表叔

biaozhi 标志

Biesan 瘪三

bu weisheng 不卫生

bu wenming 不文明

canlan de Zhongyuan wenhua 灿烂的中
　原文化

Chuanqing 穿青

chuantong 传统

chusheng di 出生地

da de minzu 大的民族

Daluren 大陆人

Danmin 蛋民

danwei 单位

dao 道

Daomin 岛民

datong 大同

dezhi 德治

Di 狄

difang tedian 地方特点

difang wenhua 地方文化

diqu wenhua 地区文化

diyu wenhua 地域文化

Dongbei Dahan 东北大汉

Dongbeiren 东北人

duo yuan yi ti 多元一体

Duomin 墮民

fada 发达

Fan 番

Fanyi 番夷

fazhi 法治

fenbu guang 分布广

fengjian 封建

fengsu xiguan 风俗习惯

fensan guang 分散广

gaihu 丐户

Gangba 港巴

Gangpian 港片

Gansu Yangyudan 甘肃洋芋蛋

gongsuo 公所

guangfan de renwen lishi 广泛的人
文历史

Guanhua 官话

guannian 观念

Guazi 瓜子

gulao de chuantong wenhua he xisu
古老的传统文化和习俗

guo 国

guofu 国父

guojia 国家

guxiang 故乡

haipai wenhua 海派文化

Hakka 客家 (pronunciation in Hakka)

Han 汉

Hanfu yundong 汉服运动

hang 行

Hanguo 汉国

Hanhua 汉化

Hanren 汉人

Hanren shequ 汉人社区

Hanyu 汉语

Hanzi 汉字

Hanzu 汉族

Hanzu cisheng jituan 汉族次生集团

Hanzu yaqunti 汉族亚群体

Hanzuren 汉族人

henan 河南

Henan Bangzi 河南帮子

Henanren 河南人

Hokkien, Hoklo 福建 (pronunciation in
Minnan dialects)

Hua 华

Huaxia 华夏

Hubeilao 湖北佬

huiguan 会馆

Huimin 回民

hukou 户口

hukou zhidu 户口制度

hunxue 混血

Huo Lei Feng 活雷锋

hutong wenhua 胡同文化

jia 家

Jiangbei 江北

Jiangbei Zhuluo 江北猪猡

Jiangbeiren 江北人

jiangjiu Zhongyong zhi Dao 讲究中
庸之道

Jiangnan 江南

Jiangnan Pianzi 江南骗子

Jiangnanren 江南人

jianmin 贱民

jiashen 家神

jiaxiang 家乡

jiaxiang guannian 家乡观念

jiazhangzhi 家长制

jiazu guannian 家族观念

jiguan 籍贯

jimi zhengce 羁縻政策

Jing Youzi 京油子

Jiumaojiu 九毛九

Jiutouniao 九头鸟

Jiuzhou 九州

keji 客籍

Kejia 客家

Kejiaren 客家人

kemin 客民

kuai 鬼 (pronunciation in Cantonese)

Kuazi 侉子

laihua 来化

Lao Beijing 老北京

Lao Shanghai 老上海

laojia 老家

laoxiang 老乡

laoxiang guanxi 老乡关系

Laoxi'er 老西儿

lau 佬 (pronunciation in Cantonese)

li 礼

liangmin 良民

Long de Chuanren 龙的传人

luan 乱

Lunyu 论语

luohou 落后

Luren 鲁人

Man(zi) 蛮(子)

mangliu 盲流

mei sha tedian 没啥特点

meiyou wenhua 没有文化

meiyou zongjiao 没有宗教

min 民

minxi 民系

minzu 民族

Minzu Shibie 民族识别

mixin 迷信

Nan man bei kua 南蛮北侉

Nan Manzi 南蛮子

Nanfang 南方

Nanfang wenhua 南方文化

Nanren 南人

nei 内

Ncimengren 内蒙人

Nongmin 农民

nongmingong 农民工

pianpi 偏僻

Pingdiren 平地人

Punti 本地 (pronunciation in Cantonese)

Putonghua 普通话

qianwei 前卫

qunti 群体

quyu wenhua 区域文化

ren 人

ren duo di guang 人多地广

renke 认可

renqun 人群

renzhong 人种

Rong 戎

ronghe 融合

Rujia daode 儒家道德

sangzi 桑梓

Sannong Wenti 三农问题

Semuguan 色目官

Semuren 色目人

Shaanxi Lengwa 陕西楞娃

Shabi 傻逼

Shamao 傻冒

Shandiren 山地人

Shandong Dahan 山东大汉

Shandong'er 山东儿

Shanghai Bendiren 上海本地人

Shanghai Yazi 上海鸭子

shanyu jieshou xin de shiwu 善于接受新
的事物

shaoshu minzu 少数民族

sheng 生

shenghuo jiezou 生活节奏

shenghuo xiguan 生活习惯

shi 氏

Shiji 史记

shimin 市民

shu 熟

shuangyu jiaoyu 双语教育

siwei 思维

sixiang 思想

sixiang geng kaifang 思想更开放

Subei 苏北

Subeiren 苏北人

suzhi di 素质低

Taibazi 太巴子, 太佰子

tedian 特点

tianxia 天下

tongxiang guannian 同乡观念

tongxianghui 同乡会

tongyi 统一

tongyuan 同源

tongzhi 同质

Tufei 土匪

wai 外

waidi 外地

Waidiren 外地人

wei shibie de minzu 未识别的民族

wen 文

wenhua 文化

wenhua fenwei nong yidian 文化氛围
浓一点

wenhua shang de qiangda 文化上的强大

wenhua shuiping 文化水平

wenhua shuiping di 文化水平低

wenhua shuiping gao 文化水平高

wenhua suzhi 文化素质

Wenzhou Xiao Laoban 温州小老板

woguo ge minzu 我国个民族

Wu xiaojia 吴小家

Wuyu wenhua 吴语文化

Wuzu Gonghe 五族共和

Xia 夏

xiang 乡

Xiangbalao 乡巴佬

Xiangxiaren 乡下人

xianjin 先进

Xiao Shimin 小市民

Xiao Sichuan 小四川

Xiaobie 小瘪

Xiaochilao 小赤佬

xiaoshun fumu 孝顺父母

Xilairen 西来人

xing 姓

xingge 性格

xingshi 姓氏

Xueqiu: Hanzu de renleixue fenxi
雪球: 汉族的人类学分析

Xuzhou de 徐州的

yan 人 (pronunciation in Cantonese)

Yi 夷

yiban 一般

yong putong de fangfa lai zuoshi 用普通的方法来做事

yong Xia bian Yi 用夏变夷

you tese 有特色

you wenhua 有文化

yuanji 原籍

yudie 玉牒

Yueyu wenhua 粤语文化

Yunnan Daduxiao 云南大毒枭

yuyan wenhua 语言文化

zhangwo le xuduo xianjin jishu 掌握了许多先进技术

zhi 质

Zhi si Yi ru niu ma zhi shou jimi 制四夷如牛马之受羁縻

zhong 种

Zhongguo 中国

Zhongguo de Jipusairen 中国的吉普赛人

Zhongguoren 中国人

Zhonghua 中华

Zhonghua minzu 中华民族

Zhongwen 中文

Zhongyuan 中原

zhongzu 种族

zhuliu wenhua 主流文化

zouhun 走婚

zu 族

zui xiandai 最现代

zuji 祖籍

zunzhong quanwei 尊重权威

zuqun 族群

REFERENCES

Anagnost, Ann. 1997. *National Past-Times: Narrative, Representation, and Power in Modern China*. Durham, NC: Duke University Press.

Anderson, Benedict. 1983. *Imagined Communities: Reflections on the Origin and Spread of Nationalism*. London: Verso.

Anderson, Eugene N. 1972. *Essays on South China's Boat People*. Asian Folklore and Social Life Monographs 19. Taipei: The Orient Cultural Service.

Barabantseva, Elena. 2010. *Overseas Chinese, Ethnic Minorities, and Nationalism: De-Centering China*. London: Routledge.

———. 2012. "Who Are 'Overseas Chinese Ethnic Minorities'? China's Search for Transnational Ethnic Unity." *Modern China* 38 (1): 78–109.

Barth, Fredrik. 1994. "Enduring and Emerging Issues in the Analysis of Ethnicity." In *The Anthropology of Ethnicity: Beyond "Ethnic Groups and Boundaries,"* edited by Hans Vermeulen and Cora Govers, 11–32. Amsterdam: Het Spinhuis.

———. 1996 (1969). "Ethnic Groups and Boundaries." In *Theories of Ethnicity: A Classical Reader*, edited by Werner Sollors, 294–324. Houndmills, UK: Macmillan.

Bass, Catriona. 1998. *Education in Tibet: Policy and Practice since 1950*. London: Zed Books.

Bauer, Wolfgang, ed. 1980. *China und die Fremden*. Munich: C. H. Beck'sche Verlagsbuchhandlung.

Bentley, G. Carter. 1987. "Ethnicity and Practice." *Comparative Studies in Society and History* 29 (1): 24–55.

Bhabha, Homi K. 1990. "Introduction: Narrating the Nation." In *Nation and Narration*, edited by Homi K. Bhabha, 1–7. London: Routledge.

Bjorklund, E. M. 1986. "The Danwei: Socio-Spatial Characteristics of Work Units in China's Urban Society." *Economic Geography* 62 (1): 19–29.

Blake, C. Fred. 1981. *Ethnic Groups and Social Change in a Chinese Market Town*. Asian Studies at Hawaii 27. Honolulu: University Press of Hawaii.

Blum, Susan D. 2001. *Portraits of "Primitives": Ordering Human Kinds in the Chinese Nation.* Lanham, MD: Rowman and Littlefield.

Bourdieu, Pierre. 1991. *Language and Symbolic Power.* Cambridge, MA: Polity Press.

Bourdieu, Pierre, and Jean-Claude Passeron. 1977. *Reproduction in Education, Society and Culture.* London: Sage Publications.

Bray, David. 2005. *Social Space and Governance in Urban China: The Danwei System from Origins to Reform.* Stanford, CA: Stanford University Press.

Brewer, M. B. 1993. "Social Identity, Distinctiveness, and In-Group Homogeneity." *Social Cognition* 11 (1): 150–64.

———. 1999. "Multiple Identities and Identity Transition: Implications for Hong-Kong." *International Journal of Intercultural Relations* 23 (2): 187–97.

Brown, Melissa J. 1996. "On Becoming Chinese." In *Negotiating Ethnicities in China and Taiwan,* edited by Melissa J. Brown, 37–74. Berkeley: Institute of East Asian Studies, University of California.

———. 2004. *Is Taiwan Chinese? The Impact of Culture, Power, and Migration on Changing Identities.* Berkeley: University of California Press.

Brubaker, Rogers. 2004. *Ethnicity without Groups.* Cambridge, MA: Harvard University Press.

Calhoun, Craig. 1994. "Social Theory and the Politics of Identity." In *Social Theory and the Politics of Identity,* edited by Craig Calhoun, 9–36. Cambridge, MA: Blackwell.

Carrico, Kevin. 2012. "Recentering China: The Cantonese in and Beyond the Han." In *Critical Han Studies: The History, Representation, and Identity of China's Majority,* edited by Thomas S. Mullaney, James Leibold, Stéphane Gros, and Eric Vanden Bussche, 23–44. Berkeley: Global, Area, and International Archive / University of California Press.

Chan, Kam Wing, and Will Buckingham. 2008. "Is China Abolishing the *Hukou* System?" *China Quarterly* 196:582–606.

Chan, Kam Wing, and Li Zhang. 1999. "The Hukou System and Rural-Urban Migration in China: Processes and Changes." *China Quarterly* 160:818–55.

Chao, Wei Yang. 1986. "Evolutionary Theory and Cultural Diversity: A Study of the Ethnology of China's National Minorities." PhD diss., University of California.

Chen, Zhihong. 2012. "'Climate's Moral Economy': Geography, Race, and the Han in Early Republican China." In *Critical Han Studies: The History, Representation, and Identity of China's Majority,* edited by Thomas S. Mullaney, James Leibold, Stéphane Gros, and Eric Vanden Bussche, 73–91. Berkeley: Global, Area, and International Archive / University of California Press.

Chen Shisong. 1999. *Tianxia Sichuanren* (Sichuan People: Folk under heaven). Chengdu: Sichuan Renmin Chubanshe.

Cheng Yinghong. 2011. "Dangdai Zhongguo de zhongzuzhuyi yanshuo" (Racism in contemporary China). *Wenhua Zongheng* (Cultural cross-currents) 4. www.21bcr .com/a/shiye/guancha/2011/0420/2640.html.

———. 2012. "*Gangtai* Patriotic Songs and the Racialized Chinese Nationalism." Paper presented at the conference Construction of Race and Racism in East Asia, East-West Perspectives. University of Armed Forces, Munich, Germany, September 12–14.

Chin, Tamara T. 2012. "Antiquarian as Ethnographer: Han Ethnicity in Early China Studies." In *Critical Han Studies: The History, Representation, and Identity of China's Majority,* edited by Thomas S. Mullaney, James Leibold, Stéphane Gros, and Eric

Vanden Bussche, 128–46. Berkeley: Global, Area, and International Archive / University of California Press.

Ching, May-bo. 1996. "Literary, Ethnic or Territorial? Definition of Guangdong Culture in the Late Qing and the Early Republic." In *Unity and Diversity: Local Cultures and Identities in China*, edited by Tao Tao Liu and David Faure, 51–66. Hong Kong: Hong Kong University Press.

Chio, Jenny. 2014. *A Landscape of Travel: The Work of Tourism in Rural Ethnic Guizhou*. Seattle: University of Washington Press.

Choi, Chi-Cheung. 1995. "Reinforcing Ethnicity: The Jiao Festival in Cheung Chau." In *Down to Earth: The Territorial Bond in South China*, edited by David Faure and Helen F. Siu, 104–22. Stanford, CA: Stanford University Press.

Chow, Kai-wing. 1997. "Imagining Boundaries of Blood: Zhang Binglin and the Invention of the Han 'Race' in Modern China." In *The Construction of Racial Identities in China and Japan: Historical and Contemporary Perspectives*, edited by Frank Dikötter, 34–52. London: Hurst and Company.

———. 2001. "Narrating Nation, Race, and National Culture: Imagining the Hanzu Identity in Modern China." In *Constructing Nationhood in Modern East Asia*, edited by Kai-wing Chow, Kevin M. Doak, and Poshek Fu, 47–83. Ann Arbor: University of Michigan Press.

Chu, Yiting. n.d. "The Power of Knowledge: A Critical Analysis of the Depiction of Ethnic Minorities in China's Elementary Textbooks." Unpublished paper.

Clothey, Rebecca. 2005. "China's Policies for Minority Nationalities in Higher Education: Negotiating National Values and Ethnic Identities." *Comparative Education Review* 49 (3): 389–409.

Cohen, Abner. 1996. "Ethnicity and Politics." In *Ethnicity*, edited by John Hutchinson and Anthony D. Smith, 83–84. Oxford: Oxford University Press.

Cohen, Myron L. 1993. "Cultural and Political Inventions in Modern China: The Case of the Chinese 'Peasant.'" *Daedalus* 122 (2): 151–70.

———. 1994. "Being Chinese: The Peripheralization of Traditional Identity." In *The Living Tree: The Changing Meaning of Being Chinese Today*, edited by Tu Wei-ming, 88–108. Stanford, CA: Stanford University Press.

———. 1996 (1962). "The Hakka or 'Guest People': Dialect as a Sociocultural Variable in Southeast China." In *Guest People: Hakka Identity in China and Abroad*, edited by Nicole Constable, 36–79. Seattle: University of Washington Press.

Cole, James H. 1982. "Social Discrimination in Traditional China: The To-Min of Shaohsing." *Journal of the Economic and Social History of the Orient* 25 (1): 100–11.

———. 1996. "Competition and Cooperation in Late Imperial China as Reflected in Native Place and Ethnicity." In *Remapping China: Fissures in Historical Terrain*, edited by Gail Hershatter, Emily Honig, Jonathan N. Lipman, and Randall Stross, 156–63. Stanford, CA: Stanford University Press.

Cole, John W., and Eric R. Wolf. 1999 (1974). *The Hidden Frontier. Ecology and Ethnicity in an Alpine Valley*. Berkeley: University of California Press.

Constable, Nicole. 1996. "Introduction: What Does It Mean to Be Hakka?" In *Guest People: Hakka Identity in China and Abroad*, edited by Nicole Constable, 3–35. Seattle: University of Washington Press.

Crossley, Pamela Kyle. 1987. "Manzhou Yuanliu Kao and the Formalization of the Manchu Heritage." *Journal of Asian Studies* 46 (4): 761–90.

———. 1990a. *Orphan Warriors: Three Manchu Generations and the End of the Qing World*. Princeton, NJ: Princeton University Press.

———. 1990b. "Thinking about Ethnicity in Early Modern China." *Late Imperial China* 11 (1): 1–35.

———. 1997. *The Manchus*. Cambridge, MA: Blackwell.

———. 1999. *A Translucent Mirror: History and Identity in Qing Imperial Ideology*. Berkeley: University of California Press.

Dautcher, Jay. 2009. *Down a Narrow Road: Identity and Masculinity in a Uyghur Community in Xinjiang China*. Cambridge, MA: Harvard University Asia Center.

Davis, Sara. 2005. *Song and Silence: Ethnic Revival on China's Southwest Borders*. New York: Columbia University Press.

Day, Alexander F. 2008. "The End of the Peasant? New Rural Reconstruction in China." *boundary 2* 35 (2): 49–73.

———. 2013. *The Peasant in Postsocialist China: History, Politics, and Capitalism*. Cambridge: Cambridge University Press.

Deglopper, Donald R. 1977. "Social Structure in a Nineteenth-Century Taiwanese Port City." In *The City in Late Imperial China*, edited by G. William Skinner, 633–50. Stanford, CA: Stanford University Press.

Denby, David. 2005. "Herder: Culture, Anthropology and the Enlightenment." *History of the Human Sciences* 18 (1): 55–76.

Dikötter, Frank. 1992. *The Discourse of Race in Modern China*. London: Hurst and Company.

———. 1996 (1990). "The Idea of 'Race' in Modern China." In *Ethnicity*, edited by John Hutchinson and Anthony D. Smith, 245–54. Oxford: Oxford University Press.

———. 1997. "Racial Discourse in China: Continuities and Permutations." In *The Construction of Racial Identities in China and Japan: Historical and Contemporary Perspectives*, edited by Frank Dikötter, 12–33. London: Hurst and Company.

Ding Yifu. 2002. *Dongbeiren shi zayangde: Dui Heitudiren xingge de jiedu* (Who are the Northeasterners: An assessment of the Black Soil People). Beijing: Jincheng Chubanshe.

Documents of the 16th National Congress of the Communist Party of China. 2002. Beijing: Foreign Languages Press.

Duara, Prasenjit. 1993. "De-Constructing the Chinese Nation." *Australian Journal of Chinese Affairs* 30:1–26.

———. 1995. *Rescuing History from the Nation: Questioning Narratives of Modern China*. Chicago: University of Chicago Press.

Eberhard, Wolfram. 1942. *Kultur und Siedlung der Randvölker Chinas*. Leiden: E. J. Brill.

———. 1962. *Social Mobility in Traditional China*. Leiden: E. J. Brill.

Ebrey, Patricia. 1996. "Surnames and Han Chinese Identity." In *Negotiating Ethnicities in China and Taiwan*, edited by Melissa J. Brown, 19–36. Berkeley: Institute of East Asian Studies, University of California.

Elliott, Mark. 2012. "Hushuo: The Northern Other and the Naming of the Han Chinese." In *Critical Han Studies: The History, Representation, and Identity of China's Majority*, edited by Thomas S. Mullaney, James Leibold, Stéphane Gros, and Eric Vanden Bussche, 173–90. Berkeley: Global, Area, and International Archive / University of California Press.

Elvin, Mark. 1977. "Market Towns and Waterways: The County of Shang-hai from 1480 to 1910." In *The City in Late Imperial China*, edited by G. William Skinner, 441–73. Stanford, CA: Stanford University Press.

Eriksen, Thomas Hylland. 2002. *Ethnicity and Nationalism: Anthropological Perspectives*. London: Pluto Press.

Fairbank, John King. 1968. *The Chinese World Order*. Cambridge, MA: Harvard University Press.

Fan Chuo. 1961. *Manshu* (Book of the southern barbarians). Edited by Giok-Po Oey. Ithaca, NY: Cornell University Southeast Asia Program.

Faure, David, and Helen F. Siu, eds. 1995. *Down to Earth: The Territorial Bond in South China*. Stanford, CA: Stanford University Press.

Fei Xiaotong [Fei Hsiao-tung]. 1980. "Ethnic Classification in China." *Social Science in China* 1:94–107.

———. 1988. *Minzu yanjiu wenji* (Collection of essays on *minzu* studies). Beijing: Renmin Chubanshe.

———. 1989. *Zhonghua minzu duo yuan yi ti geju* (The pattern of plurality and unity in the Chinese nation). Beijing: Zhongyang Minzu Xueyuan Chubanshe.

———. 1992. *Hsiang T'u Chung-Kuo: From the Soil, the Foundations of Chinese Society*. Berkeley: University of California Press.

Feld, Steven, and Keith H. Basso, eds. 1996. *Senses of Place*. Santa Fe, NM: School of American Research Press.

Ferguson, James. 1994. *The Anti-Politics Machine: "Development," Depolitization, and Bureaucratic Power in Lesotho*. Minneapolis: University of Minnesota Press.

Finnane, Antonia. 2008. *Changing Clothes in China: Fashion, History, Nation*. New York: Columbia University Press.

Fitzgerald, John. 1995. "The Nationless State: The Search for a Nation in Modern Chinese Nationalism." *Australian Journal of Chinese Affairs* 33:75–104.

Flick, Uwe. 1998. *An Introduction to Qualitative Research*. London: Sage Publications.

Foucault, Michel. 1972. *The Archeology of Knowledge and the Discourse on Language*. New York: Pantheon.

———. 1990. *The History of Sexuality*. Vol. 1, *An Introduction*. New York: Vintage.

———. 1991. *Discipline and Punish: The Birth of the Prison*. London: Penguin.

Friedman, Edward. 1994. "Reconstructing China's National Identity: A Southern Alternative to Mao-Era Anti-Imperialist Nationalism." *Journal of Asian Studies* 53 (1): 67–91.

Gernet, Jacques. 1988 (1979). *Die Chinesische Welt*. Frankfurt am Main: Suhrkamp Taschenbuch Verlag.

Giersch, C. Patterson. 2012. "From Subjects to Han: The Rise of Han as Identity in Nineteenth-Century Southwest China." In *Critical Han Studies: The History, Representation, and Identity of China's Majority*, edited by Thomas S. Mullaney, James Leibold, Stéphane Gros, and Eric Vanden Bussche, 191–209. Berkeley: Global, Area, and International Archive / University of California Press.

Gladney, Dru C. 1991. *Muslim Chinese: Ethnic Nationalism in the People's Republic*. Cambridge, MA: Harvard University Press.

———. 1994. "Representing Nationality in China: Refiguring Majority/Minority Identities." *Journal of Asian Studies* 53 (1): 92–123.

———. 1995. "China's Ethnic Reawakening." *Asia Pacific: Analysis from the East-West Center* 18:1–8.

———. 1998. *Ethnic Identity in China: The Making of a Muslim Minority Nationality*. Case Studies in Cultural Anthropology, edited by. George Spindler and Louise Spindler. Fort Worth, TX: Harcourt Brace College Publishers.

———. 1999. "Making Muslims in China: Education, Islamicization, and Representation." In *China's National Minority Education: Culture, Schooling, and Development*, edited by Gerard A. Postiglione, 55–94. New York: Falmer Press.

Gong Yin. 1992. *Zhongguo tusi zhidu* (Tusi system in China). Kunming: Yunnan Minzu Chubanshe.

Goodman, Bryna. 1992. "New Culture, Old Habits. Native-Place Organization and the May Fourth Movement." In *Shanghai Sojourners*, edited by Frederic Wakeman Jr. and Wen-hsin Yeh, 76–107. Berkeley: Institute of East Asian Studies, University of California.

———. 1995. *Native Place, City and Nation: Regional Networks and Identities in Shanghai, 1853–1937*. Berkeley: University of California Press.

Gu Xiaoming. 2002. "'Shanghairen' de zulei neihan he 'Xin Shanghairen'" (Shanghainese: Connotations of the category and the phenomenon of "New Shanghainese"). In *Shanghairen* (Shanghainese), edited by Shanghai Zhengda Yanjiusuo, 173–79. Shanghai: Xuelin Chubanshe.

Guldin, Gregory Eliyu. 1996. "Desakotas and Beyond: Urbanization in Southern China." *Ethnology* 35 (4): 265–83.

Guojia Tongjiju Renkou he Shehui Keji Tongjisi (National Bureau of Statistics of China, Department of Population, Social, Science, and Technology Statistics), ed. 2002. *Zhongguo renkou tongji nianjian 2002 / China Population Statistics Yearbook*. Beijing: Zhongguo Tongji Chubanshe.

Gupta, Akhil, and James Ferguson. 1992. "Beyond 'Culture': Space, Identity, and the Politics of Difference." *Cultural Anthropology* 7 (1): 6–23.

Hansen, Mette Halskov. 1999. "Teaching Backwardness or Equality: Chinese State Education among the Tai in Sipsong Panna." In *China's National Minority Education: Culture, Schooling and Development*, edited by Gerard A. Postiglione, 243–80. New York: Falmer Press.

———. 2005. *Frontier People: Han Settlers in Minority Areas of China*. London: Hurst and Company.

Hanson, Marta. 1998. "Robust Northerners and Delicate Southerners: The Nineteenth-Century Invention of a Southern Medical Tradition." *positions* 6 (3): 515–50.

Harrell, Stevan. 1989. "Ethnicity and Kin Terms among Two Kinds of Yi." In *Ethnicity and Ethnic Groups in China*, New Asia Academic Bulletin 8, edited by Chien Chiao and Nicolas Tapp, 179–97. Hong Kong: New Asia College.

———. 1995. "Languages Defining Ethnicity in Southwest China." In *Ethnic Identity: Creation, Conflict, and Accommodation*, edited by Lola Romanucci-Ross and George De Vos, 97–114. London: Sage Publications.

———. 1996a. Introduction to *Negotiating Ethnicities in China and Taiwan*, edited by Melissa J. Brown, 1–17. Berkeley: Institute of East Asian Studies, University of California.

———. 1996b. "The Nationalities Question and the Prmi Prblem." In *Negotiating Ethnicities in China and Taiwan*, edited by Melissa J. Brown, 274–94. Berkeley: Institute of East Asian Studies, University of California.

———. 2001. *Ways of Being Ethnic in Southwest China*. Seattle: University of Washington Press.

Harrell, Stevan, and Ma Erzi (Mgebbu Lunze). 1999. "Folk Theories of Success: Where Han Aren't Always the Best." In *China's National Minority Education: Culture, Schooling and Development*, edited by Gerard A. Postiglione, 214–41. New York: Falmer Press.

Harrison, Henrietta. 2000. *The Making of the Republican Citizen: Political Ceremonies and Symbols in China, 1911–1929*. New York: Oxford University Press.

———. 2001. *China. Inventing the Nation*. London: Arnold; New York: Oxford University Press.

Hayes, James. 1995. "Notes and Impressions of the Cheung Chau Community." In *Down to Earth: The Territorial Bond in South China*, edited by David Faure and Helen F. Siu, 89–103. Stanford, CA: Stanford University Press.

Heberer, Thomas. 1984. *Nationalitätenpolitik und Entwicklungspolitik in den Gebieten nationaler Minderheiten in China*. Bremen, Germany: Uni Bremen.

———. 1989. *China and Its National Minorities: Autonomy or Assimilation?* Armonk, NY: M. E. Sharpe.

Hirsch, Francine. 2005. *Empire of Nations: Ethnographic Knowledge and the Making of the Soviet Union*. Ithaca, NY: Cornell University Press.

Ho Ping-ti. 1966. "The Geographic Distribution of Hui-Kuan (Landsmannschaften) in Central and Upper Yangtze Provinces." *Tsing Hua Journal of Chinese Studies* 5:120–52.

Hoffman, Curt, and Nancy Hurst. 1990. "Gender Stereotypes: Perception or Rationalization?" *Journal of Personality and Social Psychology* 58 (2): 197–208.

Honig, Emily. 1992a. *Creating Chinese Ethnicity: Subei People in Shanghai, 1850–1980*. New Haven, CT: Yale University Press.

———. 1992b. "Migrant Culture in Shanghai: In Search of a Subei Identity." In *Shanghai Sojourners*, edited by Frederic Wakeman Jr. and Wen-hsin Yeh, 239–65. Berkeley: Institute of East Asian Studies, University of California.

———. 1996. "Native Place and the Making of Chinese Ethnicity." In *Remapping China: Fissures in Historical Terrain*, edited by Gail Hershatter, Emily Honig, Jonathan N. Lipman, and Randall Stross, 143–55. Stanford, CA: Stanford University Press.

Horowitz, Donald. 1975. "Ethnic Identity." In *Ethnicity: Theory and Experience*, edited by Nathan Glazer and Daniel P. Moynihan, 111–40. Cambridge, MA: Harvard University Press.

———. 1985. *Ethnic Groups in Conflict*. Berkeley: University of California Press.

Huang Guangxue. 1995a. "Woguo de minzu shibie" (The project of *minzu* classification in our country). In *Zhongguo de minzu shibie* (*Minzu* classification in China), edited by Huang Guangxue, 360–68. Beijing: Minzu Chubanshe.

———, ed. 1995b. *Zhongguo de minzu shibie* (*Minzu* classification in China). Beijing: Minzu Chubanshe.

Huang Shuping. 1998. "Guangdong yu Xianggang de quyu wenhua yanjiu / A Study on Regional Cultures of Canton and Hong Kong." In *Renleixue yu xinan minzu / Anthropology and the Peoples of Southwest China*, edited by Wang Zhusheng, Lin Chaomin, and Yang Hui, 385–99. Kunming: Yunnan Daxue Chubanshe.

Jenkins, Richard. 1997. *Rethinking Ethnicity: Arguments and Explorations*. London: Sage Publications.

Johnson, Bonnie, and Nalini Chhetri. 2002. "Exclusionary Policies and Practices in Chinese Minority Education: The Case of Tibetan Education." *Current Issues in Comparative Education* 2 (2): 142–53.

Joniak, Agnieszka, and Peter Lüthi. 2001. "'Since they have never been to school, they do not know who they are': An Analysis of Ethnic Identity in Zuosuo (Southwest China)." MA thesis, University of Bern and Adam Mickiewicz University.

Joniak-Lüthi, Agnieszka. 2009. "The Han in the People's Republic of China: Discourse of Unity and *De Facto* Diversity." *Linguistic and Oriental Studies from Poznań* 9:149–66.

———. 2013. "The Han *Minzu*, Fragmented Identities, and Ethnicity." *Journal of Asian Studies* 72 (4): 849–71.

———. 2014. "Han Migration to Xinjiang Uyghur Autonomous Region: Between State Schemes and Migrants' Strategies." *Zeitschrift für Ethnologie* 138:155–74.

Jost, John T., and Mahzarin R. Banaji. 1994. "The Role of Stereotyping in System-Justification and the Production of False Consciousness." *British Journal of Social Psychology* 33:1–27.

Kaiser, Robert. 1997. "Nationalism and Identity." In *Geography and Transition in the Post-Soviet Republics*, edited by Michael J. Bradshaw, 11–30. Chichester, UK: John Wiley and Sons.

Keyes, Charles F. 1991. "The Proposed World of the School: Thai Villagers' Entry into a Bureaucratic State System." In *Reshaping Local Worlds: Formal Education and Cultural Change in Rural Southeast Asia*, edited by Charles F. Keyes, 89–130. New Haven, CT: Yale University Southeast Asia Studies.

Kymlicka, Will. 1995. Introduction to *The Rights of Minority Cultures*, edited by Will Kymlicka, 1–27. New York: Oxford University Press.

Leach, Edmund Ronald. 1970 (1954). *Political Systems of Highland Burma: A Study of Kachin Social Structure*. London School of Economics Monographs on Social Anthropology no. 44. London: Athlone Press.

Lei, Guang. 2003. "Rural Taste, Urban Fashions: The Cultural Politics of Rural/Urban Difference in Contemporary China." *positions* 11 (3): 613–46.

Leibold, James. 2006. "Competing Narratives of Racial Unity in Republican China: From Yellow Emperor to Peking Man." *Modern China* 32 (2): 181–220.

———. 2007. *Reconfiguring Chinese Nationalism: How the Qing Frontier and Its Indigenes Became Chinese*. New York: Palgrave Macmillan.

———. 2010. "More Than a Category: Han Supremacism on the Chinese Internet." *China Quarterly* 203:539–59.

———. 2012. "Searching for Han: Early Twentieth-Century Narratives of Chinese Origins and Development." In *Critical Han Studies: The History, Representation, and Identity of China's Majority*, edited by Thomas S. Mullaney, James Leibold, Stéphane Gros, and Eric Vanden Bussche, 210–33. Berkeley: Global, Area, and International Archive / University of California Press.

Leong, Sow-Theng. 1997. *Migration and Ethnicity in Chinese History: Hakkas, Pengmin, and Their Neighbors*. Stanford, CA: Stanford University Press.

Leyens, Jacques-Philippe, Vincent Yzerbyt, and Georges Schadron. 1994. *Stereotypes and Social Cognition*. London: Sage Publications.

Lin Wenxun. 2001. *Chengduren* (The People of Chengdu). Chengdu: Sichuan Wenyi Chubanshe.

Lin Yutang. 1998 (1935). *My Country and My People / Wuguo yu wumin*. Beijing: Foreign Language Teaching and Research Press.

Lipman, Jonathan N. 1996. "Hyphenated Chinese: Sino-Muslim Identity in Modern China." In *Remapping China: Fissures in Historical Terrain*, edited by Gail Hershatter, Emily Honig, Jonathan N. Lipman, and Randall Stross, 97–112. Stanford, CA: Stanford University Press.

———. 1997. *Familiar Strangers: A History of Muslims in Northwest China*. Seattle: University of Washington Press.

Liu, Zhiwei. 1995. "Lineage on the Sands: The Case of Shawan." In *Down to Earth: The Territorial Bond in South China*, edited by David Faure and Helen F. Siu, 21–43. Stanford, CA: Stanford University Press.

Liu Jianping. 2003. "Xin Shanghairen xingxiang yundong" (Shifts in the image of the New Shanghainese). *Nanfang zhoumo*, February 27.

Liu Xiaochun. 2003. *Beijingren shenmeyang?* (What are the Beijing People like?). Beijing: Xueyuan Chubanshe.

Liu Yexiong. 2002. *Ala Shanghairen* (We the People of Shanghai). Shanghai: Shanghai Renmin Chubanshe.

Lovell, Nadia. 1998. "Introduction: Belonging in Need of Emplacement?" In *Locality and Belonging*, edited by Nadia Lovell, 1–24. London: Routledge.

Lu, Hanchao. 2010. "Small-Town China: A Historical Perspective on Rural-Urban Relations." In *One Country, Two Societies: Rural-Urban Inequality in Contemporary China*, edited by Martin King Whyte, 29–54. Cambridge, MA: Harvard University Press.

Lü, Xiaobo, and Elisabeth J. Perry, eds. 1997. *Danwei: The Changing Chinese Workplace in Historical and Comparative Perspective*. New York: M. E. Sharpe.

Lu Yilong. 2008. "Does *Hukou* Still Matter? The Household Registration System and Its Impact on Social Stratification and Mobility in China." *Social Science in China* 29 (2): 56–75.

Lunyu / Analects of Confucius. 1994. Beijing: Huayu Jiaoxue Chubanshe / Sinolingua.

Ma, Rong. 1992. "The Development of Small Towns and Their Role in the Modernization of China." In *Urbanizing China*, edited by Gregory Eliyu Guldin, 119–54. New York: Greenwood Press.

———. 2014. "Reflections on the Debate on China's Ethnic Policy: My Reform Proposals and Their Critics." *Asian Ethnicity* 15 (2): 237–46.

Ma Shuo. 2002. *Henanren re shui le?* (Who did the Henan People offend?). Haikou: Hainan Chubanshe.

Malkki, Liisa. 1992. "National Geographic: The Rooting of Peoples and the Territorialization of National Identity among Scholars and Refugees." *Cultural Anthropology* 7 (1): 24–44.

Mao Tse-tung [Mao Zedong]. 1954. *Selected Works of Mao Tse-Tung*. Vols. 1–3. London: Lawrence and Wishart.

———. 1968–69. *Ausgewählte Werke (Band I–IV)*. Beijing: Verlag für Fremdsprachige Literatur.

Martiniello, Marco. 1995. *L'ethnicité dans les sciences sociales contemporaines*. Paris: Presses Universitaires de France.

Medrano, Juan Díez, and Paula Gutiérrez. 2001. "Nested Identities: National and European Identity in Spain." *Ethnic and Racial Studies* 24 (5): 753–78.

Morgan, Lewis H. 1976 (1877). "Ancient Society." In *Karl Marx: Die Ethnologischen Exzerpthefte*, edited by Lawrence Krader, 124–360. Frankfurt am Main: Suhrkamp Verlag.

Moser, Leo J. 1985. *The Chinese Mosaic: The People and Provinces of China*. Boulder, CO: Westview Press.

Mullaney, Thomas S. 2011. *Coming to Terms with the Nation: Ethnic Classification in Modern China*. Berkeley: University of California Press.

Mullaney, Thomas S., James Leibold, Stéphane Gros, and Eric Vanden Bussche, eds. 2012. *Critical Han Studies: The History, Representation, and Identity of China's*

Majority. Berkeley: Global, Area, and International Archive / University of California Press.

Müller, Claudius C. 1980. "Die Herausbildung der Gegensätze: Chinesen und Barbaren in der frühen Zeit (I. Jahrtausend v. Chr. bis 220 n.Chr.)." In *China und die Fremden,* edited by Wolfgang Bauer, 43–76. Munich: C. H. Beck'sche Verlagsbuchhandlung.

Naquin, Susan, and Evelyn S. Rawski. 1987. *Chinese Society in the Eighteenth Century.* New Haven, CT: Yale University Press.

Navaro-Yashin, Yael. 2012. *The Make-Believe Space: Affective Geography in a Postwar Polity.* Durham, NC: Duke University Press.

Nima, Badeng. 2008. "The Choice of Languages in Tibetan School Education Revisited." *Chinese Education and Society* 41 (6): 50–60.

Nimni, Ephraim. 1995. "Marx, Engels, and the National Question." In *The Rights of Minority Cultures,* edited by Will Kymlicka, 57–75. New York: Oxford University Press.

Oakes, Penelope J., S. Alexander Haslam, and John C. Turner. 1994. *Stereotyping and Social Reality.* Oxford: Blackwell.

Oakes, Penelope J., and Katherine J. Reynolds. 1997. "Asking the Accuracy Question: Is Measurement the Answer?" In *The Social Psychology of Stereotyping and Group Life,* edited by Russell Spears, Penelope J. Oakes, Naomi Ellemers, and S. Alexander Haslam, 51–71. Oxford: Blackwell.

Paasi, Anssi. 1996. *Territories, Boundaries and Consciousness: The Changing Geographies of the Finnish-Russian Border.* Chichester, UK: John Wiley.

Perry, Elisabeth J. 1995. "Labor's Battle for Political Space: The Role of Worker Associations in Contemporary China." In *Urban Spaces in Contemporary China: The Potential for Autonomy and Community in Post-Mao China,* edited by Deborah S. Davis, Richard Kraus, Barry Naughton, and Elizabeth J. Perry, 302–25. Washington, DC: Woodrow Wilson Center Press.

Pieke, Frank N. 2003. "The Genealogical Mentality in Modern China." *Journal of Asian Studies* 62 (1): 101–28.

Ramsey, S. Robert. 1987. *The Languages of China.* Princeton, NJ: Princeton University Press.

Rawski, Evelyn S. 1988. "A Historian's Approach to Chinese Death Ritual." In *Death Ritual in Late Imperial and Modern China,* edited by James L. Watson and Evelyn S. Rawski, 20–34. Berkeley: University of California Press.

Rhoads, Edward J. M. 1974. "Merchant Associations in Canton, 1895–1911." In *The Chinese City between Two Worlds,* edited by Mark Elvin and G. William Skinner, 97–117. Stanford, CA: Stanford University Press.

———. 2000. *Manchus and Han: Ethnic Relations and Political Power in Late Qing and Early Republican China, 1861–1928.* Seattle: University of Washington Press.

Roosens, Eugeen E. 1989. *Creating Ethnicity. The Process of Ethnogenesis.* Frontiers of Anthropology 5. Newbury Park, CA: Sage Publications.

Rowe, William T. 1984. *Hankow: Commerce and Society in a Chinese City, 1796–1889.* Stanford, CA: Stanford University Press.

Rudelson, Justin. 1997. *Oasis Identities: Uyghur Nationalism along China's Silk Road.* New York: Columbia University Press.

Sautman, Barry. 1997. "Myths of Descent, Racial Nationalism and Ethnic Minorities in the People's Republic of China." In *The Construction of Racial Identities in China and Japan: Historical and Contemporary Perspectives,* edited by Frank Dikötter, 75–95. London: Hurst and Company.

———. 2001. "Peking Man and the Politics of Paleoanthropological Nationalism in China." *Journal of Asian Studies* 60 (1): 95–124.

Schein, Louisa. 2000. *Minority Rules: The Miao and the Feminine in China's Cultural Politics.* Durham, NC: Duke University Press.

Scott, James C. 1998. *Seeing Like a State: How Certain Schemes to Improve the Human Condition Have Failed.* New Haven, CT: Yale University Press.

Segawa, M. 1996. *Zupu: Huanan Hanzu de zongzu, fengshui, yiju* (Ancestral records: Patrilineal clans, fengshui and migration of the southern Han). Translated by Qian Hang. Shanghai: Shanghai Shudian Chubanshe.

Sherif, Muzafer. 1967. *Group Conflict and Co-Operation: Their Social Psychology.* London: Routledge and Kegan Paul.

Siegel, Brian. 1989. "The 'Wild' and 'Lazy' Lamba: Ethnic Stereotypes on the Central African Copperbelt." In *The Creation of Tribalism in Southern Africa*, edited by Leroy Vail, 350–71. London: James Currey; Berkeley: University of California Press.

Siu, Helen F. 2007. "Grounding Displacement: Uncivil Urban Spaces in Postreform South China." *American Ethnologist* 34 (2): 329–50.

Skinner, G. William. 1977. "Introduction: Urban and Rural in Chinese Society." In *The City in Late Imperial China*, edited by G. William Skinner, 253–73. Stanford, CA: Stanford University Press.

———. 2001. *Marketing and Social Structure in Rural China.* Ann Arbor, MI: Association for Asian Studies.

Spears, Russell, Penelope J. Oakes, Naomi Ellemers, and S. Alexander Haslam. 1997. Introduction to *The Social Psychology of Stereotyping and Group Life*, edited by Russell Spears, Penelope J. Oakes, Naomi Ellemers, and S. Alexander Haslam, 1–19. Oxford: Blackwell.

Stalin, J[osef]. 1948 (1913). *Marksizm i natsional'nyĭ vopros* (Marxism and the national question). Leningrad: Gosudarstviennoje Izdatel'stwo Politicheskoĭ Literatury.

———. 1950. *Werke.* Band 2, *1907–1913*. Berlin: Dietz Verlag Berlin.

Sun Yat-sen. n.d. *San Min Chu I: The Three Principles of the People, with Two Supplementary Chapters by Chiang Kai-Shek.* Taipei: China Publishing Co.

Swain, Margaret Byrne. 2001. "Native Place and Ethnic Relations in Lunan Yi Autonomous County, Yunnan." In *Perspectives on the Yi of Southwest China*, edited by Stevan Harrell, 170–91. Berkeley: University of California Press.

Tajfel, Henri. 1969. "Cognitive Aspects of Prejudice." *Journal of Social Issues* 25:79–97.

———. 1981. *Human Groups and Social Categories.* Cambridge: Cambridge University Press.

Tajfel, Henri, M. G. Billig, R. P. Bundy, and Claude Flament. 1971. "Social Categorization and Intergroup Behaviour." *European Journal of Social Psychology* 1(2):149–78.

Tang, Wenfang, and Gaochao He. 2010. *Separate but Loyal: Ethnicity and Nationalism in China.* Honolulu: East-West Center.

Tapp, Nicholas. 1995. "Minority Nationality in China: Policy and Practice." In *Indigenous Peoples of Asia*, edited by Robert H. Barnes, Andrew Gray, and Benedict Kingsbury, 195–220. Ann Arbor, MI: Association for Asian Studies.

———. 2002. "Cultural Accommodations in Southwest China: The "Han Miao" and Problems in the Ethnography of the Hmong." *Asian Folklore Studies* 61:77–104.

Tapper, Richard L. 1988. "Ethnicity, Order and Meaning in the Anthropology of Iran and Afghanistan." In *Le fait ethnique en Iran et en Afghanistan*, edited by Jean-Pierre Digard, 21–34. Paris: Editions du CNRS (Colloques Internationaux).

Thierry, François. 1989. "Empire and Minority in China." In *Minority Peoples in the Age of Nation-States*, edited by Gérard Chaliand, 76–99. London: Pluto Press.

Tong Enzheng. 1989. "Morgan's Model and the Study of Ancient Chinese Society." *Social Sciences in China* 10:182–205.

Vasantkumar, Chris. 2012. "Han at *Minzu*'s Edges: What Critical Han Studies Can Learn from China's 'Little Tibet.'" In *Critical Han Studies: The History, Representation, and Identity of China's Majority*, edited by Thomas S. Mullaney, James Leibold, Stéphane Gros, and Eric Vanden Bussche, 234–55. Berkeley: Global, Area, and International Archive / University of California Press.

Wallman, Sandra, ed. 1979. *Ethnicity at Work*. London: Macmillan.

———. 1983. "Identity Options." In *Minorities: Community and Identity*, edited by Charles Fried, 69–78. Berlin: Springer-Verlag.

Wan Zengwei. 2002. "'Xin Shanghairen' yu 'Lao Shanghairen'" ("New" and "old" Shanghainese). In *Shanghairen* (The People of Shanghai), edited by Shanghai Zhengda Yanjiusuo, 96–99. Shanghai: Xuelin Chubanshe.

Wang Feng. 2010. "Boundaries of Inequality: Perceptions of Distributive Justice among Urbanites, Migrants, and Peasants." In *One Country, Two Societies: Rural-Urban Inequality in Contemporary China*, edited by Martin King Whyte, 219–40. Cambridge, MA: Harvard University Press.

Wang Jianmin, Zhang Haiyang, and Hu Hongbao. 1998. *Zhongguo minzuxue shi, 1950–1997, Xia Juan / The History of Ethnology in China, 1950–1997, Part 2*. Kunming: Yunnan Jiaoyu Chubanshe.

Watson, James L. 1988. "Funeral Specialists in Cantonese Society: Pollution, Performance, and Social Hierarchy." In *Death Ritual in Late Imperial and Modern China*, edited by James L. Watson and Evelyn S. Rawski, 109–34. Berkeley: University of California Press.

———. 1993. "Rites or Beliefs? The Construction of a Unified Culture in Late Imperial China." In *China's Quest for National Identity*, edited by Lowell Dittmer and Samuel S. Kim, 80–103. Ithaca, NY: Cornell University Press.

Watson, James L., and Evelyn S. Rawski, eds. 1988. *Death Ritual in Late Imperial and Modern China*. Berkeley: University of California Press.

Watson, Rubie S. 1988. "Remembering the Dead: Graves and Politics in Southeastern China." In *Death Ritual in Late Imperial and Modern China*, edited by James L. Watson and Evelyn S. Rawski, 203–27. Berkeley: University of California Press.

Weng Dujian. 2001. *Zhongguo minzu guanxi shi gangyao* (Outline of the history of relations between the Chinese *minzu*). Beijing: Zhongguo Shehui Kexue Chubanshe.

Whyte, Martin King, ed. 2010. *One Country, Two Societies: Rural-Urban Inequality in Contemporary China*. Cambridge and London: Harvard University Press.

Wicker, Hans-Rudolf. 1974. *Zur Frage der asiatischen Produktionsweise im alten China: Ein Beitrag zur Marxistischen Formationenlehre; Veröffentlichungen des Seminars für Ethnologie der Universität Bern, Nr. 4*. Bern: Universität Bern, Seminar für Ethnologie.

———. 1997. "Introduction: Theorizing Ethnicity and Nationalism." In *Rethinking Nationalism and Ethnicity: The Struggle for Meaning and Order in Europe*, edited by Hans-Rudolf Wicker, 1–42. Oxford: Berg.

Wong, Siu-lun. 1979. *Sociology and Socialism in Contemporary China*. London: Routledge and Kegan Paul.

Xiang, Biao. 2005. *Transcending Boundaries. Zhejiangcun: The Story of a Migrant Village in Beijing*. Translated by Jim Weldon. Leiden: Brill.

Xiong, Yuezhi. 1996. "The Image and Identity of the Shanghainese." In *Unity and Diversity: Local Cultures and Identities in China*, edited by Tao Tao Liu and David Faure, 99–106. Hong Kong: Hong Kong University Press.

Xu Jieshun. 1999. *Xueqiu: Hanzu de renleixue fenxi / [Snowball:] An Anthropological Analysis of Han Nationality*. Shanghai: Shanghai Renmin Chubanshe.

——. 2012. "Understanding the Snowball Theory of the Han Nationality." In *Critical Han Studies: The History, Representation, and Identity of China's Majority*, edited by Thomas S. Mullaney, James Leibold, Stéphane Gros, and Eric Vanden Bussche, 113–27. Berkeley: Global, Area, and International Archive / University of California Press.

Yan Ruxian. 1982. "A Living Fossil of the Family: A Study of the Family Structure of the Naxi Nationality in the Lugu Lake Region." *Social Sciences in China* 3 (4): 60–83.

——. 1989. "Marriage, Family and Social Progress of China's Minority Nationalities." In *Ethnicity and Ethnic Groups in China*, New Asia Academic Bulletin 8, edited by Chien Chiao and Nicholas Tapp, 79–87. Hong Kong: New Asia College.

Yang Dongping. 1994. *Chengshi jifeng* (City monsoon). Beijing: Dongfang Chubanshe.

Yang Guorong. 2002. "Shanghairen: Lishi yu xiandai" (The Shanghainese: Past and present). In *Shanghairen* (The People of Shanghai), edited by Shanghai Zhengda Yanjiusuo, 73–80. Shanghai: Xuelin Chubanshe.

Ye, Xian'en. 1995. "Notes on the Territorial Connections of the Dan." In *Down to Earth: The Territorial Bond in South China*, edited by David Faure and Helen F. Siu, 83–88. Stanford, CA: Stanford University Press.

Yi Zhongtian. 2002. *Xibei feng dongnan yu* (In the northeast it winds, in the southeast it rains). Shanghai: Shanghai Wenhua Chubanshe.

Yuan Jiahua. 1983 (1960). *Hanyu fangyan gaiyao* (Outline of Han language dialects). Beijing: Wenzi Gaige Chubanshe.

Yuan Yida and Zhang Cheng. 2002. *Zhongguo xingshi: Qunti yichuan he renkou fenbu* (Chinese family names: Inheritance and distribution). Shanghai: Huadong Shifan Daxue Chubanshe.

Zhang, Li. 2001. *Strangers in the City: Reconfigurations of Space, Power, and Social Networks within China's Floating Population*. Stanford, CA: Stanford University Press.

Zhang Qi. 2000. *Beijingren he Shanghairen qutan: Zhongguo shuangcheng ji* (Beijing People and Shanghai People talk: Notes from the twin cities). Beijing: Jincheng Chubanshe.

Zhao, Gang. 2006. "Reinventing China: Imperial Qing Ideology and the Rise of Modern Chinese National Identity in the Early Twentieth Century." *Modern China* 32 (1): 3–30.

Zheng Zhenman. 2001. *Family Lineage Organization and Social Change in Ming and Qing Fujian*. Honolulu: University of Hawai'i Press.

Zhonggong Zhongyang Wenxian Yanjiushi and Zhonggong Xinjiang Weiwu'er Zizhiqu Weiyuanhui (Chinese Communist Party Central Committee's Document Research Office and the Chinese Communist Party Committee of Xinjiang Uyghur Autonomous Region), ed. 2010. *Xinjiang gongzuo wenxian xuanbian, 1949–2010* (Selection of working papers on Xinjiang, 1949–2010). Beijing: Zhongyang Wenxian Chubanshe.

INDEX

Anagnost, Ann, 6, 43, 87, 106, 151
Anderson, Benedict, 6, 43, 131
Aqsu, 17, 61
"Asiatic mode of production,"
    150–51n46
associations of fellow locals (*tongxiang-hui*), 68–69
asymmetric power relations, 47, 62, 107

"barbarians" (also "barbarian other"),
    26–27, 30–32, 105, 145n6, 148n20. *See also* "savages"
Barth, Fredrik, 92, 131–32
Beifang. *See* North
Beijing, 12, 68, 70, 73, 75, 93, 101, 110–11,
    117; as a fieldwork location, 9, 15–18,
    45, 56–58, 62, 110, 134
Beijing Person/People (Beijingren),
    4, 10, 14, 71–74, 77, 80–81, 83, 92,
    96–98*table*, 98, 99*table*, 100–102, 114,
    129, 135
Bendiren, 77, 94, 96*table*, 109. *See also*
    Local; Native
biaozhi (symbols), 45. *See also* markers of
    Han-ness
"bilingual education" (*shuangyu jiaoyu*),
    153–4n20

biopolitics, 6, 8, 90, 138, 146n7
Boat People (Danmin), 30, 32, 113, 127,
    130, 149n30, 32
boundaries (also boundary-making),
    37, 92, 94; ethnic, 131–32, 149n34; of
    ethnicity, 14, 132; *minzu*, 4–5, 7, 24,
    42, 55, 65, 81, 133–37; intra-Han, 5, 9,
    14, 16, 25, 42, 64–65, 71, 81, 89, 91, 101,
    105, 109–11, 113, 115, 120–23, 131, 135–
    36, 142; of contemporary Han-ness,
    4, 5, 20, 22–23, 32, 45–47, 55, 63, 87, 131;
    of premodern Han-ness, 6, 20, 22–23,
    25–29, 32–33, 128
Bourdieu, Pierre, 53, 58, 62, 92

Cantonese (Guangdongren), 14, 30,
    98–100, 102, 124–25, 127, 130, 135,
    154n8, 155n17
Chinese language/script (Zhongwen),
    31, 53, 152n8. *See also* Han language;
    Putonghua
Chinese national identity, 9, 22, 35,
    65, 81–82, 87, 158n15. *See also*
    Chinese-ness
Chinese-ness: as a national identity, 9,
    65, 80–83, 86, 137, 158n15; in overseas
    communities, 146n14. *See also*

Chinese-ness *(continued)*
  Han-ness/Chinese-ness intertwine-
    ment; Han-ness/Chinese-ness in
    premodern China
coerciveness of identities, 11, 83–84,
  87–88
collective identity label (also identifier),
  24, 26–27, 33, 55–56, 76, 90–91, 94, 98,
  101, 105, 109, 127, 130, 145n4, 155n15.
  See also Han identifier; socionym
common/collective place *(gongsuo)*, 68
critical Han studies, 18, 140
culture. *See wenhua*
culture-wildness/barbarism paradigm, 7,
  25–29, 31, 37, 40, 51, 128, 145n6

Danmin. *See* Boat People
danwei (working unit), 107
decent people. *See liangmin*
degree of ethnicity, 13, 14, 133, 137–39
demeaned people. *See jianmin*
"density" (of identities), 14, 20, 24, 116,
  136–37
difang tedian (local characteristics), 125
diqu wenhua. See regional cultures
discrimination: intra-Han, 11–12, 32,
  73–74, 76, 80, 86, 112, 114–16, 126,
  149n32
diyu wenhua. See regional cultures
duo yuan yi ti ("plurality in unity"), 140
Duomin. *See* Fallen People

education (as transmitter of Han-ness
  and Chinese-ness), 56–61, 64–65, 72,
  87, 90, 120, 153n20, 155n12
"essence" *(zhi)*: construction of, 121–6;
  Han, 79, 86, 115, 118, 121–23, 126; and
  "regional cultures," 124
ethnic group, 43, 127–28
ethnicity, 13–14, 26, 55, 69, 92, 112, 116,
  127–28, 131–33, 137–39; and Han
  minzu, 55, 137–39
evolutionary model of social
  development: Morgan's, 39–40, 58,
  151nn47,48; Stalin's, 39–40, 58
exclusivity/nonexclusivity (of identities),
  130–34, 136, 138

Fallen People (Duomin), 130, 149n32
Fan, 27
Fanyi, 27
Fei Xiaotong, 20, 29, 33, 58, 67, 123, 125,
  140, 147n17, 154n6
fellow locals. *See laoxiang*
flexibility (of identities), 55, 134–35, 138
Foucault, Michel, 57, 60, 64
fragmentation (of "the Han"), 4, 12, 19,
  44, 89, 113, 115, 118, 121–22, 125–27, 131,
  135, 140–41
Fujian (province), 32, 99, 101–3, 149n31

Gladney, Dru C., 12, 20, 21, 42, 55, 72, 124,
  127, 131
gongsuo. See common/collective place
Guangdong (province), 16, 30, 32, 77, 101,
  103, 117, 125, 130, 145n6, 149n31, 158n11
Guangdongren. *See* Cantonese
Guanhua. *See* Officials' Speech
guild/guild hall *(huiguan)*, 68–69
guxiang (home place), 10–12, 66–67, 69–71,
  77, 79. *See also* home place; *jiaxiang*

Hakka (Kejia), 13, 32, 75–76, 91, 98*table*,
  99, 113, 124–5, 127, 130, 149n31,
  155nn17,18
Han (ethno)nationalism, 34–36, 52, 54,
  144
"Han, the": as a *minzu*, 119–21, 128; as a
  narration, 5–8, 20, 43, 45, 54, 64–65;
  as a nation, 7, 14, 22, 34–36, 38, 41, 49;
  as the "core" of the nation, 3, 7, 36–38,
  119–20, 122, 129–30, 150n44; as the
  "unifier of nationalities," 8, 39, 79,
  129; as an "invented tradition," 8, 20;
  teleological/organic representations
  of, 7, 19, 37, 43, 101, 123–26, 140; as a
  racial community, 22, 33–37, 53–54,
  101, 128, 152–3n12; Communist-era
  narration of, 38–42; Republican-era
  narration of, 34–8; as an unmarked
  category, 50, 63. *See also* Han-ness;
  "snowball"; "unifier of nationalities"
Han becoming "minorities," 25, 56,
  147n17, 158n12
Han identifier, 21, 23–24, 112

Han in ethnic minority areas, 56–59, 143

Han language (Hanyu), 49, 53–54, 59, 61–65, 146n15, 152n8,10; as a language of instruction in ethnic minority areas, 59, 62, 65, 153n20. *See also* Chinese language; Putonghua

Han/Chinese culturalism, 22, 35, 54

Hanguo ("country of the Han"), 9

Hanhua (Hanification), 27

Han-ness/Chinese-ness intertwinement, 8–9, 14, 24–25, 33–38, 41–42, 145n6, 152n8, 158n15

Han-ness/Han identity: and ethnicity, 13–15, 26, 43, 51, 55, 127–29, 131–39; and whiteness, 50–51, 152n4; and Confucianism, 26, 30, 49, 51–52, 118; contemporary, 45–55, 78–80, 119–22; distribution of, 56–65; historical contingency of, 6, 19–24, 113, 140–41; in the Republican period, 34–37; invisibility of, 47, 48*table*, 50, 63–64, 115–16; limits of Han-ness, 141–43; premodern/imperial, 6, 24–33, 145n6; state interventions in, 55, 119–22, 126, 133–38; under the Communists, 39–42, 54–55, 128; vis-à-vis other collective identities, 9, 63–65, 71–72, 78–81, 84–89, 115–18, 121–23, 133–39, 141–43

Hanren shequ ("communities of Han People"), 127

Hansen, Mette Halskov, 55, 58, 60, 147n17, 152n9, 156n18, 158n12

Harrell, Stevan, 8, 19, 24, 30, 50, 56, 58, 120, 128, 131–32, 151nn54,57, 152n7, 155n17

Henan (province), 12, 73–75, 92, 97*table*, 103, 107, 111, 155n14

Henan Person/People. *See* Henanese

Henanese (Henanren), 74, 81, 93, 98–100, 103, 110–12, 155n15, 157n211; stigmatization of, 111

hierarchization/verticalization of identities, 12, 15, 21, 53, 79, 86, 111, 142, 158n16. *See also* intra-Han hierarchies of power; social positioning strategies

Hokkien, 32, 113, 127, 149n31

home place, 10–12; definitions of, 67–71, 76–78, 84–86; and discrimination, 12, 73–75, 110–12; flexibility of, 11, 70, 74, 76–78, 85–86; hierarchies of, 12, 157n19; identity, 10–12, 22, 71–76, 79, 84–88; multiple, 11–12, 76–78, 85–86, 98; politics of, 11, 28, 73–74, 78, 86; and social organization, 33, 67–69, 88, 112, 154n8, 157n19. *See also* associations of fellow locals; guild; *guxiang*; *jiaxiang*; *laoxiang*; *laoxiang guanxi*

"home-place-determined mind-set" (*jiaxiang guannian*), 91, 94, 141

Hongkongese (Xianggangren), 91, 97*table*, 98–101, 103

household registration (*hukou*), 12, 69, 78, 107–8, 113, 141, 154n10; as an identity, 11, 78, 83–84, 87

Hua, 6, 19, 21, 24, 26–27, 37

Huaxia, 6, 19, 24, 26–27

huiguan. *See* guild

hukou. *See* household registration

identifier. *See* collective identity label; socionym

identity networks, 10, 90, 116, 138

"imagined community," 6–7, 131–32; Han as a, 14, 22–23, 26, 43, 115, 118, 129, 133, 135, 140

imperial examinations, 31–32, 51, 107, 147n15

"inappropriate other," 106–7. *See also* Rural Han; rural strangeness

Inner Mongolia, 4, 12

Inner Mongolian/Mongol (identity label, *minzu*), 53, 56, 73–75, 86, 93, 134, 152n3

intra-Han hierarchies of power, 12, 90–92, 101–2, 109, 112, 114. *See also* hierarchization/verticalization of identities; social positioning

jia (identity), 13, 15, 128–30, 133–39, 144, 154n3, 157n5, 158n9,15

Jiangbei (North of the River), 75, 111

Jiangnan (South of the River), 75, 111, 155n14, 157n19
Jiangsu (province), 75, 110, 117, 157n19
jianmin (demeaned people), 32, 130
jiaxiang (home-place), 10–12, 67–71. See also guxiang; home place
jiaxiang guannian. See "home-place-determined mind-set"
jiguan (ancestral home-place), 67, 78, 148n24
Jiuzhou, 26–27

keji (registered as guests), 76
Kejia. See Hakka
kemin (migrating farmers), 68

labeling, 91–94, 101, 109–10. See also naming
laihua (transformation by proximity), 27
laojia (old home), 154n3
laoxiang (fellow locals), 68–69, 85, 142
laoxiang guanxi (networks of fellow locals, home-place networks), 68–69, 112, 142
Leach, Edmund, 122
liangmin (decent people), 32
Lin Yutang, 67, 152–3n12
"living fossil," 40, 151n49
Local (identity label), 4, 10, 14, 91, 96–97table, 100–1, 109–13, 138, 142. See also Bendiren; Native
locality: social construction of, 70, 75–6, 94, 101, 109–14; –outside-ness differentiation, 91, 104, 109–14, 133, 141. See also Local; Native; nativity
Lower Yangzi basin, 68
Lugu Lake (region), 40, 158n13

Mainlanders-Taiwanese/Hongkongese differentiation, 91, 97table, 100–101, 136
majority-minority differentiation, 20, 42, 45, 47, 48table, 59, 61, 63–64, 141, 143
Manchu: as "the other" of the Han, 7, 22, 34–36, 105, 149n34
markers of Han-ness, 6, 19, 45–46; popular, 48–54; in premodern period, 25–33; in Republican period,

39–42; since the 1950s, 39–42; channels of transmission of, 57–62; in Zuosuo, 56–57. See also biaozhi; Han-ness; tedian
Migrant (identity label), 14, 109–10. See also Outsider; Stranger, Waidiren
migrant ruralness/strangeness, 110, 112
migrant workers, 69, 86, 100, 105, 111, 154n10
min (identity), 13, 15, 128–31, 133–36, 138, 144, 158n15
"minor minzu." See "minorities"
"minorities": as the "other" of the Han, 47, 52, 58–63, 141, 143, 152n3
"minority cultures," 61, 126
minxi (branches; "branches within the minzu"), 125, 127
Minzu Classification Project (Minzu Shibie), 5, 8, 15, 23, 38, 40, 42, 55, 90, 105, 114, 120, 128, 158n13
Minzu Shibie. See Minzu Classification Project
minzu switches, 55, 134, 138, 147n17
"mixed blood" (hunxue), 151n54
Morgan, Lewis Henry, 39–40, 58, 151n47
Mosuo. See Na

Na (Mosuo, Mosuoren), 40, 56–57, 59, 62, 134, 158n12
naming, 90–92, 94, 112; politics of, 101. See also labeling
Nanfang. See South
nation: Stalin on, 39; Marx and Engels on, 150n44
"national unifier." See "unifier of nationalities"
nationality: Stalin on, 39, 150n45; Marx and Engels on, 150n44
Native (identity label), 9, 91, 96table, 109, 112, 114. See also Bendiren; Local
native place, 10, 66–70. See home place
native-place networks. See guanxi; laoxiang
nativity, social construction of, 91, 109–13, 133, 149n31, 156n18. See also locality: social construction of
nativity-outside-ness differentiation. See locality: –outside-ness differentiation

"nesting" of identities: politics of, 130, 138, 142, 158n15,16

Nongmin. *See* Peasant

non-*minzu* identities. See *ren*; *jia*; *min*

North (Beifang), 28, 104, 112–13, 116–17, 124–25, 135, 158n11

Northeasterner (Dongbeiren), 75, 79, 95*table*, 98, 99*table*, 136

Northerner (Beifangren), 10, 77, 95*table*, 98, 100*table*, 103–5, 112, 114, 124, 136, 158n11

North-South differentiation, 102–5, 113, 116

Nuosu (Yizu), 56, 59–62, 153n18,19

Officials' Speech (Guanhua), 148n29

Outsider (identity label), 9, 10, 91, 96–97*table*, 100–101, 109–14, 142. *See also* Migrant; Stranger; Waidiren

outside-ness (also as outsider identity), 104, 111, 116, 133–34, 137, 141

"participants' primordialism," 87, 119–20

patriotic education, 87, 120

peasant: construction of the category, 106–8, 156n10,14

Peasant (Nongmin): as an identity label, 98, 99*table*, 195, 129

Peking Man, 35

"plurality in unity." See *duo yuan yi ti*

primordial "givens," 84, 119–20

Prmi, 56, 134

Punti, 32, 113, 149n31

Putonghua (common speech), 38, 53, 57, 61, 99*table*, 146n15, 152nn8,10. *See also* Chinese language; Han language

qunti (group), 127

quyu wenhua. *See* regional cultures

regional cultures (*diqu wenhua, diyu wenhua, quyu wenhua*), 117–18, 121, 123–26

regional differentiation, 91, 102–5, 112, 117–18, 157n1

relationality of identities, 5, 10, 66, 115, 123, 137

ren (identity), 13, 15, 128–31, 133–36, 144, 150n43, 157n5, 158n13,15

renqun (human groups), 127

reversed Orientalism, 88

"roots" (also "origins"), 28, 72, 74, 76, 78, 85, 91, 101, 117, 123, 132–33, 152n5, 155n20

Rural Han (Ruralite, identity label), 4, 9–10, 14, 98, 99*table*, 101, 105–6, 112–13, 129, 135, 138

rural strangeness, 110, 157n22. *See also* migrant ruralness

rural-urban differentiation (also rurality/ urbanity differentiation), 91, 100–101, 104–10, 112, 133–34, 137, 141

"savages," 26–27, 52. *See also* "barbarians"

scales of interaction, 4, 10, 15–16, 20, 80, 82, 84, 87, 112, 114, 118, 120, 123, 132, 135–38, 157n1, 158n15

school curriculum: narratives of Han-ness and nation in, 58–60, 65, 153n20

"secondary cultural differentiation" (also "secondary" identities), 14, 119, 120, 122, 123–26, 133. *See also* "essence"

Shanghai, 12, 75, 93–94, 100, 110–11, 114, 117, 154n8, 157n19; as a fieldwork location, 9, 15–18, 56–57, 73, 101

Shanghai Person/People. *See* Shanghainese

Shanghainese (Shanghairen), 4, 72, 74, 77, 79, 80, 81, 92, 94, 96–97*table*, 98, 99–100*table*, 102, 103, 105, 109–11, 127, 130, 135–36

shaoshu minzu. *See* "minorities"

Sichuan (province), 12, 17, 40, 56, 58, 68, 86, 92, 117, 117

Sichuan Person/People. *See* Sichuanese

Sichuanese (Sichuanren), 95, 98, 99–100*table*, 102–3, 112, 124, 127, 129, 135

sinicization, 27, 147n13

situationality (of identities), 10–12, 63, 65, 88, 115, 132, 135–36, 141

"snowball" (*xueqiu*), 20, 123, 125, 140. See also *duo yuan yi ti*

social positioning strategies, 8–9, 11–12, 25, 61, 64, 78, 90, 101, 136. *See also*

social positioning strategies *(continued)*
hierarchization/verticalization of
identities; intra-Han hierarchies of
power
socionym, 90–94, 98, 100–101, 103,
105, 110–13, 128, 145n4; examples
of, 95–98*table*. *See also* collective
identity labels
soil: discourse of, 73, 77, 85, 87, 94, 101.
See also "roots"
South (Nanfang), 28, 77, 104, 112–13,
116–17, 124–5, 135
Southerner (Nanfangren, Nanren), 10,
68, 77, 98, 100*table*, 101–5, 112, 124,
136
spatial kinship, 67–68, 71
spatiality of Han-ness/Chinese-ness, 26,
37, 40, 47, 54, 76, 95–97*table*, 147n10
Stalin, Josef, 3, 39, 40, 58, 129, 150nn44,45
stereotyping (also stereotypical characteristics), 91–94, 98, 99–100*table*,
100–12. *See also* markers of Han-ness;
tedian
Stranger (identity label), 91, 96–97*table*,
101, 109–11, 138. *See also* Migrant;
Outsider; Waidiren
Subei, 12, 73–75, 86, 110–11, 157n19
Subei Person/People (Subeiren), 73–74,
79, 86, 93, 98, 99–100*table*, 100,
110–12, 114, 155n15, 157n20
subethnic groups/distinctions, 127
"subgroups of Hanzu" (Hanzu *cisheng
jituan*, Hanzu *yaqunti*), 127
Sun Yat-sen, 22, 34–36, 52, 137
Sunan (Southern Jiangsu), 157n19

Taiwanese, 91, 97*table*, 99–100*table*,
100–103, 136
Tajfel, Henri, 92–93
tedian (stereotypical characteristics), 45,
57, 91, 125, 156n1. *See also* markers of
Han-ness; stereotyping
Tibetans, 33, 36, 38, 47, 56, 58, 60, 134, 136,
143, 152n3, 158n15
tongxianghui. *See* associations of fellow
locals
transitory ethnicity, 14, 18, 138–39, 143

"unifier of nationalities" (*obedinitel
natsionalnostei*), 39, 129. *See also*
"Han, the": as the "unifier of
nationalities"
Urbanite/Urban Han (identity label), 4,
9–10, 13–14, 93, 105–9, 112, 114, 116, 135,
138, 142
urbanity (also as urban identity), 12, 91,
101, 104, 109, 112–13, 115, 129, 133–34,
137, 141
urbanity-rurality differentiation. *See*
rural-urban differentiation
urban-rural divide. *See* rural-urban
differentiation
Uyghur, 9, 18, 47, 61–62, 153nn17,20,
158n15; -Han interactions, 87, 135–37,
143, 152n7; as an "other" of the Han,
47, 136–37, 152n3

verticalization of identities. *See*
hierarchization of identities

waidi (outside, outer place), 111
Waidiren, 97*table*, 109. *See* Outsider;
Stranger
Wallman, Sandra, 122, 131
wenhua: usage of, 30, 48–49*table*, 53, 56,
99*table*, 103, 116–17, 125
wildness-culture paradigm. *See* culture-
wildness/barbarism paradigm
Wuzu Gonghe (the Republic of Five
Races), 36

Xia, 6, 21, 24, 27, 123
Xinjiang, 4, 9, 17–18, 58, 61–62, 65, 87,
134–35, 143, 153n20, 156n18
Xu Jieshun, 20, 23, 125
xueqiu. *See* "snowball"

Yangzi River, 67, 75, 111, 117, 124
Yellow Emperor, 7, 22, 35, 150nn38,39
Yellow River, 117, 124
Yi ("savages"), 26–27
Yi (Yizu, Nuosu), 30, 151n54, 153n18. *See
also* Nuosu
yong Xia bian Yi ("transformation of Yi
savages by the ways of the Xia"), 27

Yuanmou Man, 35
yudie (imperial genealogies), 149n34
Yunnan, 22, 40, 55, 156n18

Zhejiang Person/People (Zhejiangren), 68, 73, 77, 98, 99*table*, 101–2, 114, 136
Zhongguoren, 19, 21, 24, 26–27, 33

Zhonghua, 6; *minzu* (Chinese nation), 5, 24, 33, 36, 49*table*
Zhongyuan (Central Plains), 75, 125
Zuosuo village (Sichuan-Yunnan border), 17–18, 56–57, 59–61, 64, 134, 153n18
zuqun (ethnic group, lineage group), 127